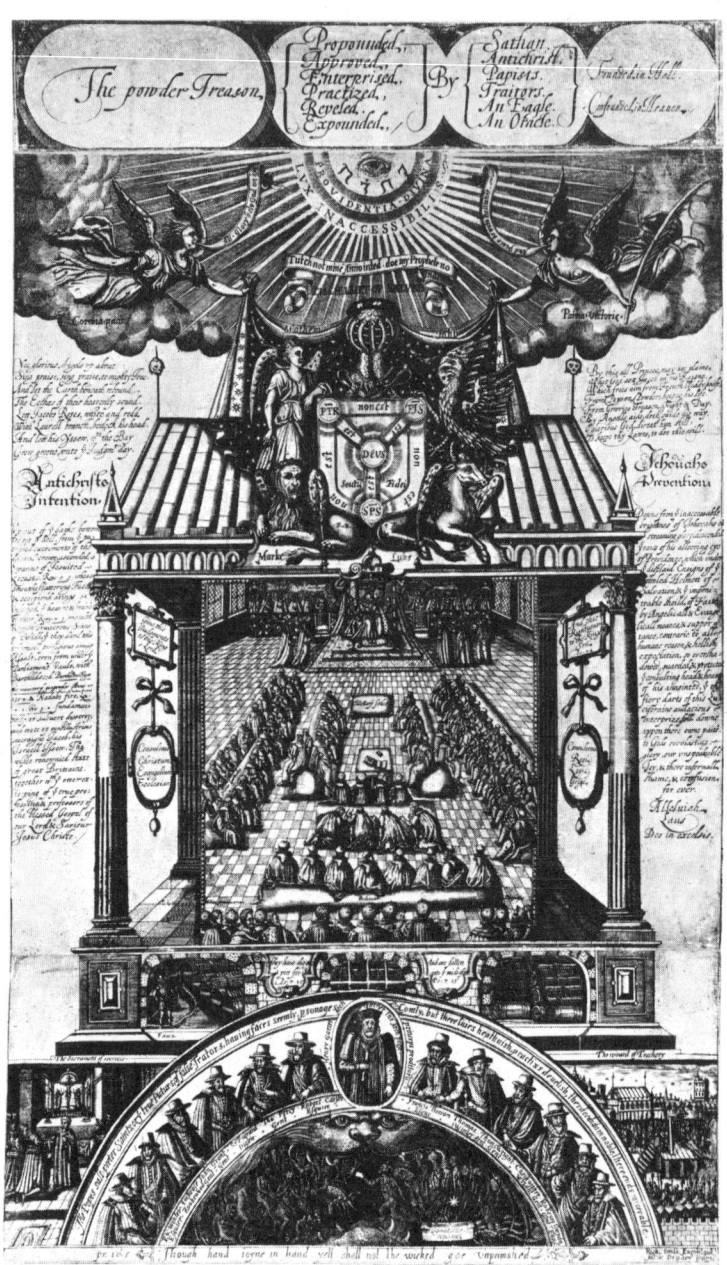

'THE POWDER TREASON'

THE
GUNPOWDER PLOT

*The Narrative of Oswald Tesimond
alias Greenway*

Translated from the Italian
of the Stonyhurst Manuscript,
edited and annotated by
FRANCIS EDWARDS
S.J., F.S.A., F.R.Hist.S.

THE FOLIO SOCIETY

London 1973

PRINTED IN GREAT BRITAIN
by W & J Mackay Limited, Chatham

Contents

Illustrations

The publishers would like to thank Stonyhurst College, the Ashmolean Museum, Dr Dunstan Edmonston, the National Portrait Gallery, and the Trustees of the British Museum for permission to reproduce the items listed above. Reproductions of Crown-copyright records in the Public Record Office appear by permission of the Controller of HM Stationery Office.

Introduction

'*Fiction there is – and history. Certain critics of no little discernment have considered that fiction is history which might have taken place, and history fiction which has taken place. We are, indeed, forced to acknowledge that the novelists' art often compels belief, just as reality sometimes defies it. Alas! there exists an order of minds so sceptical that they deny the possibility of any fact as soon as it diverges from the commonplace. It is not for them that I write.*'

André Gide, LES CAVES DU VATICAN
(*Dorothy Bussy's translation, London, 1952*)

THE PROBLEM of the man with the dark lantern, like the other man of mystery in the iron mask, has baffled and intrigued many generations of professional historians and amateur sleuths alike. Perplexity concerning the gunpowder plot is likely to continue for an indefinite time to come. While the evidence known to survive is not sufficient to enable us to reach full certainty, there is too much to permit an admission of simple ignorance as to what happened under parliament on that more than ordinarily obscure November night in 1605. New scraps of evidence still come to light. New interpretations of what we had still suggest themselves. The hunt for more goes on. Many well-informed people, however, may wonder if this tally-ho is not an outmoded cry. Memory harks back, perhaps, to 1897, when John Gerard, S.J., asked a question 280 pages long: *What was the Gunpowder Plot?* Did not the redoubtable Dr

S. R. Gardiner reply with *What Gunpowder Plot was*? In fact, a fine display of late nineteenth century self-confidence allowed too few question-marks to appear in his reply. This answer was published, with incredible promptitude, in the same year as the question. Perhaps the Victorians moved too fast. Certainly, a running contest continued in *The Athenaeum* until the average spectator grew tired of trying to keep pace.

Half a century later, however, Mr Hugh Ross Williamson usefully reminded the world with his scholarly study that the pursuit was by no means over. Gerard's original questions had not been answered to everyone's satisfaction. Controversy must still continue until, later rather than sooner, all the relevant documents are published – as many as possible in facsimile – so that the difficulties and possibilities of the surviving evidence become more widely obvious. We are still at the stage when scholars and students who wish to understand what happened must ideally go back to the original documents, many of which, even now, are unpublished. Nevertheless, since the days of Gerard and Gardiner, publication of further important documents and studies has proceeded steadily. The reader is no longer quite so dependent on the views of specialists as formerly. One cannot attempt here an adequate review of plot literature to date, but some mention of works recent and less recent seems desirable in order to place the present document in its historical and historiographical context. Mr Ross Williamson's book made good use of two important calendars of original documents at Hatfield, published in 1938 and 1940 respectively. It also included an excellent bibliography. Before this, Donald Carswell usefully republished in 1934, the King's Book, and contemporary, official accounts of the trials of the plotters, and of Henry Garnet, S.J.

The present work belongs to a group of original, contemporary manuscripts at Stonyhurst, significant items of which were published by John Morris in *The Troubles of our Catholic Forefathers*. The three volumes appeared between 1872 and 1877. The first volume included an unfinished autobiographical account of Father Oswald Tesimond's landing in England in 1597.* Tesimond was better known, perhaps, under his alias of Greenway. His hand produced the

---

* pp. 143–83; from C. Grene, *Collectanea C*, ff. 176 (b)–188 (a).

manuscript now before us in translation.* He does not appear to have been the author of the original story, which was probably in Latin and sent to Rome, or written there, for the better information of the jesuit authorities, especially Father Robert Persons and the General. The original author was probably a secular priest, but he cannot at the moment be identified, any more than the date of his original manuscript.†

From this original Latin, John Gerard, S.J., as we may conjecture, prepared his version in English, adding, omitting and altering as his own experience suggested. This was probably intended for circulation among the English community in Rome and elsewhere. Tesimond prepared a similar document in Italian, likewise editing and altering according to his own knowledge and experience. This was presumably intended for circulation among his Italian friends of whom, by the time of writing, he may well have had a considerable number. A Yorkshireman, Tesimond was educated with Guy Fawkes and John and Christopher Wright at the free school by 'Le Horse Fayre' on the outskirts of York itself. Thus his acquaintance with the plotters began early. Tesimond's earlier religious affiliation may have been as confused as theirs. At all events, he had begun to make up his mind by 1580, when, as a lad of seventeen, he made his way to study at the English College, Rome. He entered the Society on 13 April 1584, and proceeded, after his novitiate, to train in theology at Messina, Sicily. In 1597, he returned to England as a Jesuit priest. He was now thirty-four years old. A man of resource, Father Oswald managed to elude the authorities successfully for the next few years; until the aftermath of the plot in fact, in which his name became so much involved that he was obliged to escape abroad. 'He was safely conveyed to Calais in a small boat laden with dead pigs, of which cargo he passed as the owner.'‡ Tesimond eventually found his way back to Rome, and then to Sicily in 1621 as Prefect of Studies in the Messina seminary. He was known on the continent as Philip Beaumont, Beaumond or Bémont. He subsequently went to teach theology at the English

---

* Stonyhurst MS, A.IV.4.
† The question of authorship, and a fuller discussion of the MSS involved is given in *JSA*, Vol. 4, No. 2 (October 1970), pp. 96–108.
‡ John Morris, *The Troubles* . . ., I, London, 1872, p. 143.

College, Valladolid, and after further work at Florence and Naples died in 1635.

The proclamation for his arrest, issued on 15 January 1606, described him as 'of a reasonable stature, black hair, a brown beard cut close on the cheeks and left broad on the chin, somewhat long-visaged, lean in the face but of a good red complexion, his nose somewhat long and sharp at the end, his hands slender and long fingers, his body slender, his legs of a good proportion, his feet somewhat long and slender. His apparel of cloth, hose and jerkin much after the Italian fashion, the jerkin buttoned on the breast, his cloak buttoned down before with ribands hanging down on his breast, his hat narrow-brimmed with a small band and a broad, full crown, as now the fashion is.'*

Tesimond, then, was reasonably well equipped by personal knowledge, taste and education to write an Italian narrative of the plot. However, his narrative shows signs of haste, and of having been broken off about two-thirds of the way through. It has all the appearances of a first draft for a more polished effort which presumably never materialized. As a historical document, this gives it the advantage of a certain spontaneity and air of candour which might have been lost in an essay more carefully elaborated. The Italian, again very plausibly, is that of a man who has grown rather rusty. He had been some ten years away from it if he began to write in 1607 or 1608; that is, almost immediately on his return to Europe, if not Italy. A contemporary Italian colleague of the translator's, Father Michele Garofalo, S.J., of the Naples Province, kindly consented to examine the narrative from the linguistic viewpoint. He concluded, 'The Italian rendering is very poor; i.e. (1) wrong spelling of many words. (2) continual faults in the construction of sentences. (3) over-use of Latin terms or Latin endings of the words' – this, of course, confirms the surmise that the writer was following a Latin original – '(4) it needs very careful reading in order to get the meaning of each paragraph.'

After the Gerard narrative† this account from Greenway's hand is the longest, and, up to a point, most authentic which we have of

* ibid., p. 144.
† Published by John Morris in *The Condition of Catholics under James I*, London, 1871.

the gunpowder plot. It was written by someone moving in the circle of the plotters. It was not produced by an official or member of the government of the time who might well have had it in mind to deceive us. It descends to circumstance and tries to provide a flowing narrative from evidence which is much of the time disjointed and not infrequently contradictory. To what extent it can be confirmed or challenged from sources elsewhere will, it is hoped, be evident from the foot-notes. Undoubtedly, it is an important piece of evidence, and although it has provided material for most writers on the plot to date, it has never before been published in its entirety. The narrative is far from being a full and final revelation. The writer was as much in the dark as his reader concerning a great many events. In the presence of documents he could never have seen, we are in a better position to assess the truth of his own statements and judge them in the fitful light of our own theories. Archbishop Mathew, reviewing the modest work of the present translator's on the subject, succinctly classed theories on the plot under three heads: 'according to the orthodox, old-fashioned view Salisbury *discovered* the conspiracy, a second judgement is that he *nourished* and a third that he *invented* it'.*

The narrator takes, on the whole, the view that the government of the day merely discovered the plot. This, at any rate, argues considerable honesty, since he himself most strongly disapproved, and could only feel embarrassment at the involvement of apparently bona-fide catholics. The present translator inclines strongly to the view that the first Earl of Salisbury ultimately concocted it, or the significant part of it. This merely makes the gunpowder plot one in rather a long series which began quietly enough in 1564, if not earlier,† and ended with almost a bang in 1605.

Some of the long series of so-called catholic plots have been investigated. Others still remain to be analysed in detail. Those that the present writer has so far examined do not stand up to serious investigation. They suggest rather an ingenious political contrivance to deal with special difficulties on the part of Sir William Cecil and his son Sir Robert. They constituted an effective way of getting rid of enemies, rivals and unwelcome policies by the very

---

* *Sunday Telegraph*, 2 November 1969.
† See M. D. R. Leys, *Catholics in England; 1559–1829*, London, 1961, pp. 15–16.

method of manoeuvring them into the fatal category of the treason-
able. The gunpowder plot is thus the last episode, at least for a
time, in the age of treason which preceded reason. The people and
events of the time are, happily, as remote from most of us as Belfast
from Piccadilly, but the Greenway narrative touches on problems of
human nature and politics that in one form or another will always
be with us.

Note on the text

NOTHING HAS BEEN omitted from the original text without the usual indication of three dots, except for the opening of the Narrator's Preface and Chapter I. Passages omitted were either strictly theological in context – illustrations of points from Scripture &c. – or else were repetitive or rhetorical. Also omitted was a rather long preamble in the beginning of the first chapter on the general course of the Reformation from the time of Henry VIII up to the end of Elizabeth's reign. Its terms are general, and seemingly contain nothing new. Apart from this, every effort has been made to preserve and translate in the sense of the narrator whatever was of historical significance, or that he considered to be so.

The greater part of the narrative is delivered in the third person, but the narrator frequently breaks in with reminiscences and observations in the first person. This seems to confirm the idea that he was working from another narrative and documents before him. Sometimes he quotes letters almost in their entirety. All of which lends a certain vividness to his style, but it must be confessed, it does not always make for easy reading. Fortunately, the story is fairly straightforward as Greenway tells it, and so confusion is less than might be expected. The fact that the narrative is unfinished, with numerous cancellations and alterations in the original, suggests that this was an early or even a first draft. Doubtless, the author would have revised much if he had ever got round to a re-writing. Meanwhile, every effort has been made to recast phrases in short, modern sentences, avoiding the Ciceronian cadences of the original. To have done more than this, even in the all-important

cause of readability, would surely have involved serious infidelity
to the original.

ABBREVIATIONS

Manuscript Sources:

AAW	Archives of the Archbishop of Westminster.
Add:	Additional MSS (BM).
ARSJ	Archivum Romanum Societatis Jesu.
E	Exchequer.
GPB	Gunpowder Plot Book (PRO, SP14/216).
SIM.E:	Archivo General de Simancas: Estado.
SP 12	State Papers, Domestic; Elizabeth I.
SP 14	State Papers, Domestic; James I.
SP 38	Docquet Books.
SP 77	State Papers, Flanders.

Printed Sources:

BM	British Museum.
CRS	Catholic Record Society.
CSP	Calendar of State Papers.
DC	Donald Carswell, *Trial of Guy Fawkes and others* (*The Gunpowder Plot*), London, 1934.
DJ	David Jardine, *A Narrative of the Gunpowder Plot*, London, 1857.
DNB	Dictionary of National Biography, 1889 edition.
EGF	Francis Edwards, S.J., *Guy Fawkes: the real story of the Gunpowder Plot?*, London, 1969.
GBM	George Blacker Morgan, *The Great English Treason* . . ., Oxford, 1931, 2 vols.
GIL	Joseph Gillow, *Biographical Dictionary of the English Catholics*, 5 vols, London, 1885.
HFR	*Records of the English Province of the Society of Jesus*, Henry Foley, S.J., 8 vols, London, 1877–83.
HHS	H. H. Spink, *The Gunpowder Plot and Lord Monteagle's Letter*, London, 1902.
HMC	Report of the Historical Manuscripts Commission.
HRW	Hugh Ross Williamson, *The Gunpowder Plot*, London, 1951.

JG	John Gerard, *What was the Gunpowder Plot?* London, 1897.
JSA	Journal of the Society of Archivists.
PD	Paul Durst, *Intended Treason*, London, 1970.
PRO	Public Record Office.
PS	Philip Sidney, *A History of the Gunpowder Plot*, London, 1905.
R.HIST.S.	Royal Historical Society.
SAL.CAL.	M. S. Giuseppi, *Calendar of the MSS of the Most Honourable the Marquess of Salisbury . . . preserved at Hatfield House*, part XVI, London, 1933; part XVII, for 1605, 1938; part XVIII, for 1606, 1940 (HMC Reports).
SRG	S. R. Gardiner, *What Gunpowder Plot was*, London, 1897.
STC	A. W. Pollard and G. R. Redgrave, *A Short title Catalogue of books printed in England, Scotland and Ireland, and of English Books printed abroad, 1948.*
VAUX	Fr. Godfrey Anstruther, O.P., *Vaux of Harrowden*, Newport, Mon., 1953.
WIN	Edmund Sawyer, *Memorials of Affairs of State . . . from the Original Papers of . . . Sir Ralph Winwood . . .* 3 vols, London, 1725.
WTL	William Thomas Lowndes, *The Bibliographers' Manual of English Literature, published in 4 vols,* in London, 1834.
YAJ	Yorkshire Archaeological Journal.

The Narrative of
Oswald Tesimond
alias Greenway

Narrator's Preface

SUCH ARE HUMAN AFFAIRS that even when they are most deserving of praise they are often the subject of calumny and sinister interpretation by those who like to sit in judgement on the interior state of others. Sometimes misunderstanding arises through chance circumstances and unexpected accidents. Although these may be the fault of a few, they are often attributed to all the members of a group by those who know little about it or are otherwise unfavourable. We can believe that this has happened to us in our own day. We papists are not only condemned by some for being inconstant in our labours and sufferings, we are also accused of impatience. So either way we are worthy of blame, or at least scarcely deserving of sympathy. This is mainly because of a plot in England which was brought about in the last few months by a number of catholic gentlemen and knights. There is no question that its impudence calls for blame. However unreasonable it may have been, I trust that anyone who reads the following account will see quite clearly that it was the damnable mistake of only a few individuals. Furthermore, it must be blamed only on to those who have already paid the price. In no sense should it be ascribed to any other particular persons, and still less to the catholic community.

ONE

QUEEN ELIZABETH came to the end of her days after many
evils and miseries endured by the catholics with much
patience. Those unhappy people scarcely had time or opportunity,
even now, to think that good days had returned to them, or to hope
that God would say to them, 'Lift up your heads for now your salvation draws near.' Certainly, they hoped that after the long and
damaging flood of unrelenting persecution, some bird of good omen
would bring them the olive branch of peace, with word of land where
they could set their feet and enjoy for the future that peace so long
desired. They had eyes and minds fixed on the king then reigning
in Scotland; James, the first of that name now reigning in England.
They thought they had good reason to expect much of him. In the
first place, he was the son of a mother who had lived not only as a
catholic, but with the reputation of a saint living a long time among
people depraved and perverse. One could say that she died in
defence of her faith. They would never have believed that the
mother's merits would fail to win from God the grace of His true
knowledge for her son . . .

Furthermore, they would never have believed that the king
would take up so intimately and confidently with those, and indeed
only those, who had betrayed his mother, and in the end killed her
after long imprisonment. It was through their means, indeed, that
his own father had been assassinated. And the king himself had been
detained in his own kingdom for many years at best like a schoolboy
but for much of the time as little more than a prisoner. To this one
could add that it seemed reasonable to the catholics that the king

would not be bound to follow the footsteps and example of Queen Elizabeth. She had been persuaded by her council at the beginning of her reign that for reasons of state, it was necessary to break with the Holy See. Making herself the head of the new church, she must defend herself with her adherents against the old. She knew well that the pope was fully cognizant of the invalidity of her mother's marriage to Henry VIII. She also knew that the Holy See greatly esteemed and favoured Queen Mary, both at the time when she was Queen Dowager of France, and later when she came to peaceful possession and rule of her kingdom of Scotland. For that reason, she was feared, hated and envied by Queen Elizabeth as the legitimate and proximate heir to her kingdom. The catholics of England showed whole-hearted affection for Mary, not only as a fellow-papist, but also as one whom they recognized in right and conscience as the true heir of Henry VIII, and who had a very real interest in the kingdom. It was this more than anything that induced Elizabeth to give herself out as a defender of heresy and bitter enemy of the catholics.

Now as regards James I, who was the successor and undisputed progeny of his mother, nothing of what was said above could stand as an obstacle to him. Nor could he reasonably doubt the favour, even affection, with which the Apostolic See regarded him. Of this he had received no small demonstration while he was still reigning in Scotland, and openly professing a heresy much opposed to catholicism. Indeed, the favours shown him had been considerable enough to suggest an affection nothing less than paternal. Who could have supposed that the manifold example of powerful and devout kings his ancestors would now fail to move him sufficiently to unite himself to the church . . ? While those kings obeyed that church, they were always regarded among the first in Christendom for honour, might and wealth. It seemed to many catholics, and indeed to many of the other communion, that in order to have a firm and lasting peace with the Princes of Christendom, he could do no less. If only for reasons of state, James should agree with them in the profession of identical faith. For where there is disagreement on so basic and essential a point, social harmony and firm peace cannot last long. But hardly anyone thought that he would take to persecuting the catholic community. For this very reason the late queen had been very much disliked by nearly everybody. Following this path, James would appear to want the whole world for his enemy. Doing this he would virtually declare himself an enemy of other rulers who were catholics. The queen had been anxious, as far as she could, to extirpate catholicism not only in England but everywhere else as well. On the other hand, catholics allowed hope to grow thanks to the good report given of James by men who knew him in the queen's time when he was reigning as King of Scotland. These people broadcast optimistic facts about him not only in England but also at the more important vantage-points abroad. I know that the first and foremost potentates of Europe remember it well even to this day. They enlarged on the rare gifts, natural qualities and the affection he showed particularly to those who had given faithful service to his mother. He himself bears witness to this in his little book called *Basilicon Doron*.* There he gave the same precept to the prince, namely that he should show himself most affectionate and appreciative towards those who had shown more complete fidelity and unswerving loyalty to his parents. To this they added his peaceable disposition and natural humanity which were opposed, as they thought, to every kind of persecution and cruelty. Especially so when it was aimed at catholics, whose religion he willingly conceded to be the oldest in Christendom; that of the Mother Church. However, there were many things in it which did not please him, and so he had not embraced it.

Perhaps it will occur to some that these reasons were either too general, or not sufficiently weighty, to justify our having placed as much hope as we claim in the present king. I would ask them to ponder the details which follow. We know for certain that many men were sent off to different places in the royal name with letters to this effect, namely that christian rulers could expect from the christian king of Scots liberty of conscience for catholics. They would be able to live under him without molestation. Many letters of this kind were sent the same year from France into England, translated from French into our common tongue. We have seen them. We also know for certain that, as soon as the queen fell ill of her last sickness, a

---

* Βαδιλιχον Αωρον in 3 books. First published at Edinburgh in 1599 in a limited edition of seven copies (WTL, II, p. 1011). On the point of James's promises, see D.J., pp. 15–16.

number of catholics of position and reputation, and also some priests, went post-haste to Scotland carrying the news to the king. They assured him at the same time of their sympathy and affection. They begged His Majesty that, in exchange for this affection, he would be pleased to give them that consolation which he knew would be most dear and welcome. That is, they should be treated in the same way as his other subjects. They should continue to be free from that most burdensome persecution suffered for so many years. He granted them as much as they asked for without denying any part of their request. Furthermore, he promised them that in their own houses they should enjoy complete freedom, keeping their priests and receiving the sacraments in accordance with their own tastes. The priests who received this promise from the king have declared to many that this was the truth; in addition, that the king, for their greater security, pledged his royal word. This was something which up to that time he had never contradicted. I can myself bear witness to having heard this from those who themselves understood it from these same priests; and moreover from one who was present at the very time, and in whose hands the king himself confirmed it with an oath. I scarcely need to mention that I have heard the same thing from many others worthy of belief, men of good family, who received from the king similar promises, and perhaps greater still, both for themselves and for catholics in general. What more could they look for, or desire from the king, than this? Or what more could he do for them as one who had not yet entered into actual possession of the Kingdom of England?

The catholics, for their part, soon showed how much hope they placed in the king. As soon as the queen was dead, they publicly proclaimed him king with the utmost alacrity through all the counties of England.* In fact, they took up his cause with so much joy that some of the protestants were moved by this demonstration

* Before Elizabeth's death, the catholics tended to divide in their sympathies between the Infanta of Spain and James VI of Scotland. See L. Hicks, 'Sir Robert Cecil, Father Persons and the Succession, 1600–1601', article in *Archivum Historicum, Societatis Jesu* An. XXIV, Fasc. 47 (Jan–June, 1955, pp. 3–47). For a good example of catholic alacrity in acknowledging James's English accession, see '1603, March. Memoranda by Sir Thomas Tresham, of his proclamation of King James I, at Northampton, March 25, 1603, in HMC, Various III, London, 1904, pp. 117–23 (Clarke-Thornhill MSS).

to wonder if the king did not after all incline to the catholic religion. I will not attempt to detail the vast expense incurred by the papists to show their affection for him, and how much they hoped from him when they took up his cause. There were some who set barrels of wine in public places, and others who threw down in the streets from their windows considerable sums of money. I could not easily describe the sums laid out by catholics everywhere to provide rich liveries, costumes, and similar marks of welcome for the king first of all, and then for his queen and the prince. Those who did not see it could not easily imagine it. So much so that the king himself used to say that he felt himself much cheered and encouraged by this universal applause from the catholics.

But it is better to hope in the Lord than trust in princes . . . How great was the grief and bitter the anguish of those poor folk who had suffered for so many years under the harsh yoke of Elizabeth when they began to see hope vanish once more from before their eyes. They now saw snatched from their hands the many alleviations which they had not only begun to hope for but actually thought they possessed. I do not say that not all, I say that not even one, of the promises made to them was kept. Without delay, the king gave ear and belief to people who were sworn and open enemies of catholics. He gave his confidence to those very same people who had been the authors and ministers of the most bitter persecution inflicted in the time of the queen. Not only did he allow himself to be persuaded by them to confirm and renew all those heartless and more than tyrannical laws which she had promulgated against us, but he added new and even more cruel measures in his first parliament. He did more against us than Elizabeth had done in many years. The papists began to wonder, reasonably enough as it seemed to them, whether the little finger of the king was not now heavier than the shoulders of the queen. Instead of the queen's scourges, they were now to be flogged with the king's scorpions. Not many weeks after his arrival in England, James revealed in his discourses a mind altogether adverse to catholics.* This gave them reason to

* For an optimistic view of James I's relations with the papists at this time see D. H. Willson, *King James VI and I*, London, 1956, pp. 148–9, 218–19. But see also the Venetian Ambassador, Nicolo Molin's view, C. S. P. Venetian, 1603–7, pp. 509–14, quoted in R. Ashton, *James I by his Contemporaries*, London,

suspect what might follow. In his first parliament he made a speech – one can read it today in print – which indulged in so much vehemence and bitterness, particularly against the Apostolic See, that he made it clear enough what could be expected of him for the future.*

The catholics earnestly desired that James would make some mention of his mother, as people generally expected of him, and in accordance with the everlasting honour and memory which she so much deserved. For her enemies had poured out vituperation against her in that very place, and when she died she had lain neglected without mark of respect. They hoped that the king would at least honour her with the usual monuments and inscriptions due to princes from their sons and successors. Perhaps one day he would realize the danger of putting off this natural duty indefinitely. It could injure his reputation considerably in the eyes of a world which can still raise its eyebrows when gratitude seems too long overdue. At least those who had belonged to the household of this great and holy queen while she lived, and who had served her with so much perseverance and fidelity, should have received from the son the reward due to them. Not even these, and others who mentioned his mother to him were, I will not say rewarded, but even kindly regarded or made welcome. So noticeable was this neglect that people concluded that even the bare memory of her was unwelcome at court. The hidden reasons for this are not known. Before long no one dared to make or offer memorials on behalf of services done to that queen, not even when those services had been considerable, and of a kind that well deserved to be recognized and rewarded. I will only mention here two or three such cases briefly so that the reader can form his own judgement.

After the Queen of Scots had been captured and kept in prison in England, two knights and a gentleman of ancient house and much honour resolved on a plan to set her free and restore her to her own

---

* See J. R. Tanner, *Constitutional Documents of the Reign of James I, 1603–25*, Cambridge, 1952, pp. 24–30; an abridgement from James I, *Works* . . ., 1616 edition, pp. 485–97.

1969, p. 9; and Lucy Aikin, *Memoirs of the Court of King James I*, vol. I, London, 1822, pp. 201–2.

Kingdom of Scotland.* This affair, although it was handled with proper secrecy, was revealed by the gentleman's son. All three were put in the Tower of London, but only the gentleman was condemned to death since the Privy Council had not sufficient evidence against the two knights. All the same, the latter were obliged to pay out huge sums of money and even to sell part of their estates to disengage themselves and to be freed from prison. Eventually, by means of his friends, the gentleman was also released, but with the loss of everything that he possessed.

After this episode, and some twenty years before Queen Elizabeth died, fourteen gentlemen – Anthony Babington and friends of his – men of good family, wealthy, and not lacking courage, agreed among themselves to bring about the liberation of the Queen of Scots.† This project too was uncovered. All the gentlemen in question were most cruelly executed. They protested as they died that their sole motive had been to free that long-suffering lady from prolonged imprisonment; and by her means to bring relief at one and the same time to the miserable state of catholics generally. On this occasion, one of the two knights above-named was re-taken on suspicion of favouring Mary's cause. After two years' imprisonment in the Tower, and very much expense, he was eventually liberated since they had no proof against him.‡

* For this Rolston-Hall plot of 1570, see F. Edwards, *The Dangerous Queen*, London, 1964, pp. 193–221.

† See Alan Gordon-Smith, *The Babington Plot*, London, 1936: J. B. Black, *The Reign of Elizabeth 1558–1603*, 2nd edition, Oxford, 1959, chapter X. Antonia Fraser, *Mary Queen of Scots*, London, 1969, pp. 475–501. The latest and most detailed study of Mary's last years is by Dr John Paul, but is still in manuscript at the time of writing.

‡ This apparently refers to Sir Thomas Gerard of the Bryn, Lancashire. As 'Sir Tho: Jarrett Knighte', he heads a list of 'Prisoners after the Babington plot, September, 1586' (BM Harleian MS 360, f. 44r: published in CRS, 2 (1906), p. 257). For the varied spellings of the surname, see C. W. Bardsley, *Our English Surnames* . . ., London, 1873, p. 25. In 'The Attorney General's lists of priests and other prisoners, 25 September, 1586', 'Sir Thomas Gerrard' again heads the list (PRO, SP 12, 193, No. 66; CRS, ibid., p. 259, and p. 264). He was still in the Tower on 2 July 1588, having been there since 23 August 1586, one year and eleven months, and 'indicted of treason' (ibid., p. 281). On 16 October, he was transferred to the 'Cownter in Wood Street', another prison (ibid., p. 284). He was apparently released before 1595, since his name is not on a list of that date (ibid., pp. 284–7).

While the above-mentioned fourteen gentlemen were lying in prison, another man was with them who was also suspected of the same design. This was Thomas Abington, whose brother Richard was one of the fourteen. He was killed along with them. In Thomas Abington's house two priests were found a few months ago [see below, p. 170]. Instead of paying this man an indemnity for the losses suffered in consequence of his devotion and service given to the king's mother, they have condemned him to death. All his goods and possessions have been confiscated including one of the finest houses in England.

Anyone can judge whether these, and other catholics innumerable did not rather deserve for their great sufferings and services, praise, affection, and even some kind of remuneration as an outward mark of esteem. Instead of which they received what in fact they suffered. Surely they had at least the right to compassion and sympathy? Instead of which we still see them harassed, persecuted and hated to the last degree by one who should have loved them . . . The bitter experience of these hardships and many other inflictions imposed from hour to hour, and one could almost say from moment to moment, after the king's accession led eventually to so much anguish and revulsion in the hearts of the catholics that, casting aside vain hopes, they began to reflect more deeply on the miseries which engulfed them. They saw that their present afflictions were incomparably greater than anything they had suffered in the queen's time. For then those who persecuted them remained in some doubt as to who would succeed after her death. For that reason they and others who differed from catholics in religion stepped with a certain care and moderation. They tempered their hatred towards them thinking of what might happen to them if the course of events radically altered. With this in mind, many of them took care to maintain friendship with the more important catholics, thinking it very probable that with the end of the queen's life would come also the end of persecution. But now fear for the future has been removed; the obstacle in the way of self-interest set aside. Everyone follows his own whim, freely showing the hatred he feels. He can lean on the arm and support of the prince. They do not fear the changes that may come after him since the succession is assured by his numerous progeny. His children have been reared and thoroughly instructed in the opinions and doctrines of the father. What is more, they have grown up and been nurtured in hatred of catholics and their religion. To this full sum of miseries could be added the fact that where before they had some hope in the promises made by the king, it now seems to the king's catholic subjects, as has been said, and not only to them but to the rulers of other kingdoms, that these promises were never made. They are not only denied but whoever affirms that they were ever made is liable to heavy and exemplary punishment. The greatest of all evils, and that which has most completely destroyed all hope in the catholics, has been to see with how much readiness the king in his first parliament agreed to confirm all the laws and statutes made against them in the time of the queen. All this without even the least word in their favour: without even saying that he would have liked more time for mature reflection, or words of that kind. In addition to this, new laws and statutes passed in that parliament place a fresh burden on their shoulders, and only aim to increase persecution. Admittedly, the immediate application of these laws was put off, but from parliament the puritans came forth in triumph. These are men renowned for their perversity, and as being most fervent and stubborn in their own views . . . Anyone can understand with the utmost ease the large sorrow and small hope that remained after that time for the unhappy and more than ever afflicted catholics.

Here we can take note of the great malice and cunning with which our enemies have so far proceeded against us. Not content with seeing us in the midst of great persecution and extreme misery, they have goaded us on with threats of even greater evils to come. In this way, they would drive us to abandon all hope of remedy so that with the further assistance of evil means they could the better justify before the world the unlimited persecution which was already taking place, and which, as we shall see, increased every day. Credibly enough, they imagined that one day trampled patience would rise up in fury. This precisely they desired so that they could claim reason and legitimate cause in the eyes of christian princes for this malice and hatred of theirs. At the same time, they took care to make them understand that in fact no persecution was going on in England even when in truth it had never been greater. For this purpose they continually sent out men to spread the idea and maintain this opinion. By sending information to Venice and other parts of Europe they insured that the news-sheets should publish the selfsame thing everywhere. Already they appeared to have persuaded christian rulers that the catholics, who in fact were more hardly pursued and persecuted than ever, really enjoyed peace and rest.★ They strove all the more to this end since they wanted the catholics to conclude that the rest of the christian world would not only fail to sympathize with them in their afflictions but would do nothing to bring about a remedy. In their disillusion they would begin to think how they could find their own remedy for their woes.

Those who speak more discerningly about these recent disturbances in England think that the deception of foreign rulers in this way was one of the principal causes which goaded on those gentlemen to extremes. For it was this which led to catholics losing all hope of being assisted at least by the charity and fellow-feeling of members of their own persuasion. This drove the spur into their flanks, and made them rush headlong down the furious course of their outlandish plot. They now thought to open up a road to new hope by putting a mine under king and nobility together. This amounted to open rebellion against those who, as they realized, had determined to root up the catholic faith root and branch through the harshest kind of persecution. There was no prince or potentate to offer assistance since they were otherwise occupied and pre-occupied, and in any case deceived in the manner indicated. As part of their plan, the plotters decided to enthrone one of the king's sons, whom they would take care to bring up as a catholic. Doubtless, they would never have embarked on such a course if they had been persuaded that christian rulers would take pity on them and the catholic church in their country, and offer their mediation with the king to remedy their evils and help their church. Instead the princes were taken in by false reportage, and thought that either there was no need of any such thing, or at least not that extreme need which in fact existed. This will become clear in the next chapter.

★ See W. K. Jordan, *The Development of Religious Toleration in England, 1603–40*, London, 1936, pp. 66–9; S. R. Gardiner, *What Gunpowder Plot was*, London, 1897, pp. 157–8.

TWO

EVEN THOSE WHO POSSESS only average knowledge of the present state of England know that the most fervent and most stubborn of all the new sects which now prevail in that kingdom are called puritans. They often differ in little or nothing from those who are commonly called protestants or calvinists. Nevertheless, on account of the incredible hatred they bear for the Catholic and Roman Church, they are regarded more than the others as the capital enemies of catholics and of all the rites and ceremonies which they use in divine service. For this reason they burn with desire to uproot completely ecclesiastical hierarchy, and to introduce in its place a popular form of government, or rather confusion, as they have it in Geneva, Scotland and other places where they have already introduced it. They have already tried to do as much in England on several occasions but without success. The violence of their unquiet spirit makes them odious to the rest of the kingdom. They are especially feared by the bishops, whose total extermination they go proclaiming through every street and thoroughfare. They hope to extinguish with them the appearances of tradition and the image of the Catholic Church which, alone among the lands pestered by these new sects, remain in the clergy and form of government in England. In order to beat down catholicism and eradicate its profession, the chief commission was given to them right at the beginning of the king's reign to persecute the catholics.

The puritans were well aware that they were neither welcome to the king nor acceptable to the state. On the contrary, by reason of their frequent rebellions and turbulent way of proceeding against him in Scotland, the king hated them above every other sort of men.

He himself admitted this, and still admits it. All the same, in order to increase our miseries and afflictions, they were set above us like overseers in Egypt, being men without pity or feeling in our regard, full of rancour and intent only on our destruction.

The puritans then, accepted with the utmost willingness the labour of our persecution. This was not only to satisfy furious zeal but because they were persuaded that, once they had conquered us, it would be no great matter for them to achieve the final victory in their designs against the protestants and bishops. These they consider inferior to themselves both in doctrine and in their manner of persuading the people, through the ordinary channels of teaching, so different from the methods of the sects. They well know that there is no other way of overcoming the catholics except by harrying them out of the land by persecution, and driving them on before them. They know that their doctrine is well founded and their constancy beyond reproach. Only the catholics can put up an adequate resistance to them since their methods alone of teaching and persuading are sufficiently effective. Among the protestants there are those who foresee and fear precisely this. For which reason they could well be content to see the catholics still on their feet, but in such a way that their numbers do not become excessive, which would happen if they were allowed too much liberty. But certainly persecution should not be so violent as to extinguish them altogether. Rather should they remain as a counterbalance and first line of defence against the fury of the puritans. However, the sectaries, generally speaking, are afraid that the catholic faith will one day prevail to the loss of puritans and protestants alike. At the same time, there are some individuals who now govern the kingdom whose hatred for us is so implacable that, provided the evil which they desire against us prevails, they are not much worried for the rest what progress the puritans make. Even less, perhaps, since they are considered to favour in their secret hearts the opinions and intentions of the puritans.★

★ For names of influential puritans, and their weight with the king and Privy Council about this time, see Patrick Collinson, *The Elizabethan Puritan Movement*, London, 1967, pp. 443–67. R. Cecil's public views on religious matters were given clearly enough in his letter to Cambridge University of December 1604 (HMC, Sal. Cal., XVI, pp. 389–91).

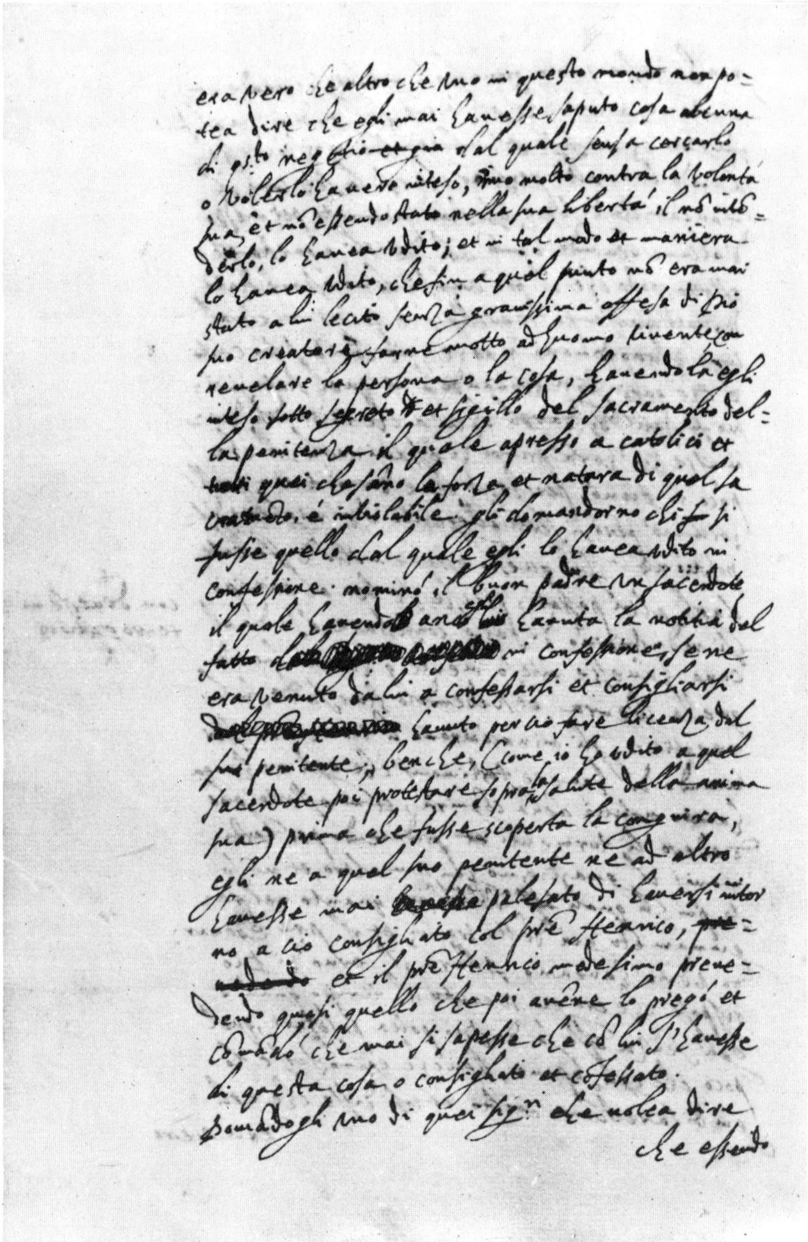
era vero che altro che uno in questo mondo non po=
tea dire che egli mai havesse saputo cosa alcuna
di qsto negotio et gia dal quale senza cercarlo
o volerlo havendo inteso, anzi molto contra la volontà
sua, et no essendo stato nella sua libertà il no inte=
derlo, lo havea udito; et in tal modo et maniera
lo havea udito, che fin a quel punto no era mai
stato a lui lecito senza gravissima offesa di Dio
suo creatore farne motto ad huomo vivente con
revelare la persona o la cosa, havendola egli
inteso sotto secreto et sigillo del sacramento del=
la penitenza il quale apresso a catolici et
tutti quei che sanno la forza et natura di quel sa
cramento, è inviolabile. gli domandorno chi si
fusse quello dal quale egli lo havea udito in
confessione. nominò il buon padre un sacerdote
il quale havendo [illegible] havuta la notitia del
fatto d[illegible] in confessione, se ne
era venuto da lui a confessarsi et consigliarsi
[illegible] havuto per cio sue licenza dal
suo penitente, benche, come io ho udito a quel
sacerdote poi protestare sopra la salute della anima
sua, prima che fusse scoperta la congiura,
egli ne a quel suo penitente ne ad altro
havesse mai [illegible] palesato di haversi intor
no a cio consigliato col pre Henrico, [illegible]
[illegible] et il pre Henrico medesimo preve=
dendo quasi quello che poi avvene lo pregò et
comandò che mai si sapesse che co lui si havesse
di questa cosa o consigliato et confessato.
domandogli uno di quei sig.ri che volea dire
che essendo

FROM THE GREENWAY NARRATIVE

As we saw above, to these furies and professed enemies of ours, full authority and commission against us was given from the very beginning. From people of this kind the first parliament was formed. In this the laws of Elizabeth were confirmed and new ones passed. And these same puritans were the people who applied them with all rigour. Nor could better instruments than these have been found for our destruction. Indeed, for anything else they were considered useless, and even for this particular purpose clumsy enough. So they were given someone to direct them. From him they could get their venom as from its source. With it they could infect the rest of the kingdom, and poison us. The man was John Popham.* He was the Lord Chief Justice of England, member of His Majesty's Privy Council, and a man inordinately cruel and implacable where catholics were concerned. He was himself a puritan, and had been a renowned persecutor for many years before the queen died. Indeed, he had been among the foremost of those who tried to procure the death of the Queen of Scots. Please note, I say, that it was to him that the principal care and charge was given of instituting and maintaining the campaign against the catholics.

For many years now, Popham had had at his disposal men from every county in England hand-picked and practised in persecution. Once this was restarted, these men were despatched by him through the whole kingdom to carry out the with utmost rigour and cruelty the penalties imposed by laws both ancient and modern. Fully armed and bearing the authority of the first judge in the land, and supported by the law, they perpetrated wellnigh incredible acts of rapine, violence and thievery. They inflicted serious injuries to say nothing of gross indignities, and all in the shortest possible time. They did far more than the laws allowed, but certainly not more than the legislators intended, as was shown quite clearly when they began to hear the complaints arising from these

---

* Sir John Popham (1531?–1607). Educated at Balliol and the Middle Temple. Privy Councillor, 1571; Solicitor-General, 1579; Speaker of the House of Commons, 1580; Attorney-General, 1581; Lord Chief Justice, 1592; in which year he was knighted. See DNB. According to *Aubrey's Brief Lives* (O. L. Dick edition, London, 1968, p. [245]), 'He for several years addicted himself but little to the study of the laws, but profligate company, and was wont to take a purse with them'.

inflictions. The authors of them, instead of being punished, remained at the side of the magistrates with all the honour due to men
worthy of such office, and as instruments apt for the purpose intended. But we cannot complain much of these excesses committed
against us contrary to law since the laws themselves virtually left a
loophole for their cruelty. When excesses were brought to light
which could cause us even more grief and hardship they were immediately established as laws in the next parliament. They were no
longer considered excesses but measures to be put in practice for the
future as perfectly just and normal measures. In case it should seem
to some that we are trying to exaggerate our persecution, or magnify
even more with words the great deal that could be written at this
point, I will note down a few things baldly by way of example. The
reader can then see to what proportions the persecution grew in a
short time, and what hope there was of any amelioration of a situation which went from bad to worse until the discovery of these most
recent troubles. He will understand the desperation to which the
catholics were reduced by the violence of the law, or at least the
desperate state to which those gentlemen who were the authors of
the latest disturbances felt themselves to be reduced.*

Already in the queen's time there were laws imposing fines. Anyone who refused to attend the protestant churches had to pay
a £20 fine for every month's absence. In order to increase the
revenue, they considered it expedient to have 13 months in the
year, taking every month as four weeks . . . Some did not find this
sum too burdensome to pay. Others were reduced by it practically
to poverty. The catholics appealed to the king as soon as he took
possession of his new kingdom to be so good as to lift this weight
from them, and forgive them their debt. The king told them that
they would not need to pay until they received further orders; or
as some say, His Majesty was simply pleased to accede to their
request. The catholics derived great consolation from this, hoping
that it would be the fair beginning of other favours which His
Majesty might wish to show them. Before much time had passed,
however, not only was the sum legally due from them demanded

---

* For the state of persecution in England on the eve of the plot, see P. Caraman, S.J., *Henry Garnet* . . ., London, 1964, pp. 312–17; also Roland Mathias,
Whitsun Riot, London, 1963, pp. 91–110.

but also all arrears. And many who in the queen's time by various devices had escaped that penalty, and had revealed themselves openly as men sure of their future, now found themselves cut off by the returning tide and in infinite difficulties. For where they might with ease have been able to pay the said sum from year to year they could not now pay it, as they were obliged to do, together with the arrears. Nor did it help to bring up the promise made to them, or to represent the difficulties and virtual impossibility of this demand in order that the sum might be reduced, or that they might at least be allowed time and term convenient in which to pay it. They had to pay the whole sum, and immediately.★

This decision of king and council was promulgated everywhere without delay. The consternation of the catholics was only outmatched by the jubilation and rejoicing of the calvinists. These hoped that this was but the beginning of persecution; and in the event it was. For at the same time, they began to apply with the utmost rigour that other law by which those who did not pay their £20 a month lost two-thirds of their property and all their chattels. To further this, men were sent off through the whole kingdom secretly to get information on the estates and possession of every catholic, what cattle or other goods they possessed, what they had on their land and in their own homes. When that was done, they reported all to the county magistrates, and in detail. From these they received order and authority to execute the law. They not only confiscated the two-thirds of their estate, but led off their cattle and sheep. From their houses they took household goods and even things necessary for life itself. They might even snatch the very meat from the larder, which was all that the recusants and their families might have to eat. They became so greedy for prey that when they found cattle grazing on the pastures and farms of catholics, even if it belonged to friends and relatives of catholics, or even to others, they took it along with them on the pretext that in fact it belonged to catholics. From this there arose great disorder and apprehension everywhere . . .

★ Greenway seems to be the main authority for the fact that arrears of fines were demanded: See DJ, p. 23. But such a course was surely envisaged in Popham's letter to the Privy Council of 8 November 1604 (see HMC, Sal. Cal., XVI, pp. 349, 350).

Persecution begun in this way was like kindled fire growing more intense with every day that passed, and spreading all about. It arose from the watchfulness of many who whispered in the ears of king and council at court. It was chiefly due to the covetousness of so many famished men who at that time surrounded the king in his court; poor and needy men having nothing of their own to live by, but none the less trying to live according to the large and lavish expenses of the royal household. They had already spent what they had managed to get together by various means at the king's first entry. They now ran to him for new handouts. But their needs were great, and their numbers enormous. The national treasury and royal income could scarcely suffice for their necessities, thanks to the money they squandered on their high living. But for all that, either because they had come with His Majesty from Scotland, or for other services rendered, he could scarcely refuse to help them in some way. They were told to look about the kingdom, and see how they could help themselves. Finally they decided that there was no better way of feeding themselves than from the goods and assets of the catholics. Hence the practice arose that three or four catholics might be given to some as their prey, to others five or six, and so from hand to hand. Nor was there a catholic in the whole kingdom whose value they did not discover in a very short time, either to devour in a moment as much as he possessed, or to compound with him in such a way that little enough remained for his own maintenance and that of his wife and children. Those thought themselves happy who were able to contrive it so that they were given in prey to their friends, or to someone who still possessed a spark of decency and humanity. Such was the marauding avarice of these people that, not content with having found out how many catholics they could have, they drew also into their nets those whom they thought any way affected towards that religion. They would never leave them alone until they had made a public profession of reformed religion. This so wounded some in their conscience that they still bewail their great misfortune, and will continue to do so. At all events, for their own shame they can learn to sympathize with the harm done to others. How impoverished they were, how far they had fallen from their first estate, how much uneasiness possessed their minds, and how much confusion in their affairs they suffered after all these exactions and extortions many can begin to imagine but few fully comprehend.*

If God in his mercy had not revealed the bloody design of those gentlemen, who had been reduced by this inhuman and barbarous treatment to the last pitch of desperation, the land would have felt the consequences, and especially the authors of this persecution. Many is the time when I reflect to console myself on the examples of ancient times, and what must have been the condition of those outraged and hard-driven saints of the primitive church. What other comfort is there when one contemplates the continuing afflictions and persecutions of every kind which the catholics now suffer in this land? Reading of what they suffered then, I can conclude that the blood-lust of those primitive persecutors was no greater than of these in England now . . . Indeed, it seems to me that the persecution now going on in England is a good deal harsher than that of the primitive church or succeeding ages. For though the number of those killed is less, the evils we suffer are more widespread. Thanks to the incredible thoroughness of our enemies, our persecution extends everywhere and affects everybody. Our woes are such that anyone who understands them properly can see that they are much more prejudicial to the spread of our faith. Indeed, they are worse than death itself. To prove my point I will content myself with one observation. The effect of this persecution can be seen in the common cry of the catholics – well known enough – who, to free themselves from the miseries in which they live, cry out almost with one voice that they would consider it a great benefit to be simply martyred for their faith . . .

It is justly considered by everyone a great evil to live in continual fear. Sometimes the expectation of imminent evil crucifies and torments more than the evil itself when actually present. In this way, the catholics of England are of all men most miserable since there is scarcely one hour of the day or night in which they are not subject to the continual danger of having their houses besieged and searched by court officials. Also because of the unbelievable barbarities which they use nowadays, and of the great

* Grants of the 'benefits of recusancy' to courtiers and others certainly became common from the end of 1607. (See Docquet Books of the 'Signet Office'; PRO, Index 6802 and 6803).

risk which they run in being found at Mass, or with priests in the house, or having Agnus Deis* found about them, or other items of devotion. All this is worse than death because nothing more than being present at Mass or having a priest in the house involves the death penalty. Possessing even one Agnus Dei can mean life-imprisonment and confiscation of all one's property, movable and immovable. The fear that these sieges and inquisitions bring with them constitute in themselves a most cruel punishment. Because without a moment's warning, for the most part at midnight, when the enemy thinks that the wretched catholics will be safe enough for him to take more easily, they come unexpected to besiege the house and those within. If the house is some distance from town, they first occupy all the approaches so that the inmates can have no warning of what threatens them.

After they have made the occupants prisoner, the searchers proceed to examination the very same morning. First, they ask them if they are catholics, and if they are they send them off as prisoners saying that they went to hear Mass. If at the first knock on the door they do not open to them without delay, they break down the doors with such fury that those within prefer to pay up quickly rather than see themselves pillaged, or witness the carrying out, as the others describe it, of the offices of justice. After this, the pursuivants run with naked sword-blade, like men beside themselves, through the whole house, splintering and breaking down any doors which they find closed or locked. They smash the locks of chests and boxes in their search, as they claim, for church and altar stuff. But for much of the time their intent is to rob, and even kill. They can break up quickly into small groups, and go through all the rooms and doors of the house. If they find the beds empty, they feel the sheets and mattresses in case they are still warm. This they take as a sign that the priest has just left for a hiding-place. They also regard it as proof

* Agnus Dei: small wax ovals made from the remains of the Easter candle in Saint Peter's, blessed by the pope. They bore the emblem of the paschal lamb. An act of 13 Eliz. Cap. 2 (1571) declared, 'whoever shall bring into these realms any Agnus Deis, crosses, pictures or beads, and deliver or offer them to any person to be used . . . incur a praemunire . . .' See *The Penal Laws against Papists* . . ., London, 1723, p. 9. 'Receivers, aiders and maintainers' of priests, 'knowing them to be such', were made guilty of a 'Felony without benefit of clergy', by an act of 27 Eliz. Cap. 2 (1585) (ibid., p. 15).

of this if they find a jug in the room or fire on the hearth, or if no fire, then at least the cinders still warm. If the beds are untidy, or there are other tell-tale signs of the kind, they immediately rush through the whole house searching cellars and basements, sounding and striking the floor for any echo that might reveal a cavity. Likewise they make bore-holes by way of test, so that, if they come up against wood, they may find the places made to hide the priests. If their boring-rods meet with no resistance, it shows that there is some underground compartment used for this purpose. They measure up the walls to see how they meet, and ascertain their thickness. Knocking everywhere with wooden mallets they can tell whether all is solid or whether there is something hollow. They take measurements over the whole house, particularly the fireplaces, so as to find secret recesses intended for priests. They uncover beds and anything else which seems to offer the least clue of what they are searching for. They pull out panels, break up walls, and wreck entire rooms. In a word, in the midst of sound and fury, they turn everything upside down, and leave all in disarray. They pass their sword-blades through the cracks in the walls, or if the walls are panelled, as is the custom in England to beautify the houses and to keep the rooms drier, they run them through with their swords to kill anyone who might by chance be hiding behind them. They do all this with such an attitude of fierce bravado, and with such frightful noise, that it has sometimes happened that ladies have lost their wits for fear. Lady Vavasour, wife of a doctor in York, was an example whom I saw myself. It has sometimes happened that, when priests were hidden in those places, they have only just escaped being transfixed and killed by sword-thrusts.

Our woes do not end even here. If they come across any persons in bed at such times, they are first narrowly examined as to who they are. If they do not belong to the house, or if they are not very well known, if roused by indignities and injuries received they reply with some feeling, they are sent off to prison. The pursuivants take the coverings off the bed, and examine the persons there to see if they have church and devotional objects hidden with them. I know of one lady, a gentlewoman of some importance and of distinguished house, who had the clothes torn from her bed, and her shift torn from her own body, as they grabbed at the crosses and reliquaries she wore round her neck. They sometimes force others to get out of bed without even giving them time to get dressed in order to search the bed at once, and everything else on the spot. If after all these and many other efforts which hatred and malice can suggest they do not find what they are after, namely a priest, they sometimes keep the house in a state of siege for many days, and even weeks. They go on, that is, until they are convinced that he is either dead of hunger or done to death by the sheer discomfort and restrictions of the place where he was hidden; always supposing that he was hidden somewhere to begin with! They can treat a household with unbearable insolence and arrogance, just as if it were a position taken by force from an enemy, and with all the accompaniments of diabolic rage and fury. After all this, they make their departure. But it is only after they have pursued and harried wretched and innocent people, and used up everything in the way of provisions which they found in the house that they finally leave with hatred and disdain. They take with them the master of the house as their prisoner, and books, or anything else which he possessed as a catholic, for a mark of their victory and final triumph.

I would probably be too prolix if I were to add to their proud insolence and violence the foxy cunning and trickery they regularly use to discover priests. I will only note down later one of these sieges and searches, and this an example well known enough. They usually post guards on all the rooms and chambers so that nobody can possibly help a priest if by chance he is hidden. They also lock up the staff of the house all together at the same time in order to make it more certain that no help will come from them. After some time, they let it be known by talking in a voice loud enough to be heard by anyone who should by chance be hidden that they have already made a thorough search. They can find nothing and are now resolved to depart. They then go off making the kind of noise which people usually make at departure. But after a little while one or more of them comes back, and, lightly tapping the wall, he talks to the priest in a low voice, and in friendly tones, telling him that his paternity can now come out seeing that the searchers by God's mercy have finally gone off, and the house is now free of them. Many priests have learnt to their cost to be silent in similar instances, and to wait for more reliable signs. If the priest does not reply to these words, they remain in the room but very quietly. They listen carefully for any shuffling of feet coming from anywhere, or any signs of shifting round, or for breathing or sighing, or indeed any other sound or movement indicating human presence. Observing this kind of care, they have succeeded in capturing not a few. Among them was that great saint and servant of God, John Cornelius . . .* But it cannot be seen otherwise than coming from the hand and protection of God that in spite of so much diligence, very few of the great number of priests at large have been captured.

This was the stage at which persecution had arrived shortly after the king's accession. Many held the view that it could hardly increase: not because the enemy was sated with our afflictions, or lacked the will to do us more harm, but simply because it did not seem possible that he could find further means to afflict us. Even if it were possible to add to the sum total of our miseries it seemed that the king would not have allowed it, either because he would not wish to drive us to the ultimate in desperation, or else to avoid the extermination of a large number of his subjects. All the more, because as far as the vast majority of the catholics were concerned they had not entirely given up hope of the king. They allowed themselves to believe that not everything he did in public was done with his consent or by his will. Nevertheless, they gradually became disillusioned, and clear enough as to what they could expect from him in the future . . .

The king himself was, it could be said, the author of the harshest law that up to this time had been passed against us. This blow, coming from the king's own hand, was the most grievous possible, since it carried with it all the weight of supreme power in the arm of the king himself. I will therefore dilate somewhat on this point, even at the possible risk of exceeding what the brevity of this work requires. We must remember that the controversy between protestants and puritans concerning ecclesiastical government and hierarchy began to forge ahead. The people themselves remained in some doubt as to which of the two parties they should follow. This

* John Cornelius, born at Bodmin, 1557, of Irish parents. Studied at Oxford, Rheims and Rome. Returned to England as a priest in 1583. Seized at Chideock Castle, Dorset, in April 1594. Executed at Dorchester on 4 July 1594, with three others. (See HFR, vii, part I, p. 170 and iii, pp. 435 et seq.)

dissension led to some strengthening of the catholics since the controversy made it clear that the protestants had no other means of defending themselves against the puritans than the catholics had, who used the same argument against them, namely, tradition, the consensus of the Fathers, and the majesty and authority of Holy Church. Furthermore, the wiser heads noticed on the occasion of this controversy that among the catholics there had always been the utmost agreement in matters of religion, and also in their obedience to their supreme head, and his overall jurisdiction. They had to admit that this made its influence felt among the body and members of the church. It also affected the members in their relations with one another. They saw that all the bishops were subject to the pope without contradiction, the clergy subject to the bishops, and among the clergy, those inferior to those superior in an admirable order of precedence. On the other hand, they saw themselves liable to a double source of harm: first there was the division which was widening among them as a result of this controversy; and second, there was the growth of catholicism which also had this for its cause. A number of books were published written on one side or the other. The protestants showed themselves more keenly aware of the dilemma; and with reason, because they were already in possession of church property belonging to bishoprics and prelacies. But they went on wasting a great deal of time while they exhorted the puritans to perfect peace so that, living with them in fraternal charity, they could unite their forces to batter the common enemy, the papists. The puritans on their side cared nothing for the empty titles of bishops and prelates, as they regarded them, but they were very eager to share in the goods and income of the church. They exhorted the protestants to divide their possessions with them, sharing out what they had seized as their own. They all of them looked only for the progress of the Gospel, and the eradication of all papists from the face of the earth. And these, thanks to the avarice and ambition of their rivals, were growing in all directions.

And now to decide, or at least diminish, this controversy since it was prejudicial to both sides, and to pacify them as far as they could, the king was pleased that, in 1604, there should be a dispute or conference in his presence. He was to be the head of the church equally in matters temporal as in those strictly ecclesiastical, and would act as judge or moderator. The most important of the bishops were present at the conference on the protestant side, while the puritans chose a number of representatives esteemed among themselves as more sufficient and learned. It was something which the catholics had begged with great urgency for many years to be granted them as a special grace and favour, but in vain. This conference lasted several days. In the end the bishops prevailed; that is, the protestant party. But because it seems that in this land nothing can happen without doing harm to the catholics, God was pleased to allow that in this conference a beginning should be made, or more correctly a perfect consummation, of all our miseries. Acting in unison, our enemies agreed among themselves on the ultimate destruction of catholicism as far as human malice and human contrivance could bring it about.*

When the dispute was over, to prevent the puritans from departing altogether disconsolate, the king thought fit to reveal his feelings for us. He told them this in no uncertain terms. Indeed he flayed us beyond measure, and in words so full of bitterness that they would scarcely be believed by any who read them. For this and other reasons I will not give them here. Suffice it to say that he pronounced so emphatically and virulently against the catholic religion that no one could any longer suppose that he intended to show it the least favour of any kind. He protested to the parliament most vehemently that he would take it as an extreme insult if anyone imagined that either then or at any time in the past he had entertained the slightest intention of tolerating those who professed that belief. Along with much else he said, 'I know that some scoundrels to my shame wish to make me out as one who favours the papists.' With this beginning his address proceeded to class the catholics in three categories. He exhorted his bishops, reprehending them for past negligence, to make diligent inquisition about papists. The bishops must see to the severe and exact punishment of every catholic according to the rules laid down by every law ancient and modern. These words dug spurs into the steed he was coursing, and gave unbounded delight to bishops and puritans alike.

* Hampton Court Conference: Greenway erroneously gives the date as 1605 (f. 21v.). See J. R. Tanner, op. cit., pp. 61–9. D. H. Willson, op. cit., pp. 202–9. *Et alibi*.

One group of papists, said the king, consisted of those who refused to make their communion, but did not refuse to come to the churches or hear sermons. A second category refused to come to church at all during the times of public services, although they were content to hear the sermons. The third kind were those who refused in any degree whatsoever to have anything to do with others. For this reason they were given the nickname 'recusants'. In fact, it is this last kind who are alone called and considered to be catholics in England. The others are called 'schismatics'. In order to escape persecution the latter accommodate themselves at least at times to what is demanded in exterior actions. Against these, the king said, they would need to use particular and extraordinary diligence. However, it was especially necessary to have one's eye on the others, and let the law against them take its course. The lord chancellor was present during the king's discourse. In order to make it clear that he agreed with the king, and to increase his own credit with him, he added that, to afflict the papists, and by their affliction make them 'know themselves', nothing would serve better than to put in execution with all rigour and diligence the ordinary processes of law against excommunicates (*de excommunicato capiendo*). The force of this suggestion was immediately understood. Many times they had discussed the possibility of imposing this yoke on the catholics, but because it was so heavy and unbearable they had not for many reasons till that day thought of it seriously. The late queen, especially, although for the most part she was extremely hostile to catholics, would never hear a word of it. But as it says in the book published about the conference, of which I spoke above, and which was printed immediately afterwards and distributed everywhere, the king, without further answer, immediately agreed to this proposal. He further expressed his wish that it should be carried out without delay.

Who could adequately estimate the great increase in the persecution of catholics due to this one provision alone? In consequence, they were no longer able to make their wills or dispose of their goods. The effect of this law was to make them outlaws and exiles; and like such they were treated. There was no longer any obligation to pay them their debts or rents for land held from them. They could not now go to law or have the law's protection. They could seek no remedy for ills and injuries received. In a word, they were considered and treated as professed enemies of the state. They were handled worse than slaves. It was further decided that officials who dragged their feet, or failed to carry out the full force of the law, should be punished. All this was a spur to those who wished us no harm, but it was quite unnecessary for the puritans who already desired nothing so much as our total ruin. To the cruelty of the law we could add the 114 canons drawn up on purpose in the same conference, and confirmed and established by the bishops, to bring about our final destruction. We can see that our persecution grew incomparably greater than it had ever been up to that day, even when the queen raged against us causing so many deaths and martyrdoms.

Because of this, the catholics finally persuaded themselves that the bitter and vituperative invective which the king used at all times, but especially in time of recreation and eating, proceeded from a mind fully confirmed in hatred. As for the invective, I could put down many things here as they were recounted by those who heard them from the king's own mouth, and who go on retailing them with special pleasure and satisfaction thanks to the little love, or rather great hatred, which they bear us. I will content myself, however, with giving two examples here which cannot be doubted. They make abundantly clear the state of the King's mind about us at that time. Both examples are printed in the book entitled, *The Late Commotion of certaine Papists in Herefordshire*,* printed at London for I. Chorlton and F. Burton. The first of these incidents took place on 5 August 1605. Dr Bancroft, who was then Bishop of London and is now Archbishop of Canterbury, gave a sermon at Saint Paul's Cross. He told the people of a certain protestation made by the king before God and His angels. It was that His Majesty claimed to be so resolute in maintaining the religion professed publicly at that time in England that in order to defend it he would not only pour out the last drop of blood in his body but also give up all his estates and kingdoms. He would do this even if they were ten times larger than they were. The king further prayed God that, if His Divine Majesty

---

* A comprehensive bibliography, which includes the book mentioned by Greenway, is given in Mathias, op. cit., pp. 139–43. This book is a detailed study of the Herefordshire incident.

foresaw that one of his own sons would in time adopt another religion, he would be taken from the world so that their common shame could be buried with him. These words, as the author of the book asserts, were aimed by the king principally against the papists. He meant to take from them any vain and foolish hope or persuasion which they might have of any mitigation of the law, or toleration for their religion.

The other example is a discourse made by the Lord Chancellor a little before the bishop's sermon.* It was delivered in the Star Chamber, a place in London well known enough. It was on Thursday, 20 June, the same year, in the presence of the justices of the land and of the nobility and leading gentlemen. They usually assemble at that time and place before leaving London, the judges to go on circuit and the rest to return home. The Lord Chancellor spoke, as it were, with the mouth of the king and by his order. He mingled his words with threats most effectively. Egerton now made an extremely sharp attack on catholics generally, and especially on the jesuits and other priests, and on anyone else who recognized the authority of the Roman Pontiff. He issued a strict command in the name of His Majesty that all the justices in their circuit, the justices of peace in the places of their jurisdiction, the lords and gentlemen on their manors and estates, and the rest of the people wherever they were, should make diligent inquisition to seek out these people. They could then be punished as they deserved. He added further that it was the king's express wish to rouse the people, then in a state of torpor, and they should see to it that this decree of his was carefully observed. A new and extraordinary penalty was added. Any justice of the peace . . . who showed that he favoured or be-friended papists, or was considered to do so, or whose wife, sons or

---

* Thomas Egerton: born about 1540, died 1617, the year following his creation as Viscount Brackley. Following a legal career, he was appointed Attorney-General in 1592, and knighted in 1593. In July 1603, he was created Baron Ellesmere and began to function as Lord Chancellor. According to DNB, (XVII, p. 162, col. 1), 'Ellesmere proved subservient to James . . . On February 9, 1604/5, he expressed resentment at a petition from Northampton-shire demanding the restitution of deprived puritan ministers, and obtained from the Star Chamber a declaration that the deprivation was lawful, and the presentation of the petition unlawful. Three days later he directed the judges to enforce the penal laws against the catholics . . .'

servants were papists, even if he professed the contrary religion himself, should be deprived of office as a man unworthy of his place.

After speaking at length to this effect, the Lord Chancellor ended with the same point which the bishop was to make later in his sermon. We have referred to it above. This was that the catholics hoped in vain if they thought that the laws made against them would be mitigated. He added to this, as the book said, a speech of the king's on the subject of the foolishness of the papists who without rhyme or reason of any kind had allowed themselves to imagine that nothing of the sort would ever proceed from him. He said further that His Majesty had made a vow in the presence of his royal council that if it came to his knowledge that any of his children had it in mind to adopt that religion he would pronounce his curse upon them in the very same instant. The catholics were no longer surprised at these or similar words coming from the king.

It was now normal for the king at meal times, especially when he found himself near someone who gave him an opportunity to talk against the catholics, to let fall from his mouth what they were waiting for. A certain Montague, Dean of the Chapel Royal, now supplies this prompting for the most part.* Although he was formerly a puritan, he is now ready, nevertheless, to adapt himself to protestant ceremonies rather than lose a position which brings him so much honour and reward. Our enemies make considerable use of him since he has easy access to the king almost whenever he wishes, and can suggest to him whatever he pleases. His method is to carry some catholic author with him in his breast pocket with the page marked. He then begins to talk about religion – the usual subject of the king's conversation at table. Montague then emphasizes to the king some point of controversy which displeases him. For the most part, his friends see to it that it is about some aspect of the pope's jurisdiction

---

* James Montagu or Montague: 1568(?)–1618. Educated at Cambridge, and later Master of Sidney Sussex College. In 1603 he was Dean of Lichfield, and in 1604 of Worcester. Subsequently he became Dean of the Chapel Royal, and in 1608 he was made Bishop of Bath and Wells. He edited and translated the works of James I published in English in 1616. Translated to Winchester on 4 October this year. Died at Greenwich. See DNB. Also Francis Godwin, *De Praesulibus Angliae Commentarius . . .*, Cambridge, 1743, pp. 390–1; J. Le Neve, *Fasti Ecclesiae Anglicanae*, vol. I, Oxford, 1854, p. 145.

in church affairs, and the superiority of his power in some matters above that of princes. They know very well that teaching of this kind is anathema to the king. Hence it arises that, after the discussion begins, his excitement grows gradually, and at last ends in rage. He will then speak with so much vehemence against the teachings of our faith, and in particular against the pope, that anyone unacquainted with his customs and manners would be dumbfounded. In these moods of exaltation he will talk slander and vituperation against his catholic subjects. The same persons who saw to it that he would be led on to this also make his sayings public. In this way, they come to diminish the reverence, the respect, to say nothing of the love, that the subject should feel for his prince. The object of those people who are so ready to goad the king to words of this kind is precisely that afterwards they may spread them abroad. So they kindle and fan the flame of mutual hatred.

The people who do this also intend that their adversaries should be reduced to desperation. Instead of using restraint and patience, they will have recourse to foolhardiness and anger, and in this way hasten their own destruction. Thus we know for certain how that most wretched and miserable plot came about of which we shall speak. Those gentlemen heard from day to day how the king grew more incensed against the catholics, and the sort of language he used against them at all times and in all places. In particular, he was used to calling them traitors. This is a name which is hated in England more than anything else, and more, perhaps, than in other lands. This was for no other reason than the profession of their religion. Indeed, the king would often end his talk by saying that anyone who knew what was due to his native country and still believed in the articles of faith of the Roman Church could not be a loyal subject. On the contrary, he must be a traitor and an enemy to his prince. I am well aware that there are some who will scarcely believe that the king would use such biting words, which must seriously prejudice and touch to the quick so many catholics who for long years have made themselves known to the world for patience and fidelity. Therefore, in order to make my words credible, and that readers may see and sympathize with our miseries, I consider myself obliged to confirm what I have said by one example chosen from many that proves the point in detail.

FROM THE ARMADA TO THE GUNPOWDER PLOT

The Attorney-General was Sir Edward Coke,★ a man known and esteemed more than most for his knowledge of the common law. After the king's accession, he wrote a book in which he troubled himself to prove that all catholics and recusants in the land were traitors, people guilty of *lèse-majesté*. To prove his point, he gave an account of the various laws and statutes of this country. Apart from the incredible malice, falsehood and errors to which he resorts in this book, he clearly shows how great is his hatred and malevolence for us. Or perhaps one should say how filled and blinded he is by his ambition and avarice, for in fact he cares little about any religion. With profound hypocrisy and dissimulation, he shows himself a great zealot for that sect which he knows pleases the king, but for which, otherwise, he cares little enough. This man presented his book to the king. James not only accepted it with gratitude – he showed this by the dignities and honours which he conferred on Coke – but went on to sing great praises for the theme of the book, its argumentation, and the doctrine it contained. In the presence of many of the leading men of the realm and others, the king confirmed with an oath that he was already convinced in his innermost being that all the catholics were traitors. This had been demonstrated in that book with very sufficient and manifest proofs. These words were received with applause; for so the words of princes are usually received. But not a few of the bystanders were displeased, who were well aware of the innocence of the catholics and their admirable patience up to that time.

That patience would have continued to the present moment if they had not been deceived by the crafty ways of the Attorney and his accomplices who were men like himself; and also if the king himself had not been deceived, and those poor gentlemen reduced to extremity and the last pitch of desperation. But apart from what

★ Sir Edward Coke: 1552–1634. Protégé of Lord Burghley, he became Solicitor-General in 1592, Speaker of the House of Commons in 1593, Attorney-General in 1594, and Chief Justice of the King's Bench, 1613. He was dismissed from the latter office in 1616. He was an able lawyer but vindictive and unscrupulous. According to Aubrey (op. cit., p. [68]) 'He will play with his case as a cat would with a mouse, and be so fulsomely pedantic that a schoolboy would nauseate it'. The work referred to seems to have been the fifth of his law reports (a series which began for the year 1572 (14 Eliz.)), since R. Persons, S.J., wrote an answer to it in 1606 (see STC, p. (121); WTL, I pp. 453-4).

has been said above, that book had another object in view, even more pernicious and more immediate. This was that, having first poisoned the mind of the king with false information and filled him with dark suspicions and consequent hatred of the catholics, it would be easy to introduce and pass legislation in the next parliament which our enemies had already drawn up and decided on among themselves. If it were needed, they could propose yet further laws of their own devising. In the second place, the estates of the realm would understand that, since the king himself approved of that book and held us to be such as the attorney described, all would now be eager to persecute us with the utmost cruelty of which they were capable by law. On the other hand, no one would dare to defend us knowing well the prejudice which that book had stirred up in the mind of the king against us. In consequence they would know the danger to which such a defence would expose them.

This, in the event, was another great spur and sufficient motive to move those gentlemen to that unhappy plot. They saw themselves already classed as traitors when they were in fact innocent. Indeed, they were already being punished as such. Hence they could not but be moved by the humiliation of so much injustice, as well as by the misery to which the malice and insatiable hatred of the enemies had reduced them. So they resolved at one and the same time to avenge themselves of all their enemies, and to free themselves from the evils which hung over them in the forthcoming parliament. All the more, because they felt that they could do nothing to worsen the state in which they then found themselves since they were already considered as traitors by the king and by those who held sway in the kingdom. . . . Their principal intention, in fact, was, as they protested when they came to die, to liberate the land from its gruelling slavery and to set at liberty all those people who, partly because of the savagery of the law, did not dare to raise their eyes to see the light of true christian doctrine; but partly because having seen it and known it they did not dare to confess it for fear of persecution.

But it is not my business here to praise any part of the intention which they may have had; and much less to excuse the deed. I will only say that the crafty contrivance of those who for self-interest, or hatred of their fellow men forced them to desperate measures, involved hazard to the state, peril for the ruler, and no little loss to the contrivers themselves . . . Did those who had been at the helm for so many years in this land of ours become a little too sure of our infinite patience . . .? Did it never occur to them that they might find some catholics among us who felt inclined to depart from the example of the rest, or from the doctrine received and practised by the vast majority . . .?

To finish this chapter, I only wish to remind our enemies that the common opinion which they and nearly everybody in the country had of us before this latest happening was the same, namely that in every adversity we showed great patience and humility . . . Finally, let them remember, that out of so many thousands of patient catholics, they have only found a few exceptions in all these years. Nevertheless, these few, out of resentment, have made very clear to the world how heavy and insupportable is the yoke which we all bear in this most cruel and inhuman persecution. Scarcely affected among those who know anything is the opinion of our innocence and the justice of the cause for which we suffer.

THREE

FROM WHAT HAS BEEN SAID, it will be clear at this point to everyone that the catholics in England had arrived at the nadir of their miseries. There was no more hope for them. Not from the king, who had forgotten his promises and changed his mind now he was secure in his new kingdom. He showed himself rather their open enemy, and the enemy of their beliefs. Nor could any hope be placed in the rest of those who governed and controlled the state since they were the selfsame men who in the time of the queen had begun, nurtured and continued the persecution. And now, finding the king so easily persuaded to harm catholics, or more exactly, so ready to persecute them, his ministers made every effort to bring the persecution to perfection. First, they got the king to pronounce catholics traitors by word of mouth. They were then referred to as such in printed books which branded and proclaimed and held them up for all in the kingdom to gape at. Adrift on such a sea of miseries, what else could have been in the mind of those afflicted and every way discomfited catholics if not the expectation that every day some new burden would be added: a further increment to the weight under which they already groaned. Certainly, the enemy continued to threaten. Experience of what they had already suffered led them to expect the exact and pitiless execution of past laws made against them . . .

The assault on their morale, which was launched against them after the death of Elizabeth, had recourse to even more violence. It was like a second persecution. But it still left the majority resolved to achieve their end with the help of patience and christian humility:

that end being a heavenly country and eternal glory . . . The attitude of the majority of catholics, and up to a point even of all, is something very obvious to anyone who remembers the great fervour which they show in spiritual matters, that is, in their recourse to the sacraments, their continued prayers in perfect resignation of their wills to the will of God. All the time they encouraged one another to expect relief from Divine Providence alone as they waited on God with true patience and fortitude, and painfully made their way through those hard times. They urged and exhorted one another so that by good example and decency they would find a way of softening the hardness in the hearts of their enemies. The worst of these were in the parliament which all were waiting for. These were the puritans. It seemed that they were elected on purpose in order to cut off every approach offering hope to catholics . . .

It is cause for wonder that there should have been for so many years and in the midst of so savage a persecution such admirable perseverance and endurance, so much patience, so much acceptance, so much dogged obedience in a nation as free-spirited as ours, and containing so many great-hearted men . . .

But to return to the story we are trying to tell. The unhappy state of affairs weighed on the minds of a few – and as we shall see there were indeed only a few. Kindled within them was a just desire, as it seemed to them, of retribution. They burned to liberate themselves and their friends from this cruel servitude and oppression. But at last they found a remedy for these evils which was no less lacking in pity and humanity than the very authors of such evil. Led by anger and desperation, they decided to open a way to new and better hopes by the utter destruction of their adversaries. They saw themselves abandoned by christian powers and potentates in the peace which they had all concluded with the new King of England. They realized finally that by false information their misery was neither known nor believed . . . They saw now that methods of open violence were unleashed against themselves so that their reasonable desires could never be fulfilled.

Not only was all government now in the hands of the enemy, but its vigilance was so great that they would have been prevented even in the first steps made to help themselves some other way. Even if they had kept their secret, not all catholics would have been of the same mind since, as has been said, the majority proceeded according to other principles and lived by other tenets. But even if the rest had found the will to unite, they would not have found a leader for their cause. Even if they had found a leader, it could not be doubted that the puritans and the protestants united against them with the forces of the king would have been superior. Because of this, and for other reasons as far as we can guess them, or more exactly, as far as they confessed them after their plot was discovered, the conspirators decided to use artifice and secrecy to carry out by means of a few what the many could not achieve. So that the reader may be fully satisfied of my accuracy in this story, I want him to know that what I say here will either be taken from the confessions made by them and put in print, or else came most reliably from themselves before they died and while they were still in the country. I have had good means of finding out all.

Mr Robert Catesby was a gentleman of good family, indeed, of a house ancient and illustrious, rich and influential. He was some thirty-four years old at the time of the plot, and was loved and esteemed not only by catholics but by the very protestants for his many unusual qualities both physical and mental.* This gentleman it was who decided after much reflection to gather together all the enemies of the catholic religion in England and get rid of them in one single blow. Liberty and religion would then be restored to catholics with no resistance. To carry out this resolve, the best way seemed to him to await the reassembly of parliament, when the three estates of the realm would all be together with the king,

---

* The writer's estimate of most of the powder-plotters is decidedly optimistic. Sir William Parker, Robert Catesby and Francis Tresham were all fined and reserved to 'her Majesty's use' after backing the wrong side in the Essex rising of February 1601 (see EGF, chapter 3, especially p. 46). Catesby himself, far from being wealthy, was obliged to sell his Chastleton estate to cover his 4,000 mark fine. He had inherited it from his grandmother in 1593. As far as religion went, he married Catherine Leigh, a Protestant; and a child, Robert, was on record in the parish register of Chastleton, as being baptized in the parish church on 11 November 1595 (DJ, p. 30). Francis Tresham, his cousin, remarked of him to his father, Sir Thomas Tresham, at Whitsun 1605, 'I was with my cousin Catesby this morning, who promiseth money tomorrow to pay the interest, but you know his promises' (HMC, Various, III, p. 148). In the translator's view, Catesby's role was that of an agent-provocateur, second-in-command to Thomas Percy.

councillors, puritans and bishops. These were all of them determined that in that time and place they would give the final death blow to the catholic cause, as we have said. In that same moment of time, the plotters hoped to bring upon their heads the evil they had designed for others. They would blow them up with a mine, and the Parliament-house along with them. In this way, the authors of those most cruel laws would be removed along with the memory of the very place where they had been made. By this means he also thought that no leader would be left to oppose the papists. These would have time to organize and unite with their friends and fellow travellers; all those who were tired of heresy, and looked for remedy, they could bring in with them. They could accomplish the task, moreover, without the help of foreign princes. It would be all the easier since Catesby intended to seize the king's eldest son,* or if he should happen to die, the second-born. He did not doubt that the forces of the kingdom would rally to the latter.

Acting together, such forces would be great enough to free the catholic nobility from threatened ruin. These would have no other course but to exercise their power and authority, which would be done without opposition and so anticipate any possible tumults. Tumults, in any case, would be few enough because there would hardly be anybody left to begin them. Few would have the hardihood to attempt opposition, since all their leaders and the protestant magistrates would have perished together at the same moment. Robert Catesby had a specially trusted friend with whom he usually shared his secrets and more important affairs. This was Mr Thomas Wintour, a young man of considerable ability and great courage.†

---

* Henry Frederick, Prince of Wales, 1594–1612. Died of typhoid. The second son was Charles, born at Dumfermline, 1600. Succeeded as Charles I in 1625.
† Thomas Wintour: perhaps the most obscure of all the principal plotters. Again, his earliest convictions, if any, seem to have been protestant. According to Philip Sidney (PS, p. 34), 'born, in 1572, he spent the greater part of the last decade of Elizabeth's reign on the Continent fighting first in the Netherlands, curiously enough against Spain . . . Before the period of the Essex rebellion, however, he had changed his politics, and I believe his religion. He was a convert to Roman Catholicism.' Unfortunately, Sidney gave no references to his source in this. My own researches at the Hague in 1965, fairly extensive if not exhaustive, uncovered no reference to Wintour. Interesting new light on his visit to Spain and plans for invading England in this period

As far as one could be at the age of thirty-four, he was a man of unusual wisdom and experience. Catesby revealed his intention to this man, and asked him if he had sufficient daring to help him with the enterprise. The young man replied that if he could persuade himself that his design was lawful, tended to the service of God, and was moreover likely to succeed, he would not refuse to expose body and life to every danger. Indeed, he had done as much already in wars of much less importance than this enterprise. 'But two things,' he said, 'deter me from it powerfully at first sight; and I am not sure that there will not be other difficulties when I have further reflected on it. The first objection is the great cruelty involved, and the quantity of blood we shall have to spill. From this will arise an enormous hatred for us, and a reputation for infamy not only in the eyes of the world, but more especially in the hearts of relatives and friends of those who have to die. The second point is whether this design could succeed since it would call for a suitable house from which to begin the mine, and many a pair of arms more than we have to finish it. In any case, who are the men whom we could trust in a matter of such importance? Add to this the risk we run, and the suspicion we shall arouse in buying so much gunpowder, and a thousand other necessary items, together with the difficulty of working underground without being heard or discovered.'

Robert Catesby replied, 'The first thing I have thought about in this project is whether it is lawful. Or is it inevitably bound up with some offence to God? I have decided in this not to consult anyone else but rather to rely on my own conscience in which I find neither hatred for particular individuals nor any regard for my own interests. Nor do I have any other object in view but to free myself and those who share my faith from the most unjust persecution in which we find ourselves, and to defend our lives and goods from the violence of other people. I can discern no law or reason which forbids this. As for what you say about the hatred and infamy which would arise from the deed, I put it in second place to the good which would follow, that is, freedom for body

comes from A. Loomie's recent study *Guy Fawkes in Spain* . . ., Bulletin of the Institute of Historical Research, Special Supplement No. 9, November 1971, pp. 4–17, 30–46.

and soul and a host of other things. In the eyes of those who are not guided by prejudice and self-interest, I cannot appear to be other than right in a cause so just. In necessity as great as ours we must repel force with force. Nor should the harshness or cruelty of the deed have any effect on us in view of the cruelty and un-bridled barbarity which our enemies use towards us. Their cruelty is far greater than anything I aim to do against them. I am only working against life. They will rob us of what is dearer than life, namely our goods, freedom, honour and every shred of hope for our posterity. In any case, they not infrequently deprive us of life, and they certainly strike at the souls of our wives and children. For this reason what man is there so lacking in religion, or so shallow in his knowledge of God, that he would not despise, for the sake of these, everything else in the world, including life itself? In a word, an evil as great as the one we seek to remedy cannot be cured with gentle medicine, or with anything less harsh than this. Or if it can, then I would like to hear one of us tell me what it is. Now as for the other difficulties which you foresee in your imagination, I do not deny that they are such, and I also see the risk involved. But once we have begun, who can forbid us trying to push on to the conclusion? I am sure that in the course of carrying out the design those difficulties which appear to us at present, not unreasonably, as insuperable would in fact be taken in our stride. To conclude, I wish for nothing more than your usual loyalty, secrecy, prudence and doggedness.'

After this conversation, it soon occurred to them that they could not carry out a work of this kind alone. They wondered with how many others they could share it. Evidently, they should be very few, and men of great courage and loyalty. Robert Catesby, how-ever, was rich in friends as well as patrimony, and from among them all he chose two. One was Mr Thomas Percy, one of the king's Gentlemen Pensioners, and a man of proved valour.* He was a cousin

---

* Thomas Percy: the least plausible of all the plotters. His function was, most probably that of principal agent-provocateur. For T.P.'s relationship with Northumberland, see R. Davies, *The Fawkes of York*, Westminster, 1850, p. 34: '. . . it has been generally assumed that T.P. was a near relative of [the Earl]; and much trouble has been taken to prove that he was a younger son of Edward Percy of Beverley, a grandson of Henry, the fourth Earl [cf. Collectanea

of the Earl of Northumberland, who was the Captain of the Pensioners, and among the leading men of the realm both for his ancient lineage and his influence and wealth. Thomas Percy, in his youth, had been rather wild and given to the gay life, a man who relied much on his sword and personal courage. However, he was reconciled to the church and became a catholic. He then changed his ways in remarkable fashion, giving much satisfaction to the catholics and considerable cause for wonder to those who had known him previously. This gentleman – whether of his own initiative or by someone else's order – went more than once to Scotland before the queen died to deal in various matters with the king. Among other things, speaking in the name of the catholics, he asked the king to receive them into his good graces, and accept them as his loyal subjects, which indeed they would be, along with the rest. For in him they placed their hopes. He told the king how readily they would receive him for their king and lord after the queen's death; that to him they looked for liberty after so many years of crushing servitude. He reminded the king of the persecution to which the catholics were then subjected, and begged him to be so good as to send him back to give him good news in his name. This would redound to his own great credit. For himself there was nothing in the world he desired to see more than the liberation one day of so many of his brethren who were completely loyal subjects and servants of His Majesty.

The king received him kindly, and also the affection of the catholics expressed for himself. He made Mr Thomas very generous promises to favour catholics actively, and not merely to free them from the bondage and persecution in which they were then living. Indeed, he would admit them to every kind of honour and office in the state without making any difference between them and the protestants. At last he would take them under his complete protection. The king promised all this and much more than I write here. Not only that, but in order to make himself more acceptable to the

Topog. et Geneal., vol. ii, p. 60]. But the evidence of this affiliation is not conclusive, and the fact of Guy Fawkes having once lived at Scotton adds considerable weight to the opinion that the conspirator was one of the Percys of that place; and if it were so, he and Fawkes must have been residents of Scotton at the same period.' But see DJ, p. 39, note (*).

catholics, the king pledged his word as a prince; he took Percy by the hand when he swore to carry out all that he had promised. It would be difficult to imagine the elation with which Percy returned from Scotland to England, bearer as he was of such good news. It would also be difficult to assess how much this did for the king, winning over as it did the allegiance of the catholics and filling them with highest hopes. Percy spread word everywhere among the catholics, though secretly, of what had passed between him and the king. I myself have heard him tell the story with his own lips, although at much greater length than what I have written down here. But he told it sorrowfully since he saw the very opposite taking place of what the king had promised the catholics before his accession to England.

Percy much bewailed the fact that he had lost his own reputation with the papists. For they must now consider him two-faced; an instrument used deliberately to deceive them. His sorrow was all the greater in view of the fact that after the king came to England, he presented him with a memorial and supplication in the name of the catholics by which he hoped to remind him in some way of all that had passed between them. The only reply he got was profound silence. He was further made aware on that occasion that the reminder of himself and what had passed between him and the king while in Scotland was unwelcome to the king now of England. For that reason, His Majesty did not look on him kindly. This sowed the seed of a great resentment in Percy's soul. The more the king drew apart from the catholics, and persecution increased, so much the more grew Percy's own grief and desire to remedy the mistake which he thought he had made in having persuaded the catholics to think well of the king. James's aversion for them was now growing from day to day. Percy thought it made up for his error in some measure, and also relieved the disappointment which he felt for the bad success of his negotiation, if he narrated what had passed between him and the king. He felt that he could atone by making clear to his listeners his own profound disappointment and grief. He lost no opportunity of doing this with persons he trusted whenever opportunity offered. Most of his opportunities for relieving his grief in this way offered themselves in the company of Mr Robert Catesby. Catesby soon sized up the situation. He realized how the mind of a

gentleman of this quality would be affected by the injury which he
thought he had received from His Majesty, and that he would be
brimming over with bitterness and disgust. He understood that he
would be ready to revenge himself, and purge the mark of infamy
with which he thought he was tainted for having roused everywhere
among the catholics the highest hopes of the king. He saw that
Percy, to redress the balance, would be ready to expose himself to
every risk.

One day, Catesby invited Percy to his house. He began to remind
him of the miserable lot of the papists. He gradually enlarged on
details and soon passed to seeking remedies. He found Mr Thomas
Percy such a ready listener that he decided it would be safe to reveal
to him, in Wintour's presence, his plan for a mine which would
bring efficacious remedy for all the evils afflicting catholics. Catesby
presented the difficulties to him as well as the plan; but he begged
and implored him, in case he should dislike the proposal, or did not
wish to help them, that as they had confided in him and revealed
their inmost thoughts, so he should swear to them on the spot that
he would never breath a word of it to any living person, or betray
their secret in any way whatsoever.★

At first Thomas Percy was dumbfounded. He wondered how it
could occur to anyone to think of anything so cruel. After further
deliberation, however, he agreed not only to keep secret what he had
heard, but to offer himself and all his resources for the enterprise.
He was further influenced by his desire that people should conclude
that what he had done to bring about the liberty of conscience for
catholics had been done truly and not according to appearances. He
was also anxious to be a means to helping the catholics towards the
peace which he had so many times promised them. I should say
that this Thomas Percy was a gentleman about forty-six years old,

★ The plot is referred to as 'the conspiracy of Percy' in an official contemporary document (Register of letters to Ambassadors: Stonyhurst MS C.II.7,
p. 39). For an account of this document, see *JSA*. Percy, as the older and more
experienced, was fitted to be the leader of the party. As Gentleman Pensioner, he was the only man with an official position at court. But thirty-four
charges of dishonesty were proved against him in 1602 (GBM, vol. I, p. 80).
Forgery and bullying tenants were further characteristic activities at least at
this time. He seems to have been neurotic (SP 14, 17, No. 16: cf. EGF, p. 30).
The narrator is, of course, reconstructing, not speaking as an eye-witness.

although, since his hair was white, he seemed to be older. He was tall and well-built, of serious expression but with an attractive manner. His eyes were large and lively. He was a man of great energy and physical courage, and pleasing in his ways. After he became a catholic, he was God-fearing and very diligent in approaching the sacraments. So much so that for his own good and that of his neighbour he always kept a priest by him in the house. If we want to say of these three gentlemen what everyone else says of them who knew them, it is that they were among the most eligible in the land, even if this plot of theirs was foolhardy and bloodthirsty.

Robert Catesby was a man of lineage and substance. His father left him an income of £3,000 ,which in this country is worth more than twice as much as elsewhere thanks to a thousand advantages which come to receivers of rent and to landowners from their lessees and from the lands themselves. Physically, Catesby was more than ordinarily well-proportioned, some six feet tall, of good carriage and handsome countenance. He was grave in manner, but attractively so. He was also considered one of the most dashing and courageous horsemen in the country. Generous and affable, he was for that reason much loved by everyone. Catesby was much devoted to his religion, as one would expect of a man who made his communion every Sunday. Indeed, his zeal was so great that in his own opinion he was wasting time when he was not doing something to bring about the conversion of the country. In this way, partly by example and partly by persuasion, he had won over to the catholic faith quite a number of gentlemen, and those among the most important, who moved in London and court circles. This in spite of the fact that because he was known to be a catholic he did not have much to do with the palace. In fact it became almost a proverb that Robert Catesby could be seen nowhere without his priest. He seemed to have much more success in converting protestants than many of the priests now to be found in England. This was due as much to his effective way of speaking and reasoning as to his not inconsiderable knowledge of the controversies between catholics and protestants. In the presence of priests, however, he used so much reticence that he would never allow himself to discuss matters of religion unless they urged him to it. The Almighty might have been better pleased if he had moderated his zeal. In that way, he could have gone on enjoying his own niche in the kingdom; and many another good and devout catholic would have done the same.

Mr Thomas Wintour was the younger brother of Robert Wintour, lord and master of the family house at Huddington in Worcestershire. We mentioned him a little while ago. Thomas had spent some years in the Flanders wars in the service of the United Provinces, fighting against the catholic king. He served as a soldier of fortune, and for his great courage as well as discretion he acquired such a reputation that in the opinion of many he could have become one of the most outstanding and widely talked-of *condottieri* in that field of war. But he came to believe that the war was unjust. Hence it was no longer permissible for him to remain there, especially as he was a catholic. Putting from him all thought of the soldier's life, he returned to England. There he gave such an account of himself and his rare qualities that in a short time he came to be considered one of the most accomplished gentlemen living in almost every field, and to vie with any who lived in London and had dealings with the court. For this reason, his company was much sought after, and enjoyed by the leading noblemen and soldiers of the kingdom. In his conversation – he delivered himself with a certain natural and pleasing eloquence – he showed much intelligence, considerable wisdom and wide experience. It seems he had studied philosophy, and his words always seemed most apt even when he was dealing with recondite and obscure matters. His intellect was always alert. He had a remarkable memory for anything to do with history either ancient or modern, especially military history. He also showed great skill in discussion, but without arrogance or affectation, and without giving any offence to his listeners.

Wintour was the special companion of Robert Catesby for whom he had a great affection, and who was much attached to him in his turn. This mutual esteem clearly indicated their common tendencies. Wintour was short of stature, but agile enough, well-built and of good carriage. His face was round but handsome, with eyes that were wide-awake and vivacious. He was a man of pleasing manners, opposed to quarrelling, but at the same time very careful of his honour and reputation. In fact, he used to say that in dealing much with people it was more difficult not to be offended than not to give offence. Indeed, he would say that the first thing one must learn in the art of conversation is to dissimulate one's own annoyance as far as possible; for making it evident that one took offence seemed to oblige the other man to maintain his own resentment. For that reason it was better to be taken at times for a man of lesser intelligence than to give signs of seeing and understanding all that passed. If he did, he ran the risk of seeing himself dishonoured and leaving a grudge behind. What was worse, by showing that he understood too well he would be obliged to defend his honour, and so come to offending his religion. To sum him up in a few words, Wintour was a man of deep faith. He had frequent recourse to the sacraments. To bring his country back to his religion he would have spared no effort, not even life itself. In this enterprise, in which he saw how much risk they all ran, it seems that the only thing he feared was that God might be offended. And this may be seen in the reply he made to Mr Catesby, and likewise in the doubts which were proposed at his instance, as we may believe, although in very obscure terms. We shall examine this later.

We have said enough about Thomas Percy, and so we will now say something about the fourth man who entered the plot. He was the second chosen by Robert Catesby and Thomas Wintour, but was no less acceptable to Thomas Percy. Indeed, he had already named him. This gentleman was a friend of all three. In a certain sense, he depended on Robert Catesby for numerous and considerable benefits received from him. On the other hand, Mr Catesby put great trust in him by reason of the great spirit of loyalty which he had already found in him. The friendship between him and Thomas Wintour had been in existence for some time. Thomas Percy had taken his sister to wife. The man we are talking about was called John Wright.* He had been renowned from his youth for his courage,

* John and Christopher Wright: descended from a protestant family at Plowden in Holderness (DJ, p. 32). Christopher, the younger brother, 'in March [1603] . . . was employed by the said Robert Catesby, Francis Tresham, Henry Garnet, and others, into Spain to negotiate with [Philip III] by the means of [Joseph] Creswell, the jesuit, and others, to proceed in that invasion which . . . Thomas Wintour had before negotiated with him [1602]' (from a contemporary printed fragment of the Act of Attainder, 1605/6, in Stonyhurst Archives, E/III/8, original in SP 14, vol. 21, No. 23). It was also claimed that on 22 June 1603 Guy Fawkes was sent by 'Sir William Stanley . . . Hugh Owen . . . William Baldwin, Jesuit, and others' from

and was considered to be one of the best swordsmen of his day. He had a good physique and sound constitution. Rather on the tall side, his features were pleasing. He was somewhat taciturn in manner, but very loyal to his friends, even if his friends were few. Before he became a catholic he was prone to quarrelling, but after he was reconciled to the church he became a man of exemplary life. He was altogether dedicated in spiritual matters, and went often to the sacraments. His house was an established haven for priests. For this reason, he and his wife had put up with great harassment and persecution for the profession of their catholic faith. The three gentlemen mentioned above had him summoned from his house in Lincolnshire where he was then staying. First they got him to make an oath of secrecy, and then they told him how much they had decided on among themselves, giving him the reasons which had moved them to this decision. It proved no difficult matter to persuade him. He was drawn along by his close friendship with them, and also by reasons which were put to him with effectiveness and vigour. His mind surrendered at last to an onrush of grief and overmastering anger. All the more so since a colouring of justice, and a pretext of devotion and zeal, accompanied the reasoning and persuasion of his friends. A fifth man was added to these four as leaders of the plot. This, however, only took place after some months, and in circumstances which we shall describe in the next chapter.

Flanders to arrange for the invasion of England. 'And . . . Guy Fawkes and Christopher Wright, though they had all the furtherance of the said Creswell', received no 'entertainment' or encouragement from Philip. Guy Fawkes received leave to go to Spain for an indefinite period on 16 February 1603 (see Archives du Royaume, Brussels, Secrétairerie d'Etat et de Guerre, vol. 21, f. 129r: many English names). Fr. A. Loomie, S.J., first noticed papers of a certain 'Anthony Dutton' of 1603 (Simancas, Estado 2512, ff. 132r-4v.). The inevitable thought occurs that this was a pseudonym for Christopher Wright: cf. Thomas Wintour's pseudonym of 'Timothy Browne'. Unfortunately, no known example of Christopher Wright's handwriting seems to have survived. See A. Loomie, *Guy Fawkes in Spain* . . . See also note *, at p. 144.

FOUR

ABOUT THIS TIME, the arrival of the Constable of Spain was expected in London to conclude peace between the Catholic King and the King of England.* This peace had already been negotiated for many months, and one could say that it was virtually concluded thanks to the labours of Don Juan de Tassis, Count of Villamediana.† All that was now needed was that the Constable should ratify and swear to the articles on behalf of His Catholic Majesty. The catholics had fervently hoped that some regard would have been had of themselves in this peace. With this in view, they had used all their influence with Villamediana. In the event, the count had not been able to get more out of the king than a few vague replies and airy promises. The gentlemen concerned with the plot followed the outcome of these peace negotiations with the greatest attention. More than others they did what they could to ensure some good outcome for the catholics. I can myself bear personal witness to this since I am very well acquainted with the particular circumstances, and the great desire they showed to achieve their end by peaceful means. With this in view they decided to send a man to Flanders. One can learn this from the confession of

* Juan de Velasco, Duke of Frias and Constable of Castile, arrived with his cortège at Dover, early in August 1604. See G. P. V. Akrigg, *Jacobean Pageant*, London, 1962, pp. 60–2.
† Juan de Tassis: his instructions, or a copy of them, dated 1603, are in the Bodleian Library (MS Lyell empt., 57, ff. 199r.–208r.). For a summary of the European context, see R. Trevor Davies, *The Golden Century of Spain, 1501–1621*, London, 1937, pp. 233–42.

Thomas Wintour which was published by order of His Majesty's councillors. The envoy's mission was to inform the Constable of the state of catholics and to beg His Excellency that they might be included in some article of the peace treaty. If this could not be done, then at least he should use his influence so that the King of England would be content to let them pay a certain sum of money wherewith they could buy off their oppression; if not for ever then at least for a time.*

The man whom they decided to send to Flanders was Thomas Wintour. 'In this way', as Robert Catesby said, 'we will leave no way untried of remedying our ills by peaceful means and without bloodshed.' Wintour told the Constable of the hope they placed in His Catholic Majesty as protector of the Catholic Church. Wintour also brought home to him their miseries, which were great enough at that moment but would become greater still when it became evident to the protestants and the English King that His Catholic Majesty attached no great importance to their need. If Philip ignored this, he would be handing them over to the persecutor. For reasons of state the King of England could do no less than take advantage of the catholics who would be abandoned to their fate by a peace made without any regard for them. Persecution would grow, and no one would be able to protest in view of the same peace. The catholics would be overpowered and uprooted before their complaints reached the ears of the catholic princes. They would be destroyed before they could be heard or believed. This would happen all the more easily when the persecutors began to tell the world that catholics were not persecuted at all, or else that persecution was only slight. Or again, that it merely consisted in letting them know that their religion was not welcome either to king or state rather than that he was harrying them in a way to give them cause for so much complaint, as they claimed. He also reminded them of the colour which the protestants had given to the persecution of catholics in the past, namely that they were friends of His Catholic Majesty and the Spaniards. In consequence, they must be enemies

* For a masterly study of the negotiations of these years, including this ransom question, see Albert J. Loomie, S.J., 'Toleration and Diplomacy: the religious issue in Anglo-Spanish Relations, 1603–5', in *Transactions of the American Philosophical Society*, new series, vol. 53, part 6, Philadelphia, 1963.

of theirs.* No one expected that the catholics would be abandoned by the Spanish King. Indeed, the common enemy of the Catholic Church had pursued them with so much implacable hatred because they looked to him. The truth was that the catholics suffered for their faith alone, and for the profession they made of it. Their enemies themselves made this clear when they left off persecuting those who were ready to dissimulate the faith which everyone knew they still held in their hearts. This did not change even if they were ready to conform by going to protestant churches. Their enemies would not have been content with this if they had persecuted them only on account of the goodwill which they showed for His Catholic Majesty . . . Indeed, the very protestants expected the Catholic King to make every effort to see that provision was made in the peace for the freedom and safety of papists. They expected it all the more since His Excellency had in his hand the direction of negotiations. Moreover, his zeal for the catholic religion was clear enough for all to see. The gentleman in question put many other considerations to the Constable, and doubtless with all the charm and manners calculated to move him. Wintour was, after all, a man of good intelligence and sound judgement, and fluent besides in Italian, French, Spanish and Latin.

The Constable replied that he was already partly acquainted with the great burden under which catholics groaned, and now he understood it much better after hearing it from him. He prayed God that His Divine Majesty would be pleased to make use of him in a matter that so much concerned His service. For the rest, and in so far as it concerned his king, it was his express will that he should do all he could to ensure peaceful existence for the catholics of that land. This had been made clear to him as one of the principal points in this negotiation for peace between the two kings. To bring it about, he would use all his influence. Indeed, he was obliged to do as much from loyalty to his king, who had laid this precise charge on him. He felt himself all the more obliged to it by the affection which any christian owes to the Catholic Church as one of its members. He was all the more moved by the fact that he saw it afflicted, persecuted and oppressed in a kingdom great and flourishing and founded in tradition like England.

* Loomie, op. cit., pp. 5–9.

With these words, and others equally full of christian sentiment, that very catholic and devout knight sent Thomas Wintour from his presence.* The latter remained well satisfied with the readiness and good will that he had discovered in the Constable to help catholics. Nevertheless, Wintour well realized that peace would be concluded without taking the catholics into account. It could not be otherwise. He was well aware how many difficulties the King of England would put in their path. So Wintour began to gather up information about Englishmen who were serving with the forces of the Archduke Albert.† He was looking for someone whose courage, knowledge of military matters, and general character were such that they could make use of his services if necessity arose. That is to say, when the Constable proved unable to effect what was desired, and had left the catholics outside the peace. Wintour well knew that after this a new persecution would be unleashed, and this in fact happened. He had received orders from Mr Catesby that if he could find such a man he should take him to England, after winning him over with promises of advancement, and even presents. However, he should tell him nothing except in general terms: that is, to say that a day might come in England when he could do better service there than he was doing at that time in Flanders.

In the end, Wintour found a gentleman by name of Guy Fawkes who left nothing to be desired for their purposes. He was a man highly skilled in matters of war, as having served in Flanders, which was then the mother of military invention and had been for many years. Fawkes had held office and command in camp.‡ He was a man

* Apart from Thomas Wintour's confession of 23/25.xi.1605 (see below, p. 137), mentioned by Greenway, there seems to be no documentary source for this information. The present editor has found nothing at Simancas to confirm or enlarge Greenway's story at this point. Nor apparently has Fr Loomie (*Guy Fawkes* . . ., pp. 4–17).

† The main sources of information on English forces in Flanders are the 'Registres des patentes, titres, ordres et depêches concernant les Trouppes . . .' in the Archives du Royaume, Brussels (Papiers d'Etat et de l'Audience), and PRO, SP 77. (See EGF, *passim*.)

‡ By 1602, Fawkes was an Alferes or Ensign, roughly a second-lieutenant. (See C. G. Cruickshank, *Elizabeth's Army*, 2nd edition, Oxford, 1966, p. 57.) 'The ensign-bearer's post was recognized to be of great importance.' All the same, 'in the normal company of 150 infantry', he came after the captain and lieutenant. According to an intercepted letter of the autumn, 1599, Fawkes

of considerable experience as well as knowledge. Thanks to his prowess he had acquired considerable fame and name among the soldiers. He was also – something decidedly rare among soldiery, although it was immediately evident to all – a very devout man, of exemplary life and commendable reticence. He went often to the sacraments. He was pleasant of approach and cheerful of manner, opposed to quarrels and strife: a friend, at the same time, of all in the service with him who were men of honour and good life. In a word, he was a man liked by everyone and loyal to his friends. Wintour took him back to England as a man altogether fitted for his purpose. He introduced him to Mr Catesby, and in a short time they understood one another so well that Mr Guy was admitted to the secret of the plot. Whether this was before the Constable's departure from England or no, I have no knowledge.

When the Constable came to England, he was on more than one occasion approached by Thomas Wintour while the peace negotiations were proceeding. Wintour spoke for the gentlemen who were his friends, but there were others also to remind the Constable to negotiate for the catholics as he best knew how, and to get the best terms he could. The end-result was that nothing would be included for them in the way of formal articles, but promises were made to His Excellency that the persecution would be mitigated, and the execution of the laws suspended. Even these promises were given with so much caution that they were not known to all, and with so much secrecy that they were never published. So it came about that those few catholics who knew about them did not trust them. They saw in it only the cunning of the persecutor, who did not wish to have even the restraint of promises put on him so that he could carry out what he intended with greater freedom. But the others saw peace concluded, and the Constable's departure, without so much as a bare mention being made of any alleviation or lightening of the burden for catholics. They now took their case to be more

was reported to be 'in great want' (EGF, p. 47). Less than four years later, he was on his way to Spain in search of better fortune. By the summer of 1603, he was recommended for a captaincy (ibid., p. 64). Nevertheless, one could wish for more confirmation of Greenway's glowing account. Fawkes does not seem to have returned to military service after his visit to Spain. Notices of him are scanty at Simancas.

desperate than ever. They knew His Catholic Majesty was a prince most zealous for the good of christianity, and a protector of the church. He was also the most powerful of all the catholic princes. All the same, he had accomplished precisely nothing with the King of England, and the catholics were left now to stew in their affliction . . .

The papists themselves correctly inferred from these beginnings what the consequences of this peace would mean for them. They saw the hardness of the king's heart, and the depth of his hatred for them and their religion. He had shown no wish to lighten the burden of their troubles even to please a reconciled friend . . . Still less did he try to win the good opinion of his many subjects subjected for so long to the harsh yoke of gruelling persecution. It made no difference that they had behaved with exemplary humility and submission. After the Constable's departure, persecution gradually increased until it reached the stage we spoke of . . . When the catholics complained, the reply came from their enemies that the time was coming, and they hoped it would soon arrive, when every papist throat would be cut. I myself well remember one time and place when this was said, but it was not said only at that one time and place. When others complained reasonably of similar grievances they returned home with retorts of the kind just given instead of remedy.

So the plotters, seeing peace concluded, catholics excluded, persecution growing, and the prospect of things getting worse, decided to carry out their design. The first and most difficult step was to find a suitable base from which to begin the mine. They therefore made a careful enquiry in the Westminster district, and more particularly round about the Parliament-building to find a house to let. They found one not very far from parliament itself, and as conveniently situated as could be desired. Mr Thomas Percy rented it on the strength of being a Gentleman Pensioner, and by reason of his office. This office kept him about the king's person and therefore the palace, since he often had to go to court. There was a garden adjoining the house. This would serve not only to keep other people at a distance but also itself prove useful for the work they were about to begin. So they rented this too, and built a fairly roomy outhouse (casetta) from which they began the mine. It occurred to them that when their neighbours heard the noises and knocking caused by digging they would come running round to find out what they were doing, and so they might suspect that they were up to no good. They therefore decided to work by day and not by night. In this way they would rouse less suspicion. After all, it would not appear strange for anyone to carry out work in his own house by day. The noise would be less noticed than by night when everything was quiet.

They bought the implements and iron tools needed, and then shut themselves up together in the house.* They first stocked themselves with hard-boiled eggs, cooked meat, pies, and other things to eat and drink so that there would be no need for coming and going. In this way, they would not be seen together, and start people talking: all the more since they were nearly all known to be catholics. If they were seen in that house it seemed likely that the protestants would suspect they had a priest there to say Mass for them secretly. This suspicion would give a pretext for the pursuivants to search the house, and so discover everything. They brought with them small-arms and other weapons so that if any should wish to search the house they would have the means of defending themselves. They were all determined to die rather than be taken alive in that enterprise. They also swore that if any of their number happened to be taken for any cause or accident whatsoever, his companions would do their utmost to free him even at risk of their own lives.

They now set to work with their digging and carting. One rested while the others laboured. Guy had the task of standing sentinel, and telling them when anyone came too near or stopped in the vicinity of the house. They would then cease work, or work in some way that attracted no attention. Guy Fawkes was given this duty, as much as anything because he was unknown. When he appeared outside he could pass himself off as a servant of Mr Thomas Percy with the task of keeping the house in order, and buying wood and other things necessary before the arrival of his master. They worked by day, digging out the earth from the mine, and throwing it into

* Accounts of the lodging in Westminster are most unsatisfactory and contradictory. According to another document, Percy's apartment was so small that there was only one bed in it, and Fawkes could only stay in it when Percy was absent (EGF, p. 112: GPB, 40). Percy normally stayed at an inn in the Strand not far from where the Earl of Salisbury had his London residence.

the outhouse which they had made in the garden. They would take it out of this shed at night, spread it over the garden, and cover it up with verdure and grass so as not to be noticed. The burdensome labour involved in this work, continued as it was with so much perseverance, came improbably from men in their walk of life, accustomed as they were to easy living. It was remarkable that they should have been able to last out so long in work to which they were not accustomed and which involved such effort. So much so that in a short time they did considerably more than men would have done who were used to earning their bread by using their hands and muscles. It must be admitted that some of them became seriously unwell. These had to stop work. The rest, however, carried on. It was also remarkable that some of them, especially Catesby and Percy, being men of unusual height, should have been able to endure the fatigue of remaining so long underground in the doubled-up position which the work demanded.

The construction called for a good deal of wood to strengthen the mine by way of propping it up. For this reason they had to have another house where the wood could be worked and to which they could carry many other things belonging to the project. This material must then be brought in secret to the mine. For this purpose they hired a house on the other side of the river. There they could also meet together since it was outside London, and could be taken as a vacation-house. What made it highly suitable from their point of view was that it was quite near parliament. Meeting together in this way they began to deliberate more carefully on their project, and take common counsel to provide for every eventuality. The first and most important point was that, if the mine venture succeeded, they would need to have a leader who would give authority to their cause, and by his authority add to their resources. They debated as to who this should be. They finally resolved that if they could get the heir-apparent into their hands, being the nearest by blood to the king, they would take him for their head. They would use his authority in everything, and gather round themselves in his name all the resources of the kingdom. They would make themselves terrible to their enemies, always supposing that anyone had the hardihood to oppose them. This would be all the less likely if no man of name or authority were left alive after the general slaughter to prevent the plotters from joining at their leisure their partisans and friends. They never doubted that in the revolution the greater part of the kingdom would take sides with them, either from a desire for change, or out of hope of better fortune. This would apply especially to the soldiers, who would be led by particular considerations of enmity or hatred, or perhaps by friendship and the good things held out to those who had rebelled. Finally, there were those who would make it an opportunity to find their way out of miseries of every kind, whether they had to do with debts, crimes or any other misfortune. The kingdom, it seems, was full of such people.

The main difficulty in all this was to carry out the first part of the plan, that is, to get the prince into their hands. The main point of the difficulty was that the prince would probably be with the king, his father, in the Parliament-house, and would die with him. If Charles, Duke of York, were also there he would likewise die along with the rest. If he were not there they would be presented with the problem of getting hold of him. This would mean fighting off those who had charge of him. The same difficulty arose in connection with James's daughter, the Lady Elizabeth. She then resided in Baron Harington's house at some distance from London.*

However, they brushed aside these difficulties, concluding that it would not be that much of a problem to get hold by brute force of whoever of them happened not to be present in the parliament. Thomas Percy had access to the palace. So on the pretext of his office and duties there it would be easy enough for him to bring in as many men as would be needed for this purpose. Horses and carriages would be on hand, strategically placed, to carry off the prisoner. 'And who will offer us any resistance,' they asked, 'at that moment of overwhelming chaos? Or rather, who will not think that we are doing a good act in saving the life of the boy, so that everyone will be ready to help rather than hinder us? For they will not know at the beginning who could have been the author of such a holocaust and devastation.' But if the prince should happen to be in a house outside London belonging to some other gentleman or nobleman of

---

* Sir John Harington: first Baron H. of Exton; created a peer at James's coronation, and given charge of Princess Elizabeth at his house, Coombe Abbey: author of *Nugae Antiquae*. Died 1613. For a sketch-map of the area showing this and the conspirators' houses, see HRW, p. 149.

the realm, they still made no difficulty about getting their hands on him. They would be able to forgather with this object in view on the day before the mine was due to be fired, on the pretext of a hunt or something else. This would take place near the house where the king's daughter or the duke was staying. They would decide on the number of men which seemed appropriate. These would get news of the main event posthaste before it was generally disseminated, and in a moment they would make themselves masters of one or other, or both royal children if they so wished.

The second point was that there would be many gentlemen in the parliament who would be friends or fellow catholics. It seemed to them an act of excessive impiety to send so many people to perdition in a moment together. They should make some distinction between innocent and guilty. To meet this objection they resolved to make every effort to save as many of the catholics and of their friends as they could without prejudice to necessary secrecy.

The third point to consider was whether they should acquaint some prince or ruler with their design so that they could avail themselves of his assistance and support when the moment called for it. They were thinking more particularly of His Holiness, at that time Clement VIII. They finally agreed not to do so. In the first place, they could not be sure that by doing this they would not chance to uncover the whole project for they could not bind any prince to secrecy by means of an oath. Indeed, this very contingency was to be expected. Doubtless, in this they were right. Secondly, they were well aware that His Holiness was very inclined to think well of the king, to whom he had always shown paternal affection. The pope hoped for good success with him since he got his information from men who did not know much about it. Indeed, the pope had lately laid his command on all to await the Divine Will and live in peace.★

It was while they were mulling over these questions and giving all their attention to the work begun that they received the news that parliament would be prorogued to a later date.† They had

★ For James's relations with Clement VIII, see Arnold Oskar Meyer, *Clemens VIII und Jakob I von England*, Rome, 1904. Vatican sources make it clear that the papacy was anxious to come to terms at this time.
† Parliament: new parliament summoned on 31 January 1604; met on 19

hoped that all would be ready for the original beginning of this parliament. However, the news caused them no dismay since it now seemed doubtful that they would have been able to finish their work properly in so short a time. Indeed, they were beginning to feel the need of more hands to help them. They decided, therefore, to take a rest over the Christmas holiday which was now close upon them. They further resolved for the future to avoid occasions when they would be seen together. In this way, by meeting less often there would be smaller risk of whispering and suspicion of what they were doing, even if speculation were far from the mark. So they gave themselves up to recreation over the holiday, everyone returning to his own house. Some would indulge in sports and pastimes, others in seasonal devotions, but it was especially agreed among them that they would never correspond with one another by letter on anything touching their plot. Still less would they use others to carry messages. With this they all retired to the country.

Robert Catesby fell to pondering all they had discussed when they were together, but more particularly the subject-matter of the second point; that is, about saving from the general conflagration those who were not open enemies, and especially those who were friends and catholics. This appeared to him as something extremely difficult. It would put the secrecy of the plot in jeopardy if it meant showing mercy to all such people. Without this, however, he could not fully satisfy his own conscience. He decided to carry out an enquiry, using general terms, and keeping from the real point, to see how much could be allowed him in this field. He would rather leave the enterprise secretly begun than put it into execution with manifest danger to his soul. However, the conviction was growing in him, thanks to certain general lines of reasoning, that he was not obliged in conscience to provide for all the innocent who would find themselves in the Parliament-house on the day when they had

March and sat till 7 July 1604 when it was adjourned by the king in person until 7 February 1605. 24 December 1604, Proclamation proroguing parliament from 7 February until 3 October 1605. 28 July 1605, Proclamation proroguing parliament from 3 October until 5 November 1605. Parliament opened on 5 November and sat until 27 May 1606. (See GBM, I, pp. 2, 148, 152, 164; R.Hist.S., *Handbook of British Chronology*, 2 (1961 ed.), p. 536.)

to blow up the mine. But to set his mind more completely at rest, and so as to be able to propound his doubts with greater plausibility, he spread the news among his friends that he had resolved to go over to Flanders to serve in the archduke's war.* He would take over a few companies of horse with him. This he spoke of with such enthusiasm that not only did word of his intention travel everywhere but it was widely believed even by his most intimate friends. Many gentlemen offered to go with him for this purpose. Seeing that this idea had succeeded altogether as he intended, he began to use the rumour for a much more important purpose, and one with far-reaching consequences. This was, to win the devotion of all the more dashing cavaliers at court, and even in the kingdom at large, so that he could make use of them when the time came without their knowing anything of his true purpose or what he really intended them to do. He contrived to bring it about in the following way.

It was one of the articles in the treaty between the Kings of Spain and England† that it should be open to any Englishman to serve His Catholic Majesty in the wars in Flanders. Taking advantage of this freedom, and using it as a pretext, Catesby not only made a show of wanting to go over to the wars, as we have said, but he encouraged many others to do the same. He pointed out that it was an honourable way of spending time. They could learn the art of war, and they would be serving a good cause. This was especially true in view of the fact that the archduke's camp was well provided with gentlemen of almost every nationality. His service was most honourable and just since it was against rebels, riff-raff, and persons of low class or no class. These latter sort of people played their own game in embroiling all Christendom in conflict.

Catesby did much by his persuasion and example, showing also a resolute desire to go over in person. As a result, the majority of

* The narrator was, no doubt, right in thinking that Catesby had no real intention of crossing to Flanders. As agent-provocateur his rôle would be complete when he had involved a sufficient number of Catholic gentlemen in what would be represented as an armed rising in the Midlands connected with an attempt to blow up parliament in London. In fact, the gentlemen in the country were doubtless forming a bona-fide company to go to Flanders, whatever their colonel intended. Hence the genuine military preparations.

† See T. Rymer, *Foedera*, Tom. VII, pt. II, Hague Comitis 1742, pp. 117–20.

those gentlemen who made a profession of horsemanship, and were considered the best soldiers in the land, decided to follow this campaign. Bold preparations were begun for recruiting a regiment of soldiers. They chose for colonel Sir Charles Percy, brother of the Earl of Northumberland, a knight of proved courage and with considerable experience behind him of the wars in Ireland. He would have captains under him, all of them Catesby's friends. Among these were three or four already involved in the plot. In this way, if the conspiracy succeeded, they would be able to make use of these men at the right moment. Recruited for the other purpose, they need know nothing of their true one till this moment. Not even the colonel himself knew anything of it, although he was a most intimate friend of Catesby.* The latter, on this pretext, provided horses, weapons, and everything else he pleased so that he could use it at the proper time without anyone suspecting his real motive. Furthermore, when the time of parliament drew near, he approached Cecil, Earl of Salisbury, who was the king's Principal Secretary. He asked for leave and passport, and by this means to have the king's permission.†Catesby was received by Cecil with a great show of affection. He received permission to leave for the wars in Flanders whenever he wished. The truth is that the Secretary and other members of the Privy Council gladly gave this gentleman leave to depart since they feared him and his followers more than any man in England. They feared him for his courage, intelligence and zeal, and for the great following of friends which he could boast.

After the report of his going to Flanders had spread about, the topic was often discussed among Catesby's friends. He himself

* For Arundell, see EGF, *passim*, and Maurus Lunn, OSB, 'Chaplains to the English Regiment in Spanish Flanders, 1605–6', article in *Recusant History*, vol. 11, pp. 133–55.

† There is no reference in the Docquet Book of the Signet Office to a passport granted to Catesby at this time. Francis Tresham received a licence to travel abroad for two years, 'with two servants, three horses or geldings, and £50 in money with all other his necessaries', granted on 2 November 1605 (PRO, Index 6802, unfoliated). Baron Arundell of Wardour received a licence to go abroad about mid-July. Lord Vaux received a licence to travel abroad for three years on 14 July. Two pages have been torn or cut out of this volume for the latter part of November. This seems to be the only mutilation of its kind in the book.

showed every sign of relishing such discourses, and was curious to know even the details. He took special care to bring the conversation round to this subject, and more frequently when he found himself in knowledgeable company. This was to satisfy himself about those doubts which gnawed at him in connection with the plot. He would first of all point out that in those wars in the Low Countries there were many catholics in the service of the states. Many of them being natural subjects of the country were, against their will, obliged to take part in many military enterprises. Was it permissible to attack and kill them or no? In order to increase the doubt that surrounded the question he would point out that it sometimes happens that the Dutch post men of this kind in the fortresses on purpose so that, to avoid harming them, the enemy shuns attacking such a fortress. In this way, he does not harm any innocent man within who is held there against his will. Proceeding from this question to others by way of disputation, Catesby would always propose by way of example what could, or usually did, happen in the Flemish wars. He would say that he was not clear in his own mind as to what he should do if he saw that the enemy, in order to escape or with some other purpose in view, should put a number of innocent catholics in the vanguard. These would of necessity be killed, unless the enemy were to succeed in his plan to the prejudice and harm of the opposing army. For it seemed to him a hard decision, and one involving great cruelty, to kill such innocent men. On the other hand, it seemed equally clear to him that if it were not done anyone could make use of this stratagem, with disastrous consequences to those who were fighting a just war. One could raise the same difficulty, as he used to say, concerning those innocent men who, finding themselves in the enemy's camp or lines, would be killed in the event of a sudden or unforeseen assault. If one were not allowed to kill these innocent men, and he was rather of opinion that one could not, many enterprises would have to be given up, and many opportunities lost, which in fact it seemed unreasonable to forgo.

By these and other doubts raised as examples in the course of conversation, Catesby made his own intentions much clearer. He had these difficulties constantly in mind so that he could turn them over, and resolve the scruples which all the time troubled him. He had the same answer to these doubts put to him by different men of learning, and in different times and places. It corresponded to what is common doctrine not only among catholics but also among pro-testants and heterodox.* That is, that in all the cases and examples proposed by him it was essential for anyone waging a just war to observe the principles of justice. But if the death of innocent people in these and similar cases was something accidental, and by no means desired by the man who was exercising his right, and if in fact he hated this consequence he could, without violation of justice, allow their death. He was not obliged to cease waging war, notwithstand-ing the damage done to innocent parties. Their death, however, was always unlawful as something intrinsically evil and forbidden when-ever it was intended. This was something made clear from many examples of history both sacred and profane. It was in accordance with the practice of all nations. It applied even to the workings of the human body from which it was often necessary to cut off a member healthy and whole to save the rest of the body from perish-ing.

Eventually, it seemed to this gentleman that by the total array of his arguments he had fully satisfied all doubts. It was clear that he and his companions did not want any harm to befall those innocent people who would find themselves in the Parliament-house. This was, as it were, the fortress which they would have to take by storm. They had justice on their side for their own defence, and for their attack on the others. For without taking the offensive they could not free themselves from the heavy hand of their enemies. One can imagine how this raw theologian would argue out these matters with his friends, instructing them in doctrine which he had heard but not well understood; forming his own conscience and theirs but not so that any of them ever thought of laying bare his thoughts in confession. Following his own course, every doubt and scruple was set aside. All the same, not long before putting his plan in execution Mr Catesby found himself still agitated by scruples springing from his cruel and overbearing intention. Even now, he

---

* This is the so-called principle of double-effect. Orthodox moralists insist on three conditions: it can only be allowed where the good effect is of the utmost importance and proportionate to the concurrent harm; the harmful effect must not be desired in any way; the good and evil effects must be simul-taneous.

was still not fully satisfied within himself. To clarify the situation
further, and to quiet his own mind once and for all, he decided at
last to reveal himself in confession, as will be said in its place.

Meanwhile, those with whom Catesby argued well remembered
his questions and doubts, or rather his lectures and discourses, after
the plot was revealed. They were not a little surprised at the skill
and artifice he used both in introducing the subject and in expound-
ing his doubts and difficulties. They wondered at the way in which
he managed to cover up his main intention so that no one ever
suspected what he was really driving at. No one surmised that he
had anything in mind apart from the crossing to Flanders. I myself
can bear witness to this since I was one of his more intimate friends
who was completely deceived. All were completely convinced that
he was going on this campaign for which he prepared horses, harness
and equipment, including valuable, embroidered saddlery.

I can say the same for that glorious martyr of Christ, a man
schooled in all virtue and learning, Henry Garnet.* He was the
Superior at that time of the Jesuit Mission in England. Even he used
to say, after that wretched plot was discovered, that he *never*†
realized the real object of the discoursed indicated above. The truth
is that Mr Catesby had never put the real case, which he kept
completely to himself, in clear terms or such as it really was. He
would have heard that there was a difference between the war in
Flanders against the rebels of a legitimate king, acting with public
authority and by commission of the state etc. [*sic*], and what he had
in mind to begin against a king who had succeeded lawfully to his
own kingdom. Catesby was only acting on private authority, personal deception and individual betrayal etc. [*sic*]. He was beside
himself with mindless fanatacism, even if he was urged on by his
ardent desire to liberate his native land from the hard yoke of
heresy, and to free his fellow catholics from the grinding persecution
which oppressed them. He had nothing else in view but to guard

* Henry Garnet: born at Nottingham, 1555. Educated at Winchester, he
joined the Jesuit novitiate in Rome in 1575. Returned to England as a priest in
1586. Superior of the Jesuits there from 1587. (See HFR, iv, pp. 35 et seq.;
P. Caraman, *Henry Garnet*, London, 1964.)
† A negative particle has been supplied here, as the sense of the Italian seems
to demand: '. . . gia sapeva a che miravano li sudetti discorsi.'

ROBERT WINTOUR

the secret of that plot by which he hoped to bring remedy to so many evils.

I must not fail to mention here something which leads me to believe that one point was not altogether hidden from this gentleman and his friends, namely that concerning the importance of legitimate authority. I am quite certain that on more than one occasion the Fathers of the Society of Jesus told them that they were forbidden by their General in every way to involve themselves, either directly or indirectly, in anything that had to do with turbulence and disturbance. Furthermore, they had the express order of His Holiness, Pope Clement, to bring to the knowledge of as many catholics as they could his clear wish that they should live in peace.* They must wait for conversion of king and kingdom from the hand of His Divine Majesty; something he himself hoped for, and not without reason, as he thought. Among other occasions, I once found myself at table with Father Henry Garnet along with others of those Fathers when Mr Catesby was also present. Before the whole company, Father Henry referred with grave words to the injunction which he had received. He told the members of the society who were there present that they should bring this command to the knowledge of their brethren of the same Order, and to all catholics known to them. In order to discharge his own conscience, and also to comply with this injunction received from his superiors, he begged all present to continue in the exercise of the patience in which they had persevered up to that time. This they had done with no less glory and praise from the catholics of England than with the satisfaction and edification of the entire christian world. For the rest, they must leave the disposition of themselves to God's goodness and Providence . . .

I well recall that when we rose from table the same Mr Catesby said, as if speaking for the others, that some were not lacking who had grown tired of putting up with ill fortune and did not give willing ear to that teaching. They were asking if there was any authority on earth that could take away from them the right given by nature to defend their own lives from the violence of others. They were saying openly that that doctrine took away from catholics spirit and energy, leaving them flaccid and poor-spirited. It put

* Caraman, op. cit., pp. 310, 313.

them in a worse position than slaves. Indeed, for that very reason they were called by their enemies out of contempt, 'God's lunatics'. I noticed that he spoke very unwillingly on this subject ever afterwards so as not to give the Fathers an opportunity for exhorting the others to patience, as they customarily did. In this way, they would make himself and his friends less acceptable. Meanwhile, in hidden ways they went about to stir up resentment in those whom they knew to be disposed to it by reason of the persecution from which they were suffering. I still remember the exact person to whom Mr Catesby said that while he was altogether pleased with the rare qualities of Father Garnet, and greatly admired the remarkable virtues he had discovered in him, he still found his lukewarmness displeasing. The person addressed said that he should speak rather of his excessive patience. It was something well known and observed by all who knew that holy priest that he was, indeed, outstanding in gentleness and patience. This was all the more noteworthy in him since he was a man of superior and penetrating intellect. His mind was lofty but wide-awake, and his judgement deep and farseeing. I say all this briefly and, as it were, in passing.

I wanted to say something here about this truly good and glorious martyr, although it is somewhat out of sequence, so that the reader can judge with how little reason our opponents in religion have tried to fasten the odium of this foolhardy and most unhappy plot on to the jesuits, and more especially Father Henry Garnet. In doing this, they have acted against reason, being moved only by crude hatred and anger against these Fathers. In the end they killed Father Garnet, with another of the same Order, together with two laymen of good life, on the false pretext that they were smeared with this contagion. There is more to be said about this later . . .

FIVE

SO FAR WE HAVE SPOKEN of the decision of the conspirators to go ahead with the plot which they had begun. We have examined the difficulties which they had to put up with, the progress they made with their mine, and certain misgivings which arose. These affected both their working operations and their attitude of mind. We have seen how they tried to allay their fears and set their minds at rest. After the Christmas holiday, they met together, as they had agreed to do, to work out what still remained to be done. The first thing they agreed on was to admit two or three more to their company so that they could help them in the mine. This was proving to be a most burdensome task. They could also buy powder and a thousand other necessary items which few could purchase without rousing suspicion, and certainly not men of their condition.

The first man chosen to join them was John Wright's brother, Christopher. He resembled his brother in all his valour and gallantry, and was a close and loyal friend of Mr Catesby. Christopher was tall and strongly built, his large features having a somewhat ruddy tan. He was discreet, a man of few words in fact, and well able to keep a secret. He was also devoted and fervent in religious matters, and after he became a catholic lived a life that was exemplary. Those other gentlemen judged him in every way suitable to assist them in what they were trying to do. Nor have I discovered that they made any difficulty about taking the oath of secrecy. The second newcomer was Mr Robert Wintour, elder brother of Thomas of whom we have spoken above. He was a gentleman of good family and line long established in Worcestershire. He was well-to-do, en-joying a large income. His wife was the daughter of Mr John Talbot who for his gentle birth, wealth and influence is far and away the first and most important gentleman of that county. Talbot* was known to be a catholic but for all that was looked up to and respected. Not that trouble had left him untouched. Indeed, both in the queen's time, and now under the king, he suffered imprisonment and many other vexations. Robert Wintour† was short, but possessed a good physique. His ways, too, were those of a sober citizen, discreet and judicious, devout and sincere in his religious practices, courteous and generous, and endowed with intrepid courage. It seems likely that his brother revealed the secret of the plot to him, and that he proved not particularly difficult to persuade. For one thing, he looked up to his brother, Thomas, as a man circumspect and cautious in everything he did; and then he cherished a great affection not only for him but also for Mr Robert Catesby.

The conspirators were now seven in number. When they took up work again in the mine they went at it with such determination and energy that they soon reached the main foundation of the Parliament-house, which was of very hard stone and some ten feet thick (16 palmi). Much labour they gave to that wall, and every blow they struck on it so resounded and re-echoed that it seemed to them that the whole neighbourhood must have heard them. The man on guard had to warn them very often to work so as to reduce the noise and echo of their strokes. They were pre-occupied by their fear on the one hand of being heard while they worked, and on the other, by the work itself of cutting the wall. This was proving excessively difficult. Then suddenly they heard a great noise and commotion over their heads. When they went to find out the cause of it they discovered that there was a cellar, and that the noise was

---

* John Talbot: of Grafton. Cousin and wealthy heir presumptive of the Earl of Shrewsbury. His son actually succeeded. Talbot's brother was Lord Windsor of Hewell. A zealous catholic, Talbot married a daughter of Sir William Petre, Mary I's secretary of state. (See HRW, pp. 74-5; DJ, pp. 109-10.)

† Robert Wintour: elder brother of Thomas, he succeeded to the family estate at Huddington. Married the daughter of John Talbot of Grafton (DJ, p. 52; HRW, p. 74). For earlier life, and possible relations with Thomas, see EGF, pp. 23-4, 29, 156-64.

caused by coal of which the cellar was full. This substance was not charcoal, but a sort of black rock which burns like charcoal to produce a very good fire.

They were considerably nonplussed by this news, fearing in the first place that the noise of their work would be easily heard by anyone who went in or out of the cellar. Furthermore, since that kind of coal was very heavy, they began to fear that it might make the floor of the cellar collapse. Then the mine would be discovered. Another difficulty was now making itself felt: the more they dug forwards, the nearer they approached the river, and so it came about that the mine sometimes filled with water. This phenomenon would increase the further they went. They had already taken up and carried out in a single night several barrels of water. This made them begin to wonder if the gunpowder would not spoil in the presence of so much dampness, and become useless for their purpose. For these reasons, they resolved to find out if the owner of the cellar would be willing to let it to them. To make their request more plausible, Thomas Percy could plead his need of it as a place to store wood and coal for his own house which stood next to the cellar.

Mr Guy did some reconnoitring in this direction.* As we have seen, he lived in the house as Mr Thomas Percy's servant. Fawkes went to the owner of the cellar and found that the coal was being taken away, so that the cellar would be empty for anyone who wished to hire it. To no one would he make it over more willingly than to Mr Thomas Percy, Fawkes's master, whom the owner was only too willing to serve and please in this as in anything else. Guy

---

* Other sources suggest that the hiring of the cellar was by no means a smooth and easy affair: (cf. EGF, pp. 111–12). It is remarkable that the idea of hiring the cellar did not occur to the miners in the first place. The narrator seems to have been entirely ignorant of the locale. The only feasible place from which to dig a tunnel was away from the river *towards* the cellar under the House of Lords. See JG, *What was the Gunpowder Plot?*, London, 1897, chapter IV, pp. 54–92, especially plan at p. 59: SRG, chapter IV, pp. 77–113. Between them Gardiner and Gerard show up the inadequacy of the records to give us a clear picture of the alleged scene of the mining operation. It is significant that no one apart from the plotters ever saw the mine or reported on it. Wintour's tale (Salisbury MS 113/54) and a confession of Fawkes (GPB, 49 and 101) are the only sources. The wetness of the cellar, as described by Greenway, would have made it quite unsuitable for a repository of gunpowder even for a few days, let alone for a matter of months.

reported to his friends how the business had gone. It was decided that he should lose no time in renting it. This he did. When they inspected the cellar they saw that it corresponded to their purpose exactly. It would serve them instead of the mine, being situated immediately under the Parliament-house. It would also be so much safer since it would occur to none to think that it served any other purpose than it usually did, that is to contain wood, coal and similar wares, which were kept there, and in other places like it, to be sold to wholesalers. Such material could also be easily transported to other places thanks to the nearness of the river.

Once they had procured the cellar, they fell to thinking how they might without suspicion bring over the barrels of powder already purchased. These were now lying in the house on the other side of the river directly opposite the Parliament-house. For this purpose they bought a boat. They rowed over by night in secrecy from one side of the river to the other. Not without danger of being seen and discovered, they succeeded nevertheless in getting the powder into the cellar. They placed some very heavy stones on top of the barrels, and all those iron (*ferri*) objects which they had used in making the mine. They covered them up with some thousands of bundles of wood. A very considerable quantity, but done in such a way that a hole or opening was left through which a man could easily introduce, when the time came, the matches on rods to fire the fuse. So as to make their deception more effective, they introduced into the cellar a large quantity of household goods such as old tables, beds, mattresses and empty barrels,* together with provision

---

* This may have been, in fact, property belonging to, or in the care of, John Whynniard, who was 'Yeoman of His Majesty's Wardrobe of the Beds' (cf. EGF, pp. 111 and 147). He had the house adjoining the Lords, part of which, at least, had been rented to Percy. According to Bishop Goodman, 'as soon as ever he heard of the news what Percy intended, he fell into a fright and died', which was seemingly on the morning of 5 November 1605 (see HRW, p. 16). S. R. Gardiner rejected Goodman's evidence on the insufficient plea that Mrs Susan Whynniard was referred to in an examination of 7 November as his wife and not his widow. But why was she not referred to as Mrs *John* W. if her husband was still alive? Why, in any case, was not John examined? He was incapacitated by illness, pleaded Gardiner. The thought that occurs to one inevitably in the 1970s is that if Whynniard died on the 5th, it was because he stumbled prematurely on something he was not supposed to know.

of wine and cider for the year. They also put a number of signs or seals at the door by the entrance whereby they would soon know if anyone with a skeleton-key had opened the cellar in their absence. They used great care in shutting and locking up the cellar. This is how things stood with the plot about the end of April, or getting on for May, in the year 1605. All they were waiting for now was for parliament to begin. But for various reasons, and to their great displeasure, it was prorogued. So to avoid the suspicion that would arise from being seen too much in one another's company they all again withdrew to their own houses. They visited one another at agreed times on the pretext of hunting or other pastimes usual among gentlemen . . .

Father Garnet had been aware for some time that Mr Catesby was holding aloof from him. Fearing that he might be gradually cooling off in his accustomed piety and matters of religion, Garnet set himself the task of finding out what he was doing. He got to know that, apart from the military preparations which he was making for his passage to Flanders, he was having frequent dealings, and that very secretly, with those special friends of his. Word was brought back to Garnet that Catesby had used words full of disgust and resentment against the king and state. Whenever they met, he read all the signs in him of a man preoccupied with grandiose and far-reaching schemes. He began to wonder whether he had not some other intention in view than what he showed outwardly. He began to watch Catesby more closely. Garnet finally concluded that something was brewing which he did not wish Garnet to know about. It might be aimed to disturb the public peace. Garnet's own letters written to his superiors in Rome show his suspicion clearly. These were later sent to me so that I could write this history practically as an eye-witness. Garnet asked for the advice and views of his superiors so that he could bring more effective remedy to the ills he now suspected. I will put down here his own words so that the reader can see, as it were in a mirror, his gentleness of spirit and how far from the mark were those calumnies which the enemies of God and himself directed against him so falsely and shamelessly . . .

First of all, here is a letter written on 25 August 1604. Peace negotiations were still in progress,* and there was still some hope

* The original of this letter seems to have been lost. The nearest known in

that the catholics might be included in it. He says that there were some who so resented the prospect of peace that they declared that anyone who claimed to be promoting it and religion at the same time were traitors, and men interfering in matters of state . . . Garnet wrote, 'In fact no one with any prudence or judgement finds the idea of peace displeasing. We certainly hope that some good will come out of it for the catholic religion, and that the catholics will continue to await results with patience.' From these words we can understand first of all how great was the desire of some to see peace concluded! There were people who could not bear the thought of relief being brought to catholics by the negotiations for peace! In the second place, one can see how much Father Henry desired to promote both. He was chiefly concerned to see peace established in the hope that it would bring some alleviation to the lot of catholics. But there were catholics who doubted how things would turn out for them after peace was restored, and so began to resent his influence. Already they showed themselves willing to use force even if peace were concluded, without regard for the others. This is why in the same letter Garnet writes as follows in cipher: 'If the negotiations for toleration do not not go well, it will be impossible to keep the catholics quiet. What can we do? The jesuits will not be able to pacify them. The pope must command all catholics not to make a move.' Could a man in so few words show greater desire of peace and quiet, or propose a more efficacious means of keeping it and preventing the disturbances he feared? But let us proceed with the story.

A month after the above was written, Garnet wrote again in reply to a letter penned by his superiors.* In this they asked to be informed whether he or any other Jesuit resident in England had shown himself opposed to peace, or given ear to unquiet spirits who were against it. They asked because a letter had been written to Padua from England containing information to this effect, although

---

* This letter, printed as of 22 September 1604, is only known from E. Joannes's version, p. 242. See note (*) p. 90.

---

date is of 29 August 1604, probably written to the chaplain of the Constable of Castile, and preserved in the Jesuit house at Loyola (English Province, S.J., Transcripts).

the writer was unknown. Father Garnet replied to the questions in these words: 'It is easy to see how far from the truth is that which has been written to Padua to the effect that the king is alienated from the catholics by reason of the indiscreet zeal of some jesuits. Both to friends and enemies, in fact, their attitude is well known. They were ever most ready to procure and forward the peace. Indeed, the negotiator (*agente*) always followed their advice in this matter, and without their help and that of their friends negotiations would not have reached this conclusion. Moreover, one of the leading men of the realm openly praised the jesuits in parliament a short while ago for their prudence, learning and right attitudes; as men, moreover, who had proved most useful in helping the peace to its conclusion. It is well known how many would have been involved in that plot of Watson's and how much peril would have been born from it, if the jesuits had not stood in the way. Although they cannot prevent everything that some wayward individual may take it into his head to devise, they are nevertheless able to bring it about that the greater and more significant section of the catholic community resign themselves to living in peace. Finally, when our enemies see the way we negotiate and proceed, they do not omit to suggest that we are flattering the king's councillors whose good opinion it seems that we have won. And so I humbly take my leave of you and our friends. This 21st September.'

It seems that a bolder defence than this could not be made, nor could the world be shown more clearly how much Garnet and his fellow jesuits loved peace. It is also to be noted that at this time they needed to defend themselves from two extremes: on the one hand from those who thought that they little favoured the peace, and on the other from those who seeing them favour it so much, thought they they were flatterers and fawners on the king and state. But the good Father knew well that the Gospel which was sown in the world and grew in it with peace needed to be maintained and preserved likewise by peace. But now we will come more closely to the subject we are dealing with. Let us see more in detail how this servant of God spoke of these affairs. To his last breath he upheld before the world, even to the grudging admiration and surprise of his very enemies, that lofty spirit of invincible patience and gentleness.

Father Garnet gradually became aware that Mr Catesby was up

to something, although he could not ascertain what it was. He therefore began to use every opportunity of persuading all and sundry to patience and long-suffering. He spoke very often on the subject both in spiritual exhortations and sermons, and with such feeling that Mr Catesby began to wonder if he were not the cause of the priest's talking so often on a subject which he found decidedly unpalatable. Catesby decided first of all to visit him less often. Subsequently, he made it very clear that he felt offended when he heard Garnet and others of the Society drumming home the same doctrine. He began to say openly, and so did others who shared his spirit, that the jesuits were getting in the way of the good that catholics could do themselves by remaining firm behind their own cause. The jesuits' insistence on papal command and authority, patience under suffering, and the vanity of hopes that relied on the intercession of princes, were undermining the common endeavour. Father Henry had information of all this, and wrote communicating it to his superiors in a cipher letter of 8 May 1605. It ran as follows:* 'It seems that the catholics have now reached a stage of desperation. Many of them are dissatisfied with the jesuits saying that they are opposed to the use of force or violence in self-defence. I have not dared to explore their thoughts too deeply so as to not to contravene Father General's order about not becoming involved in such matters.' What follows is out of cipher: 'For this reason, I cannot give you a lengthier report, and even this I have only learnt by mere chance.' Can anyone fail to see from these words how much trouble he took to hold aloof from strife? He did not even wish to know or inform himself too deeply of what he had reason to fear. His superiors likewise took great care that all the jesuits should avoid involvement in matters which could disturb the peace. So much so, that they did not wish them even to find out about such things. Certain it is that when he wrote that letter the plot was already ripe. All that concerned it materially was already put in train. They were only waiting for parliament to begin, as was said above. Of all this the good priest knew nothing right up to that time.

Now after this letter was seen and read in Rome, Father Persons

---

* This letter is only known from the printed version in Andrew Eudaemon-Joannes's, *Ad actionem Proditoriam Edouardi Coqui, Apologia pro R.P. Henrico Garneto . . .*, Cologne, 1610, p. 249.

wrote a reply in the name of His Holiness. There was also a letter from Father General to the same effect giving strict command to Father Henry that he and his fellow jesuits should continue to prevent, as far as they could, every kind of tumult and rebellion, and anything else which could embarrass king and state. Father Henry replied to these letters as follows, on 24 July of the same year, 1605:[*]

'Reverend Father, We have received your Reverence's letters with the respect which we owe both to His Holiness and to yourself. For my part, I have up to now prevented serious trouble on four occasions. No doubt we can prohibit every public manifestation of armed rising; and it is certain that there are many catholics who wish to do nothing of the kind without our approval, unless their necessity becomes most urgent. Two factors, however, cause us much worry. The first is that others in another county may fly to arms. This would force the rest, out of sheer necessity, to do likewise. For there are not a few who cannot be restrained by the bare command of His Holiness. They dared, while Pope Clement was still alive, to ask whether the pope could forbid them to defend their own lives. They claim besides that no priest has been admitted to their secret councils. They complain about us more particularly, and not a few of their friends say that we are a hindrance to them. In order to blunt their edge in some measure, and gain time in which some fitting remedy can be applied, we have begged them to send someone agreed on by themselves to His Holiness. This they have done. I have directed him to the Nuncio in Flanders who can recommend him in turn to His Holiness. I also wrote him a letter in which I explained their viewpoint, and reasons for each side of the question. The letter was written very fully and sent over by a most safe way. So much for the first danger. The second is rather more serious. There is a risk that some private endeavour may commit treason or use force against the king, and in this way all the catholics might be forced to take arms.

'In view of all this, two things are called for in my opinion. First of all, His Holiness must lay down what must be done in every case. Secondly, he must forbid under censure all recourse by catholics to

[*] This letter exists in two contemporary decipher copies of the original cipher letter, which has been lost, in ARSJ, Fondo Gesuitico, 651, 628, ff. 211r–12 v. The narrator's version is entirely faithful to the deciphers.

armed force. He must issue a public brief to this effect, the occasion of which can be the recent disturbance in Wales* which came to nothing. As for the rest, since things grow worse every day, we must beg His Holiness to provide some remedy for all our difficulties as soon as possible. Meanwhile, we can only crave his blessing and that of your Paternity. London, 24 July 1605. Your Paternity's humble servant, Henry Garnet.'

In this letter there are a number of items worthy of consideration, and which show very clearly the sincerity of this good priest. It shows how completely his conduct agreed with what his superiors ordered: that he should try to get from the pope the most effective remedy possible for an evil which every day grew more obvious. One can also see from this letter the truth of something which he told the court at his trial and when he was subjected to examination: that is, that when Mr Catesby wanted to tell him something of what he and his friends were trying to do to remedy the catholics' situation, Garnet refused to hear him. He feared that he might get to know more than he wished, or that he decently could. Perhaps it was this that moved Catesby to reveal his intention to another priest in confession. Possible he wished in this way to warn the jesuits of the evil which threatened them and many another. Or did he wish by this means to relieve his own mind of the doubts and scruples which still troubled him? But all this was a long time afterwards. One can also see the trouble that Garnet took to gain time so that any design which they had in mind should not be put in execution before His Holiness in Rome had forbidden it. To make sure of this, he saw to it that they themselves should send off a gentleman for this purpose, as it says in the letter.†

* See chapter 2, n. (*) p. 45.
† The man sent was Sir Edmund Baynham (see Win., *passim*: also article by S. E. Sprott in Recusant History, vol. 10, pp. 96–110). His mission provides an excellent example of an action, in itself ambiguous, which was given subsequently a sinister interpretation, for political purposes, by the English government. All the same, Baynham seems to fill the swashbuckling role of most of the conspirators, and may have intended to compromise Garnet. Certainly the popes of the time would not have entertained a plot of this kind (Clement VIII, 30.i.1592–5.iii.1605; Leo XI, l.iv.1605–27.iv.1605; Paul V, 16.v.1605–28.i.1621). Garnet's original letter of introduction for Baynham is in ARSJ, Anglia III, No. 56 (cf. 27.viii.1605).

It could also be that when those gentlemen realized that the priest had decided to forestall their intentions in every way possible they resolved to disarm his suspicion and fear of them. This, I think, is very probable although the resistance which the priest put up was based merely on suspicion. But when they saw him doing his best to see that other people also resisted them they realized that this could expose their secret to the risk of discovery. Already there was talk and writing going about which had to do with suspicions of this kind. What was worse, deputations were being sent hither and thither which were connected with precisely this. Perhaps after all, Garnet's would be the best method of getting better terms for the catholics. Whatever plan they now had in mind, they took pains to see that the jesuit should no longer mistrust them. He must be led to believe that they would go on waiting, as they had done hitherto, with patience and long-suffering for the help that God alone could send them.

In this they succeeded. This is evident from Garnet's letter written on 28 August the same year. This letter reports how two houses which he had occupied not far from London had been discovered and recognized by the protestants. This had forced him to take refuge here, there and everywhere until he could provide himself with another house. He also declared his intention to go on pilgrimage to a certain place which formerly had been the centre of much devotion. He writes thus:* 'As far as we can ascertain, the catholics live quietly at peace, and patiently, as is their wont. They hope that with time the king, or the son who follows him, will remedy their many grievances. The catholics grow considerably in number, and I hope that in the course of my journey I will have opportunity to do a great deal of good. God willing, I shall set out tomorrow. I hope this will be good for my health, and in any case I have no house in which to stay. I am leaving a deputy behind me etc. [*sic*].' After this he goes on to talk about his business in London and the man in whose care he had left it.

In order that we may understand the condition of the catholics at that particular time, and the persecution through which they lived, I will put down here what this good jesuit wrote in the course

* Any original or contemporary copy or decipher of this letter seems to have disappeared. This is apparently the letter in E. Joannes at pp. 255–6.

of his journey. He was an eye-witness, and lived amid the miseries he describes. The letter was written to Father Persons.*

'Good Sir, In a few days we shall be returning to London, but we are still without a house. Up to the present, we have not been able to find anything suitable; that is, a house in which we could live for any length of time. We shall have to lease some dwelling, and live after a fashion more private and retired than we have done in the past until the storm of present persecution has subsided. Examinations and searches are carried out now with unbelievable rigour. If my own hostess does not come to grief in the course of them, hers will be better fortune than has fallen to many of her neighbours. There is no comparison between the severity used at present against catholics and that of Queen Elizabeth's day. Every six weeks the courts hold session to search out catholics and their property. In many cases they deprive them of their goods against all right, seeing that sometimes the goods they take are not theirs but belong to others. They oblige the owners, when they want to recover their goods, to prove that they are indeed their own and not those of the recusants with whom they were found. It is the puritans who are appointed to the commissions in every county to hound the catholics. These men are of the lowest type and most violent, and the king would use them in no other service. The prisoners in Wisbech die of hunger.† They keep them so closely shut up that no help can come to them from their friends outside. Although the king intended that they should receive a mark every week, the gaoler, for all that, only feeds them three days a week so that he can make something out of it. If a recusant buys his goods back from the court which confiscated them, they make diligent enquiry to find out if the money with which he bought them is his own or not. If it is his own, they take even that.

'If things go on as they are, the catholics will be forced to redeem all their goods every six months, even down to the bed they sleep

* This letter, written on 4 and 21 October 1605, is preserved in AAW, old series, VIII, no. 106. Printed in M. A. Tierney, *Dodd's Church History of England*, vol. IV, London, 1841, pp. cii–cvi. Dodd attempted rather typically to give a sinister interpretation to the double-dating (p. cii).

† Wisbech Castle, belonging to the Bishop of Ely, was first used as a prison for Catholic recusants in 1580. For a scholarly account, see P. Renold, *The Wisbech Stirs, 1595–8* CRS, 51 (1958), pp. xi–xviii.

in. An example of someone who has already twice made this kind of redemption is to be found in the house where I am living at the moment.' Here he describes the person as known to Father Persons, but it would not do for me to set it down here. 'The judges give it out that the king is going to put into execution the capital laws passed against catholics. They have already martyred some in York-shire.' These, as a matter of fact, were certain laymen who had per-suaded others to become catholics. This is a capital offence. 'They say, moreover, that up to now the king has shown a measure of restraint, but from now on he will strike with the sword. He has given good demonstration of this in these martyrdoms at York. It was only after long deliberation, and in cold blood, that they finally had them killed.*

'The entire persecution has been set on foot without the catholics giving the least occasion for it. From this I very much doubt if the pope will be able to do anything to help them by using influence with the king. He should know that everything they say about the moderation being used towards catholics is all pretence and fable. In spite of all this, you may be sure that the first and foremost catholics will bear patiently all their trials and persecutions. But to what pitch of desperation such tyrannical and inhuman ways as they are now proceeding may reduce certain individuals, the experience of my pilgrimage does not allow me to say, etc. [*sic*].' Here he refers to certain incidents which happened to him in the course of his journey. They are worthy of record but cannot be written down here for the harm it could do to particular persons. However, I will not omit what he writes towards the end of his epistle in these words: 'I had a letter from Field† in Ireland' – a jesuit working

* According to VCH, York, London, 1961, p. 154, 'The fullest survey of Yorkshire recusancy was made in 1604 . . .' (See ed. E. Peacock, *A List of Roman Catholics in the Co. of York in 1604*, London, 1872: from a MS in the Bodleian; also *YAJ*, xxxvii, 24 et seq.) Many recusants were escaping from the south, and especially London, into the less persecuting climate of Yorkshire (see Archbishop Tobie Matthew to Salisbury, 18 December 1604; BM, Stowe 156, ff. 50r–51v.). The names of two laymen executed in 1604 were William Browne alias John Fulthering, and Thomas Welbourne (see HFR, III, pp. 136–7; G. Anstruther, O.P., Biographical Studies, I (1951–2), p. 115; HMC, Sal. Cal., part XVI, pp. 44–5.)
† This was seemingly Richard Field, superior about this time of the Irish Jesuits. See G. Oliver, *Collections towards illustrating the Biography of the Scotch, English and Irish members, S.J.*, Exeter, 1838, p. 226.

among the catholics there – 'which tells me that they have just
published in the last few days a most frightening edict against
ecclesiastics. In this, all are commanded to go to the protestant
churches, and there is the solemn protestation that the king never
promised, nor even had it in mind to promise, liberty of conscience
or toleration of their religion to catholics. 4 October 1605 etc.
[*sic*].'

I do not wish to say any more about this letter except to ask the
reader to notice two things worth remembering in view of what will
be said later. The first is that Father Henry, a precise observer of the
commands of His Holiness and of his own superiors, did everything
possible to restrain the catholics, even in the midst of cruel persecution, and in which a patience was needed not less than of the
saints . . . It is noteworthy that, in his opinion, the majority of the
catholics were fully resolved to possess their souls in patience,
although he could not rest assured that everyone would do so. The
other point is that, when he wrote that letter, which was on 4
October, he knew nothing of the design of those gentlemen beyond
what he had suspected originally. Perhaps his suspicion now re-
awoke in view of the violence of the persecution, which was then
growing all the time, and also because in the course of his pilgrimage
he discovered the diverse humours and dispositions of many people
of which formerly he had been ignorant. But the strongest argument that he knew nothing at that time of this plot seems to me to
be this. It had been given out that parliament would be held on 3
October.* Those gentlemen now stood alert and ready to carry out
what they had in mind. But it was at this time that the Father was
still on his journey, completely unprovided of any house or shelter,
and a long way not only from those same gentlemen but from all his
most trusted and influential friends. He was a long way, likewise,
from the other Fathers of the Society.

Garnet's total ignorance of the deed was very clearly demonstrated by his intention to return to London where he ordinarily

* The narrator has apparently overlooked the fact that the proclamation proroguing parliament from 3 October until 5 November 1605 was issued on 28
July, so that Garnet would have been aware of the prorogation nearly a month
before he set out for Holywell. This particular argument for Garnet's innocence, such as it is, thus falls to the ground. (See ch. IV, n. (*) p. 93 above.)

SIR EVERARD DIGBY

resided. This would have amounted to surrendering himself into the hands of his enemies since the projected upheaval threatened London especially. Inevitably, those who found themselves outside their houses at that time would have fallen into the hands of professed enemies of the catholics even in the course of so much confusion. This would have been especially true of anyone then on the road. They would have been the victims of a revenge wreaked upon them with every kind of cruelty in view of the frightful catastrophe still fresh in men's minds. Nor was Father Henry so lacking in judgement that he could not provide for his own safety. Nor was he so short of charity that he would not have tried to do something for the many Fathers, priests and others who were his friends, surrounded as they were by so much evil and imminent peril. He would first of all have withdrawn himself to a safe place. He would then have got warning to the others in some way so they would not be caught in the fire and horrible confusion which would have threatened them from hour to hour. He did none of these things, and many who were with him at the time can bear testimony to the fact that he did not. Nothing was further from his mind. The letter which he wrote on 4 October offers the clearest proof of this. This was the day after parliament was due to begin, when the plot would have been already accomplished. Who will dare to say that this servant of God was not completely innocent of the charge levelled against him by the heretics? Who will say that he was not entirely ignorant of what the plotters intended? . . .

So we return to the story of the plot. We shall see what happened after the conspirators, instead of using the mine, decided to use the cellar. There they placed the powder, together with everything else they needed for their purpose.

SIX

IT SEEMED TO THE PLOTTERS that by now they had overcome the greater part of the difficulties which had assailed them at the beginning of their enterprise. Indeed, it now seemed that the plan was in a certain sense completed and brought to perfection. All that was needed was that they should avoid being discovered, or even suspected, and then put the plan into execution. By now, therefore, they felt almost certain of success. All their deliberations and consultations were to do with precise circumstances, and the means they should take to have in their hands either the Prince of Wales or Duke Charles. The latter was then four years old, and resided with the queen, his mother, in the palace in London. If Duke Charles should be present in parliament at the time of firing the powder, it would be necessary to seize his sister, Elizabeth. As we have said, she was then staying with Baron Harington at a house some hundred miles from London. To make sure of this, they would need the help of more men and money. They therefore decided to let a few others into their secret in order to make use of them. Of prime importance was it that they provide themselves with munitions of war. They needed arms of other kinds than those they had. It was, therefore, necessary to take into their confidence someone of less exalted condition, who could take the waggons from London to the place where they would set up headquarters. This would be the rallying-point for their supporters.

For this purpose, they chose a servant of Mr Robert Catesby. He had seen long service with him, and Catesby had proved his sufficiency on many occasions. They knew him for a man trustworthy and close. He was called Thomas Bates.* He had long been a catholic, and for the profession of his faith had suffered hardships and persecution with great steadfastness. We shall have occasion to speak of him in greater detail later. All I wish to say about him now is that he carried out with great diligence and secrecy whatever his master commanded of him. Right up to the time that the plot was discovered, he carried himself among them blamelessly.

After Bates, they chose a gentleman called Ambrose Rookwood.† The very memory of him causes me a great deal of grief, since I knew him familiarly and loved him sincerely. This gentleman lived in Suffolk, where he had his seat, and enjoyed a very good income as the head of the family, which was both distinguished and of long standing. He was brought up from boyhood in the catholic faith, being born of catholic parents. They were thoroughly good people whose religion, goodness, and devotion he learned and imitated with great credit to himself, and amidst the universal affection of all who knew him. His house was a common refuge for priests, as it had been in the time of his father. Here his catholic neighbours could go to the sacraments, and meet often to hear sermons and talks. Nor were they prevented from this by the official visitations and frequent persecutions which he himself suffered. Indeed, he refused to be deterred by the great losses which he frequently experienced for these causes. The principal reason why the

---

* Thomas Bate or Bates: although a servant, he was in no sense, seemingly, a menial. He had his own armour, and his own man at Ashby Saint Ledgers where he lived with his wife, Martha, in a house not far from the hall where Catesby resided. He engaged in cattle-dealing (cf. GBM, I, pp. 154–6). According to John Gerard's *Narrative* . . . (John Morris, *The Condition of Catholics under James I*, London, 1871, p. 219), he was 'only for his love to his master drawn to forget his duty to God, his king, and country'.

† Ambrose Rookwood: his seat was Coldham Hall at Stanningfield. His mother was a Tyrwhitt and sister of Lady Ursula Babthorpe (see PRO, SP 14, vol. 16, No. 16: given in extenso in H. H. Spink, *The Gunpowder Plot and Lord Monteagle's Letter* . . ., London, 1902, p. 29 and pp. 308–9). Rookwood was going to fight in Flanders, it seems. About a year before the alleged plot he brought his horses to Clopton Park, near Stratford-on-Avon and John Grant's house at Norbrook, to be nearer the rendezvous (cf. Blacker-Morgan, I, pp. 171–2). Clopton belonged to Baron Carew, a trusted friend of the government.

plotters chose him was not, as I believe, simply to make use of his money, but because of their conviction that he was a man of great courage and magnanimity. He would expose himself to any danger once he was convinced that a cause was just and honourable. They were also well aware that he kept good stables, his horses being among the best in the land. Anyone could see how significant this item would be in time of need.

Rookwood was about twenty-six or twenty-seven years old. He was well-built and handsome, if somewhat short. His manner was easy and cheerful. His dealings with people were gentlemanly and courteous. He was a well-lettered man having spent his youth acquiring the humanities in Flanders. He left behind him at his death a wife who was beautiful and of gentle birth, together with two or three small children, and with them everything else he had on this earth. He preferred the companionship of this most wretched and foolhardy plot. In my opinion, one can tell from this how deep was the conviction which they cherished that the business would succeed. One can see also more of the nature of the deed itself. Certainly, men of that quality and discretion, and outstanding for goodness and judgement, would not have embarked on such a course, or faced a whole array of dangers and continuing difficulties, if they had not been convinced that it was lawful. Nor would they have allowed themselves to be consumed with so much ease by one overmastering passion.

They joined to their number another gentleman called John Grant.* His home was not very far from that of Mr Robert Wintour, whose sister he had married. This proximity was very convenient, since he was thus able to take into his house a share of the munitions and arms which they needed for the enterprise. His task was, in a sense, vital since at the right moment he had to organize a force to take the king's daughter by surprise. She lived in a house not far away, as we have seen; that belonging to Baron Harington. Moreover, the stables of a number of war-horses, which he intended

* John Grant: 'was a Warwickshire squire who had married . . . Thomas Wintour's sister Dorothy'. Norbrook, or Northbrook, Grant's home, was near Snitterfield. 'Grant was a taciturn but accomplished man, who had been likewise fined for his share in the Essex rising' (Spink, op. cit., p. 28). His religious affiliation is obscure.

to make use of at the proper time, were also near his house.★ He kept his own horses in the same place, and so could take over all others that were to be found there. In the event, as we shall see, they did just this. This gentleman was about forty years old. He was by nature taciturn, and somewhat inclined to melancholy. At the same time, he was intelligent and discreet. Apart from Latin, he knew several other languages. His way of life was admirable, and he was known to all as a good man. His courage was inferior to none in that company. This he had demonstrated often in facing up to the king's pursuivants when they came to search his house, a process which brought with it the danger of losing not only everything else he possessed but even life itself, thanks to the violence and insulting behaviour which those kind of people commonly use. On a number of occasions, he sent them packing after the kind of reception which made sure they did not trouble him again thanks to the experience they already had of him. If they did return, it was with such a company and so well equipped that they could be sure of the outcome of their encounter, and of the kind of resistance which that gentleman could put up against them. Thanks to his courage and determination, Grant won some kind of security for himself and his house, so that he was not molested quite so often by the insults and arrogance of every royal lackey, as many of the others were. For most of the time he was also able to keep a priest in his house.

The plotters chose at this time another man called Mr Robert Keyes.† It seemed that they could not expect from him any help beyond what he could give in his own person. He had neither

---

★ The stables may have been at Warwick Castle (some eight or nine miles from Snitterfield). This would explain why Catesby knew the castle sufficiently well to send Digby to collect horses during the progress across country after Dunchurch. It would also explain why Digby did it at all, believing them to be Grant's. Another example of a neutral act being given a sinister interpretation later by the government? (See EGF, p. 160).

† Robert Keyes: son of the Rector of Staveley, north Derbyshire. Like Rookwood, however, his mother was a Tyrwhitt, daughter of Sir William T. of Kettleby, Lincs., and presumably a catholic like her father (see DJ, p. 43). Nevertheless, her marriage to a Protestant parson does not argue, in the context of the age, strong convictions. Keyes was, seemingly, in indigent circumstances. His wife, Christiana, widow of Thomas Groome, was governess of Lord Mordaunt's children for a time. Keyes had a servant at the time of the plot, William Johnson (SP 14, vol. 16, No. 33, I, II, III).

possessions nor money more than what was necessary to maintain
himself and his wife. Apart from this, he was a man magnanimous and
fearless. At the time of his death, he showed, rather to the admiration and surprise of everyone, that he was a man of serious and
mature disposition, possessing good judgement and intelligence,
and also great fervour and devotion. The conspirators held him in
high esteem for the long experience they had already had of his
qualities.

This was the number of plotters at the time when they were
waiting for nothing else but the opening of parliament. As far as I
can find out, this was also their number at the time when they sent
Mr Guy to Flanders.* But they foresaw that for various circumstances it might prove necessary to increase their number. So Mr
Catesby suggested that they should give him leave, if necessity
arose, and with the permission of any two others, to choose one or
more to add to their existing ranks. Since he was the author of the
plot, and a man very circumspect in his proceedings, leave was
given. It was also at this time that the plotters sent Mr Guy, in the
company of two or three others of their number, up and down the
country to gather information on the situation and suitability of
places where in time of necessity they might build fortifications. I
got this from someone who was with these gentlemen after the plot
was discovered, and when speech was free as to what had happened.
In the course of his journey, Fawkes came across a certain number of
difficulties which, as it seemed to him, they could not resolve
adequately without first consulting men skilled in the art of fortifi-
cation. For this reason, they decided to send Guy to Flanders. He
would be able to find out if it were possible, and by what means, to
get a substantial quantity of gunpowder from those countries. This
would be needed for the war which would probably break out as a
result of the confusion and change of régime.†

They further provided a ship which was to serve for no other

---

* Nowhere else is there such a full account of the alleged reasons for Guy's
being sent back to Flanders for a time.
† It is difficult to see why it should have been necessary to obtain gunpowder
from Flanders at this time, since there is no evidence of dearth at home, at any
rate at the turn of the century. See G. Cruickshank, *Elizabeth's Army*, Oxford,
1966, p. 127; F. Edwards, article in the *London Recusant*, vol. 2, pp. 12–14.

purpose than to cross over to Flanders at the very moment of the explosion.* This was to give news of the deed to the rulers of Christendom, to forestall adverse reports put out by enemies, and to present the facts in the best light possible. They commissioned Mr Guy with other particular negotiations, but I will say no more about them, either because they are uncertain, or else because they could touch the reputation of English gentlemen still living in those parts. They themselves deny the truth of what the plotters said about them. I will satisfy myself by recounting what is certain and generally known from the confession of all. I will not relate things uncertain which, in any case, would turn to the harm of some who are still living.

In the period of parliament's adjournment, expenses went on growing. The plotters had to pour out money on a thousand things necessary to their design. Every day meant some new expense, until the time came when they could no longer find money to pay for what they needed; this in spite of the fact that they had been well supplied with money. Mr Robert Catesby therefore decided to enlist the help of one or two more who, being well supplied with funds, would be able to help out their necessity whether present or future. Apart from the provision of day-to-day essentials, present necessities included the very large expenses to which Mr Catesby was put in order to maintain all the people who depended on him, either on the pretext of going with him to the war in Flanders, or else on the plea of long-standing friendship. These he was neither able nor willing to dismiss, since he knew how much he would need them when the moment came. Meanwhile, he had to keep them. This was ordinarily in London. Sometimes he even had to furnish them with money so that something like a king's treasure was called for rather than the purse of a private person. However, since the time of parliament's assembly was not far off, he might have found some means of supplying this demand. What chiefly weighed with him, though, was the consideration that, while he had to spend money all the time in this way, when the hour of revolution arrived, it it would be more than expedient to have at hand already provided an additional and very considerable sum of money. That would be the moment when, after the death of the king and the members of

* There seems to be no other manuscript source for this statement.

parliament, all the kingdom would be up in arms. It would be necessary to pay for men, transport, and necessary provisions against anything that might happen.

Mr Catesby went over all this in his own mind. He looked in every direction for someone whom he could use for this purpose. Finally, he resolved on a gentleman who was a great friend of his, and who had all the qualities one could desire in a man. He possessed every virtue and was courageous into the bargain. What was essential to the plotters, however, was that he was rich and influential. Of the qualities and the status of this gentleman, I will say no more than what I know from the relation of those who knew him and worked with him. I do not deny that I have myself seen him many times, and even in some measure got to know him. His name was Everard Digby, a Knight of the Golden Spur,★ descendant of a very distinguished and ancient family, and moreover a man of great wealth. His ancestors had helped Henry VII with military assistance against Richard III – it was from Henry that King James was lineally descended. Such was the valour that these ancestors showed in the field that, when the battle was over, Henry VII then and there conferred knighthood on seven brothers at once. Their descendants still live at the present time in various counties enjoying considerable reputation for wealth and distinguished blood.† But Sir Everard's house, as befitted the senior line, flourished more than the others, and especially in County Rutland, where he had his principal seat, which had also been that of his ancestors. He was among the leading gentlemen of the county, although he had considerable properties and income in Lancashire and other places.‡

Sir Everard Digby was born of catholic parents who enjoyed a wide reputation for their goodness and religious sincerity. Sir

★ The 'Golden Spur' was a papal order of chivalry traditionaly associated with Constantine the Great and Pope Sylvester, but formally constituted by Pope Paul IV in 1559.
† For an account of Sir Everard's family and descendants, see DJ, p. 62.
‡ There are a number of documents relating to the Digby properties in PRO, E. 124, vol. 3 (*N.B.* ff. 238r., 268v.) and vol. 4 (*N.B.* ff. 75r., 90r., 178r.) See also PRO, E. 178, 4296 and 3574, 'The Commission to enquire in the County of Buckingham of the lands and goods of Sir Everard Digby, Knight'. E. 178 contains many documents relating to the goods of the plotters and their disposal after the plot. The list would be too long to give in full here.

Everard also inherited their piety along with their possessions and income. However, his father died while the son was still young, a mere boy in fact. Hence it came about that he was brought up in a protestant household . . . It was some time before he was old enough to make adequate judgements in religion. In fact, he did not become a catholic, or more correctly make profession of the catholic faith to which he was always strongly inclined, before arriving at the age when he had control of his own affairs, and was able to live in his own way. Up to that time, he had enjoyed much contact with the queen's court, and had every prospect of being advanced in honour and riches, thanks to the considerable satisfaction which he gave, and his rare good qualities. Nevertheless, he preferred to carry the cross with catholics in their persecution . . .

It is only giving him his bare due to say that Digby was a man so perfect in every respect that in no time at all he would win the confidence of anyone who dealt with him. He was some six feet tall. Although this was less than Mr Catesby's height, he was rather more strongly built, and somewhat more vigorous. I do not think that in the whole of England there were two gentlemen who were their equals. Digby's countenance was handsome and virile, and his eyes alert and lively. His deeds and gestures were those of a gentleman, and courtly; his manner was affable and courteous. He put himself out to please everyone, and avoid giving offence as far as he could, to anyone. He had had plenty of past opportunities to show his courage and magnanimity, and now he had not the least occasion in this latest tragedy to show the world these things more clearly. Indeed, his latest demonstration brought stupefaction to those who saw him die, as will be related later. I know someone who saw him with his other companions when they were up in arms after the discovery of the plot. He was astounded to see both him and Mr Catesby so intrepid, and lacking all fear at a time when they had nothing else to expect but death, or something even worse. They both had the accomplishments in fullest measure which are prized in gentlemen. They were also skilled huntsmen. For this purpose, Digby kept hounds, gun-dogs, falcons and horses in great number. It was he who on pretext of a big meet was to be the leader of those sent to capture the king's daughter.

Digby was an expert rider, swordsman, and played a number of

musical instruments from which he derived great pleasure. He kept
in his house a number of retainers who could play and sing together.
He was adept at all games and pastimes. Although he was only a
youth, twenty-six or twenty-seven years old, he possessed for all
that the prudence of a mature man. This he revealed in all his conversation. He was a person of sound judgement and of lively intelligence. What caused most astonishment, however, was the fact
that, although he was frequently at court, and often in the company
of young gallants ready for every prank and entirely given over to
the new religions and moral opinions, he himself was for all that a
very good-living man. Vice had no place in him. Those who looked
after his spiritual welfare at that time bore witness to this. I have
often heard them say that they derived great satisfaction from his
company, and from seeing a layman surrounded every hour of the
day by the world's distractions and bad company yet possessing so
much goodness and showing so much carefulness in his own conduct. He was extremely observant in both vocal and mental forms
of prayer, and he never passed a day without examining his conscience. He went to the sacraments once a week, and for this purpose kept a priest in his house; one of the most learned and virtuous
at that time living in England.* He also showed great zeal in helping others and trying to win them to the knowledge of his religion.
Many were converted by his means. He avoided detraction above
everything. As people noticed who indulged in it most themselves,
he knew how to change the subject with great skill when conversation tended in that direction. But whenever he heard talk against
catholic faith and practice, he did not hesitate to defend it openly,
courageously ignoring any peril that might come to him in this way.
One could give many examples, but it is not my intention to delay
the reader with what he could well regard as irrelevant to this
history. Nor in defending what was good and praiseworthy in these
gentlemen would I wish to appear to defend their deed. I only want
the reader to know that I am convinced that men of this kind would
never have staked their lives and positions in this way if they had

---

* The narrator is doubtless referring to John Gerard, S.J., who brought Sir
Everard back to catholicism, and acted as his chaplain. (See P. Caraman, *The
Autobiography of a Hunted Priest*, New York, 1955 edition, pp. 193–201, *et
alibi*.)

not been convinced in their innermost conscience that they could do so without offence to God. Undoubtedly, they put the good of their souls before all else. Neither would they have undertaken such a thing if their most cruel persecution at the hands of protestants had not obliged them to look for any sort of remedy they could to counteract the infinite evils and miseries which they suffered. And in truth no one would believe this of them who had not seen them with his own eyes or heard their words with his own ears.

Of the manner in which this gentleman came to agree to the plot I can say nothing apart from what was told me by someone who heard it from Mr Thomas Wintour after the discovery of the plot. According to this, Mr Robert Catesby first put the matter to Digby in obscure and general terms. In this way he found out what would be Sir Everard's reaction to anyone who wished to apply an effective remedy to the situation of the catholics in their present necessity. He found him ready to concur with the help that he and the others were ready to provide. Catesby told him that, in a few days, either he himself, or Mr Thomas Wintour speaking for him, would give him clearer information of their plan. Digby was content with this, and swore to keep their secret. Thus it was that, not long afterwards, Thomas Wintour sought him out and revealed the whole business to him and in what terms it stood at that time. He asked him for financial support, and to place his war-horses in readiness, and likewise hunters, hounds, falcons and gun-dogs for a hunt which would take place near Baron Harington's house. In this way, as soon as he received news of the success of the explosion, they could all without more ado seize the king's daughter. Already they should provide themselves with as many arms as they could procure. As far as I am able to find out, Sir Everard knew nothing of this plot until about a month before it was due to be put into execution. The other plotters knew nothing about him, apart from the two mentioned above and Mr Guy.★

★ There is no evidence to contradict this glowing account of Digby and for that matter, Rookwood. Their entry into this plot knowingly is scarcely plausible according to the generally accepted story. How could two gentlemen of their moral calibre willingly have become accomplices in such a crime? They do not fit the rôle of agents-provocateurs like most of the others. A suggested reconstruction of how they became involved is given in EGF, pp. 126–9.

About the same time, or a little later, they decided to share their knowledge with yet another from whom they hoped to get financial assistance. As I have said, they had a great need of money which was only commensurate with their lack of it. This other gentleman was called Francis Tresham. He too came from a very distinguished and ancient family, and enjoyed a considerable income. He lived in Northamptonshire. His father, who had died a few months previously, had suffered great persecution for his open profession of the catholic faith. There were the pecuniary penalties, and especially the monthly payment of eighty crowns, which amounted to 1,040 a year. This was due to the fact that, as we have said, they reckon the year in a new way specially for catholics which gives it thirteen months. Over and above this, Sir Thomas Tresham had to put up with frequent imprisonment and other vexations.★

We may note particularly about Francis Tresham that he was always taken to be a man of sound judgement. He knew how to look after himself, but was not much to be trusted.† This was the view even of those who were most familiar with him. For this reason, I am inclined to think that it was none other than Divine Providence which made the conspirators share their plot with him. I am all the more convinced of this because Mr Robert Catesby did not take him to be a man in whom one could place much confidence. And Mr Francis Tresham was his close relative. Catesby took him to be more interested in his own welfare and private schemes than in the common good of the catholic community, although he had always professed catholicism. Indeed, for some years before the queen died,

★ Sir Thomas Tresham, like Sir William Catesby, was converted to catholicism by the jesuit mission of Campion and Persons, about 1580. (For some account of him, see DJ, pp. 9–10.) Tresham had hoped that the accession of the new king would bring alleviation to the lot of Catholics, and lost no time in proclaiming him at Northampton in 1603. He died on 11 September 1605, and the eldest son, Francis, succeeded to his estates.

† The writer's reserve with regard to Francis Tresham is surely significant. Alone of the plotters, his character receives no general eulogy. In fact, Francis Tresham seems to have become one of the principal agents-provocateurs in the piece. His father, in spite of his own political loyalty to James I, evidently suspected, by October 1603, that Francis was going far beyond what such loyalty could normally permit. Francis was 'defaming' his own father to the king. He was also spying for the court on his catholic relations either then or somewhat later. (See EGF, pp. 52–4).

and up to that moment, he had given good satisfaction and even better hope for the future. There is no need to say more about him. It seems that Providence allowed him to enter the plot precisely so that it should be discovered. Not that it is known for certain that he revealed it, but certainly there is grave reason to suppose that it was by his means that the plot came to light. The conspirators themselves suspected that it was he alone who revealed it. Mr Robert Catesby, as is evident from Mr Thomas Wintour's confession, only a few days afterwards greatly regretted having told him.

Here I will put down what Mr Robert Catesby told a friend of mine shortly before he died, and *after the plot was discovered*.* It was that, after he had imparted this information to Mr Francis Tresham, Mr Catesby for many nights in succession woke up suddenly as if he had been called or roused by someone to do something of importance. Although it seemed to him that when he first woke up he knew very well what he had to do, yet in spite of this, when he was fully awake he could no longer remember what it was. From that time he began to wonder if some great evil were threatening them. He began to ask himself if some betrayal was not afoot among them. But as I have said, up to this day, and for all I know, there is no certain knowledge that any of the conspirators revealed the plot in any way apart from what will be described in the next chapter. Whether this was treason or chance I leave to the reader's judgement. I am fully persuaded of one thing. It was a great providence of God, and an evident sign of the Divine goodness and mercy towards the king and kingdom, who would otherwise in a moment have faced ultimate disaster . . .

I will add here something else which the same person heard at the same time from Mr Catesby's mouth. While they were working underground in the mine, and doing their utmost to pierce through the foundation-wall of the Parliament-house, they clearly heard a bell chiming in the wall itself. They were much surprised at the sound and broke off their labour to listen to it more intently. The sound lasted for quite some time. Afterwards, they went back to work. But a little later, the bell began to ring again. It lasted, as before, quite some while. The gentlemen now began greatly to wonder what it could be. Not knowing what to make of it, they

* The phrase in *Italian* is crossed out in the MS but still clearly legible.

sent one of their number to get some holy water. With this they doused the wall. The tolling ceased, but not long afterwards began again. Nor did it stop before they had sprinkled the whole wall with holy water. This went on for some days, and those who heard it attributed different meanings to it. But as it was not given to them to foresee the outcome of the plot, so likewise they were not allowed to reach the meaning of that prodigious sound. Neither do I wish to be a curious investigator of this incident. I will rest content with leaving it to the reader's judgement to decide what it was and what it meant. It is enough for me to have set down shortly and accurately the tale as I heard it told by a man worthy of belief.★

Now that the number of conspirators was complete, nothing more remained but to put in execution what they had planned. So that all would proceed smoothly and without disturbance, they carefully distributed among themselves the various duties to be carried out. They allotted to Mr Guy, the expert in that field, the tasks of firing the powder; and also, at the same moment, of passing over quickly to Flanders to spread the news. He would need to present it in such a way that it did not seem like barbarism, and so rouse the hatred of christian princes abroad, as was much to be feared.† For this purpose, they gave him in advance the principal points of letters which he should send off in all directions. It was also one of his duties to provide as much gunpowder and munitions of war as he could. At the same time, he should enlist the services of as many captains and men experienced in warfare as possible. To Mr Thomas Percy they allotted the task of seizing the prince; or if he should be in parliament with the king, his father, Percy would have to seize Duke Charles, the second-born. This would not be very

★ Prodigious elements, which only make the tale less acceptable to us, had the opposite effect on readers of the time. The miraculous was freely, and indeed, uncritically admitted as a part of even the most prosaic political occasions (cf. M. Hume, op. cit., p. 32, n. 1). Robert Cecil did his best to get the discovery of the plot accepted as divine intervention. In his letter to Sir Charles Cornwallis of 9 November 1605, he begins, 'It hath pleased Almighty God, out of his singular goodness, to bring to light the most cruel and detestable conspiracy against the person of His Majesty . . .' (Win. II, p. 170).
† Although the narrator accepts the idea that the plotters proceeded in good faith and conscience, this seems to indicate some awareness on their part that their project was morally questionable.

difficult for Percy in view of his office of Gentleman Pensioner, and his considerable knowledge and experience of the court. Thus he could enter without challenge all the rooms in the palace. For this purpose he had also assigned to his company some three or four conspirators, everyone of whom would have with him his own posse of men. These would be friends and familiars. On various pretexts but without fuller knowledge, they would go through the rooms and galleries and vestibules. When they heard the noise of the explosion in the Parliament-house, they would rush back to Mr Thomas Percy. This gentleman, under colour of saving the child, would snatch him up hastily from the palace, put him in a carriage ready prepared for this, and then, with a good guard, carry him off with the utmost speed to where the other conspirators were ready waiting for him on the road. Percy would make his way with them to Baron Harington's house. There the rest of the conspirators would be found, along with an ample company of gentlemen who had been hunting with Sir Everard Digby, although without knowing anything further until now of what was happening.

It was Sir Everard's responsibility to get his friends together at that time for a large hunting party. This was something he had done many times before. On the pretext of this meet, he would bring up a good supply of forces to his friends in the neighbourhood of Baron Harington's house where the king's daughter lived. The district lent itself very well at that time of the year to diversions of this kind, and to hunting either fowl or game. Mr Catesby had the virtual supervision of the whole operation. It fell to him to see that nothing was lacking of what was needed, and that money, munitions, arms, and horses all stood in readiness for the road: also to receive one of the princes, whether the first-born or Duke Charles. Catesby also had to see to it that all the members of the company were properly equipped. Mr Thomas Wintour was assigned to him as assistant or adjutant, although he had to be in the palace at the proper time to help Mr Thomas Percy. The other conspirators had to provide ball, muskets and pikes, laying them up with all secrecy in the country-side where they lived. Mr Robert Wintour and John Grant had the principal oversight of this detail. They used the services of Mr Catesby's servant, Thomas Bates. Being a man of ordinary condition, he could drive waggons around without rousing suspicion. No one can suppose that these men would not have carried out their appointed tasks if the main business had succeeded. Although, in fact, the essential condition was not fulfilled, the horses were all ready at the proper place and time. The hunt, as fitted the occasion, was an important meeting, and attended by a great number of gentlemen. Money was already provided. The munitions available were more than was needed either to start a war, if it had been necessary, or to defend themselves against any who might have offered opposition in the beginning of a confused revolution.

To conclude what we have said so far, Parliament was due to meet on 3 October 1605. However, by reason of the plague which was discovered in some houses in the City, it was prorogued until 5 November.* According to custom, the king gave order that this should be proclaimed in the Parliament-house with customary solemnity. The Lord Chancellor and other members of the Privy Council and noblemen met on 3 October, the day appointed, to read the decree. Mr Thomas Wintour was present in the House at that time to see if any suspected what he and his companions had in mind. He saw those gentlemen fearlessly enter the chamber beneath which the powder had already been placed. He saw them handle the business for which they had come with every sign of tranquillity. He concluded, and his fellow plotters did likewise, that at least up to that day, 3 October, their secret remained safe. It was sufficiently unlikely that the Lord Chancellor, Secretary Cecil – that is the Earl of Salisbury, the Lord Chamberlain – the Earl of Suffolk, the Earl of Northampton, and other titled men of first rank in council and kingdom, would put themselves at the tender mercy of anyone who could blow them sky high at a moment's notice. They would not have taken chances if they had known that a man might enter the room beneath them, where that great heap of gunpowder was stored, with the purpose of blowing them up.† So the con-

* The proclamation proroguing parliament from 3 October until 5 November, was issued on 28 July 1605 (*v. supra*, ch. IV, n. (†) p. 74). The reasons given were that 'the ordinary course of our subjects resorting to the City for their usual affairs at the term, is not for the most part until All-Hallowtide, or thereabouts; as also . . . there may yet remain some dregs of the late contagion' (G.B.M., I, p. 164). Plague was certainly a problem in London in February 1605 (see Sal. Cal., XVII, p. 73).
† It is sufficiently unlikely that such a quantity of powder could have been

THE MONTEAGLE LETTER

spirators assured themselves that all they had done so far was un-
suspected by anyone up to that moment. They hoped that things
would continue in this way for another month. But it pleased God
that things should turn out otherwise, as we shall relate in the next
chapter.

stored under parliament undetected. The 'cellar' was scarcely a private place,
and more than one person had access (see J.G., pp. 87–92). Gardiner (op.
cit., pp. 108–12) confirms rather than disposes of Gerard's difficulties. The
Keeper of the Palace at Westminster, at any rate from 1604, was Sir Thomas
Knyvett (see Cal. S.P. Dom., 1603–10, p. 85). He was a tried and trusted
servant of the government, and in the spring of 1605 warrants were addressed
to him as Warden of the Mint, which was then in the precincts of the Tower
(ibid., p. 211). The fact that over many months he allowed some 3,600 pounds
of powder to accumulate, and a plot to mature which was only prevented in
the nick of time, must amount to gross negligence. Far from being censured,
his career continued its very successful course without interruption. On 4
July 1607 he took his seat in parliament as Baron Knyvett of Escrick (near
York). Some attempt was made to represent him as assisting in the discovery
of the plot, but there is no evidence for it. All the same, Henry Neville wrote
to Winwood on 11 March 1604/5, referring to Knyvett, 'whose wife hath the
charge of the Lady Mary [James's infant daughter: d. 1607], and who was
himself a fortunate instrument to discover the powder' (Win. II, p. 198).

SEVEN

WHEN THE TIME for parliament to meet drew near, that is, towards the end of October, its members began to forgather in London. They included all the men of title in the kingdom, the whole bench of bishops, and those who had been elected by the people. Although the latter were for the most part gentlemen, they were, notwithstanding, the most convinced and obstinate heretics in the land. That is, they were puritans. The first intimation that this parliament would meet came not long after the king's first entry into England. Command was given by public proclamation under dire penalties that no recusant should be elected to this parliament.* That is to say, no one who refused to take the oath of supremacy, or denied that the king was head of the church and had supreme jurisdiction over it whether in matters temporal or spiritual. By this edict were excluded not only the catholics known to be such, and called recusants, but likewise all those who lived as hidden catholics and were not known as such. It also excluded those who, while they did not make open confession of catholicism, were nevertheless catholic by sympathy, and would not for anything in the world have taken so impious an oath. The puritans took occasion by this edict to make sure that, as far as they could, they alone would

* See Rymer, *Foedera*, Hagae Comitis, 1742, Tom. VII, pars I, pp. 102–4 (De Proclamatione Regis tangente Parliamentum), especially p. 103; 'we do also admonish that there be great care taken to avoid the choice of any persons, either noted for their superstitious blindness one way, or for their turbulent humours other ways, because their disorderly and unquiet spirits will disturb all the discreet and modest proceeding in that greatest and gravest council'.

be elected to represent the people. The bishops and lords take their seats as of right and without previous election.

All fell out much as the puritans had wished. In the session of the previous year, they had already demonstrated their hatred of the catholics, so that one could easily imagine what they would be capable of in the next. In this, as the event proved, they would emerge unscathed from the projected explosion. Indeed, judging from its effect, this might have been prepared by the conspirators with the precise object of sharpening their hatred and malice.* The manner in which God was pleased to free both them and the nobility, together with the king, the prince his son, and the greater part of his family, fell out in this way. At all events, this is as much as we know at the present time. Among other nobles summoned to the parliament there was one by name of Baron Monteagle. He was a catholic, or at least a catholic according to his innermost convictions.† Certainly, he was very much inclined to the catholics, and a friend of some of the plotters as well as a relative of others. Ten days before parliament was due to open, a letter was given to him in this way. Some man unknown met one of his pages by night in the neighbourhood of the baron's house. The man asked him if the baron was at home. If so, could he speak with him. When he learned that he was at supper, he begged the page to give a letter to his master, making sure that he delivered it into his own hand because it contained something that concerned him closely. The page did as he was told. The baron called one of the servants over to him and made him read the letter. The servant opened it, and found that it contained neither name of the writer nor the place from which

* This is the nearest the writer allows himself to come to suspecting that the plotters may have been agents-provocateurs.

† Sir William Parker, Lord Monteagle; son and heir apparent to Sir Edward Parker, Lord Morley: William married Elizabeth sister of Francis Tresham. His catholicism, even before the plot, was highly suspect. A letter, possibly of 1604, tells the king that he has become a protestant (BM Add. 19402, f. 146r.: mentioned in GBM, I, p. 77). His rôle was more obviously that of government agent. His name was carefully protected, and sometimes concealed. Cecil instructs Sir Edward Coke as he prepares the case for the prosecution, 'Lastly, and that you must not omit; you must deliver in commendation of my L. Monteagle words to show how sincerely he dealt, and how fortunately it proved, that he was the instrument of so great a blessing as this was.' (PRO, SP 14, vol. 19, f. 222 r. and v.)

it was written. Nor was there any date. The letter contained only these words:

'My Lord, Out of love I bear to some of your friends, I have a care of your preservation. Therefore, I would advise you as you tender your life to devise some excuse to shift off your attendance at this parliament. For God and man have concurred to punish the wickedness of this time. And think not slightly of this advertisement, but retire yourself into your country where you may expect the event in safety. For though there be no appearance of any stir, yet I say they shall receive a terrible blow this parliament. And yet they shall not see who hurts them. This counsel is not to be contemned because it may do you good, and can do you no harm: for the danger is past as soon as you have burnt the letter. And I hope God will give you the grace to make good use of it: to whose holy protection I commend you.'*

The baron read this letter, and turned it over in his mind how much danger there might be in hiding or ignoring it. This was difficult to decide since he had no idea of the writer's identity or whether he was friend or foe. Finally, he decided to take it to the Earl of Salisbury, the king's principal secretary, by name Sir Robert Cecil. Monteagle told him precisely how the letter had been given to him, and how he had ordered one of his servants to read it. The earl gave no sign that he attributed any particular importance to what the baron had told him. However, Cecil praised the latter's fidelity and obvious concern for the public good; but when he came to read the letter again, he realized that it contained a veiled threat that might be genuine. It would certainly be wise to communicate it to some other member of the council. This he did. He told the Earl of Suffolk, the Lord Chamberlain. It appeared to both alike that it could have something to do with information that was recently reported to have come from France about certain plans for stirring up tumult and rebellion threatened by the recusants. They decided to share their knowledge with three others of the council, the Earl of Worcester, the Lord Admiral, who was the Earl of Nottingham and the Earl of Northampton. They were of the opinion that, at

---

* The text is given here from HRW, p. 66. See HHS, pp. 57–91 and 229–36. PD rejects T. Ward's part in the episode (pp. 303–7). See also footnote to p. 125.

first sight, the contents of the letter could be regarded as of no great consequence. They well knew the state of the kingdom and the general disposition of the king's subjects in which one could discern only peace and tranquillity. This letter, therefore, could only have been written by someone who had a particular and personal end in view. All the same, it would be fitting to acquaint His Majesty with the letter as soon as he returned from the hunt which he was attending at that time in a place some thirty miles from London called Royston. In the meantime, it was not impossible that they would get further illumination on what the letter hinted at so obscurely. At this point, I will leave these gentlemen with their letter, and return to the subject of the conspirators.

The day following, the plotters themselves had news of this letter. It came to them by way of the gentleman who had read the letter to the baron, or by some other member of the household. We know this because a gentleman who was very familiar with the baron happened to meet Mr Thomas Wintour. He told Wintour what had passed. Even if he knew nothing of what it meant, he thought that he might be interested in the news. Thomas Wintour made a show of treating lightly what he said. All the same, he was sufficiently moved by curiosity to investigate the manner and circumstances of what had taken place. He got to know that the letter was already in the hands of the council, and that they were awaiting the king's return to give it to him. This would be in some four or five days' time. After Mr Thomas Wintour left his friend, he went straightway to Mr Robert Catesby, who was staying in London at the time. Wintour told him all that he had heard and asked his opinion as to what they should do now. By this time the plotters had already dispersed. Each of them awaited the moment to carry out his own part of the plan. Not more than three or four of them were in London, that is, the two mentioned above, Mr Guy and Mr John Wright, although I am not quite sure about the latter. All the details I set down here I had from the same man who found himself in the company of these gentlemen after the discovery of the plot.

Mr Catesby was very much disconcerted by Wintour's news. They came to offering one another conflicting advice, as usually happens in such cases. Finally, it was agreed that they should keep secret their knowledge of the letter, and also that they should find out by all means possible who had written it. When they knew the identity of the writer, they could decide whether the plot was completely discovered or not, and if so, decide on some means of getting out of the situation, both for themselves and their friends. And if this were not possible, then they would die in their own defence, making sure not to fall into the hands of the enemy. It would be easy enoug for those who found themselves in London at the time to escape to Flanders, for as we have seen, Mr Guy had a ship in readiness to make the crossing. But they were so obsessed with the desire of succeeding in the plan already begun, that they were willing to believe that whoever had written the letter had either discovered no more of the business than the letter itself suggested, or else that the privy councillors did not sufficiently understand the mystery, even if its nature were only too clearly indicated.

As a consequence of all this, they summoned Mr Francis Tresham to come without delay to meet Mr Catesby in the royal forest of Enfield Chase. There was something important to discuss with him. In fact, Mr Catesby and Thomas Wintour suspected him of having written the letter. They knew that he had always been very friendly with the baron who, in any case, was related to him since Monteagle had married Tresham's sister. Up to that time, their plans had gone forward in great secrecy; their suspicion grew from the fact that scarcely a month had passed since Tresham came to know of it when this happened. Everything seemed to point to Tresham as the indisputable culprit. Their deduction seemed to be verified later when they all came to die. The two gentlemen in question now made up their minds that if Tresham should admit to having written that letter, they would hang him then and there. At the interview, however, Tresham exonerated himself with such oaths and emphatic asseverations of innocence that his companions were convinced, at least for the time being, of his basic fidelity. But they were left even more in the dark as to what they should think about the letter. They were even more irresolute than before as to their proper course of action.

It was now Thursday, that is, six days before parliament was due to sit. It seemed to the two plotters that if the Lords of the Privy Council had guessed what was going on, they would have ordered a search to be made of the chambers where the gunpowder was. But even if they had found any, they would presumably have let out no word of it in order to catch the culprit red-handed. The plotters eventually concluded that Mr Guy should find out how things were in the cellar. He should make a careful search to see if the marks which they had put up on the door and entrance of the cellar gave some sign of having been tampered with. But they told him nothing about the letter so as not to frighten him.* They further told him that if everything seemed to be going well he should return to them at once. If he did not do so, they would take it as a sign that some misfortune had overtaken him. Guy Fawkes went off to examine and re-examine the cellar with the utmost care. He searched thoroughly every part of the cellar, but found no indication that anyone had been there. As had been previously agreed, he returned to make a complete report to his companions. These were much encouraged to understand that the house was still as it had been. They now told Mr Guy what had happened, and at the same time excused themselves for exposing him to danger. He replied that even if they had told him before, he would not have failed to do what he had done. It seemed to him that they should not say too much about that letter even among themselves. For if news of it got around, it might lead someone to stumble on the truth. Fawkes also undertook to visit the cellar from time to time to find out as much as he could of what, if anything, was going on. This undertaking he very courageously fulfilled.

Two days later, that is on Saturday and again on Sunday, they had word from the same man who had given them their first knowledge of the letter. He told them that the king had now seen it. He had returned from his hunting on the Friday in order to be in London for the opening of parliament. They were informed that the king took the letter very seriously, but the situation was being handled with great secrecy. This news greatly disturbed the plotters who happened to be in London on the Sunday. These were, Catesby, Thomas Wintour, Guy Fawkes, John Wright and Christopher,

---

* This seems to confirm what might be concluded from other evidence, namely that Fawkes was a catspaw; certainly, a subsidiary figure in the total enterprise. The story of the plotters' reaction at the letter is told plausibly but surely not convincingly. It is noteworthy that they are in touch with what is going on.

his brother. Mr Thomas Percy was expected to arrive that night or the following morning. He was riding up posthaste, and in the event arrived so late that he found himself in London only the day before parliament. Some of them thought that Mr Catesby should leave then and there for Flanders, leaving Mr Guy to look after the house. Magnanimously enough, Fawkes was quite ready to do this. In this way, when the main deed was done Catesby could put in execution the rest of the plan.

The plotters finally decided to wait for Mr Percy, and get his views on this latest proposal. They would have a further talk with Mr Francis Tresham, who was also at that time in London. Thomas Wintour went to speak with him. Tresham seemed to be a man who had lost control of himself, and told Wintour that, without doubt, the plot was discovered. In Tresham's view, Mr Catesby and his friends should seek safety in flight. This reply of Tresham's gave the others reason to suspect that Tresham knew more than he was willing to say. Certainly, he did not lack an obvious means of knowing more, thanks to his close friendship with the baron, his relative. Guy, however, had no wish to abandon a project so important, and already virtually concluded, simply on account of certain vague suspicions. Mr Thomas Percy, likewise, wished to see the end of the affair. He arrived on Sunday evening, when he had his first news of the letter. In the end, they all agreed to await the outcome, and that Mr Robert Catesby and John Wright should leave London after dinner on Monday. They would go to join Sir Everard Digby's hunt, and any other gentlemen with him. In this way, if their project did not go well, they would be in readiness to defend themselves in the most effective way possible. Certainly, they still preferred to die on the field of battle rather than let themselves be taken alive. Thomas Percy stayed in a place unknown to anybody so that, if the plot should not succeed, he could leave his companions immediately. Thomas Wintour did likewise. Guy, with great hardihood, withdrew to the house where the powder was stored.

Here I will relate something which was given out as most certain by someone who found himself with these gentlemen in the country, and indeed, heard it from Thomas Wintour's own mouth. It was this. That Saturday, Thomas Wintour dreamt that the barrels of gunpowder went off one after the other without doing any damage, and with no other result than to rouse the laughter of all those who happened to be in parliament at the time. Someone else dreamt that same night that the plot and all its circumstances had been discovered. This proved to be true, as we shall see. The fact is, we know more about the discovery of the plot than we have been told in a little book that was printed by order of the Privy Council.* Along with the confession of Thomas Wintour, there is an account of the way in which the plot was found out. I will put down here what it says there, but not in the same words.

The author of the book in question says that when the king returned from hunting, the Earl of Salisbury went to find him in the palace. He recounted the incident of the letter, and reported the views of the Lords of the Council on it. He then handed the king the letter itself. James made much of it. When the secretary realized this, he said that in his view the contents of the letter were not all that important. The writer was probably some lunatic or idiot. This he concluded from the manner of writing, and especially from the words which told him that as soon as the letter was burnt, the danger was past. The king replied, 'Moreover, from the language we can infer the nature of the threat, that is, from the statement that as soon as the letter is burnt the danger will be over. This means that we are threatened with some treason by way of fire, which will be over in a moment.' It was the king's view that they should search thoroughly all the parliament chambers, and the more carefully since it was difficult to see in what other quarter mischief was intended. For the letter threatened the members of parliament and

* It is not exactly clear which book is intended. 'His Majesty's Speech in this last Session of Parliament [9.xi.1605] as near his very words as could be gathered at the instant. Together with a discourse of the manner of the discovery of this late intended treason, joined with the examination of some of the prisoners', was published in quarto in at least two editions by R. Baker in London in 1605 (BM Catalogue, E.1940 (10) and (11)). 'A True and Perfect Relation of the Proceedings at the several Arraignments of the late and most barbarous Traitors', was printed, again in at least two editions, by Barker at London in 1606. All of these productions, covering substantially the same ground, seem to have been known as 'The King's Book'. It was reprinted in the Harleian Miscellany, vol. iv, pp. 245–67. Donald Carswell reprinted it as an Appendix to his *Trial of Guy Fawkes*, London, 1934, pp. 105–29, from Bishop Montague's first printed collection of the King's works (*v. supra*, p. 47).

all who assembled with them, although it was impossible to know who threatened and the precise nature of the threat. The king's interpretation went rather beyond the literal sense of the words quoted. At least Secretary Cecil and his colleagues thought so. All the same, they approved the king's speech, and decided to carry out his suggestion. But it was to be done quietly and without fuss, so that if nothing were found of what was suspected there would be no cause for whispering. Charge of this operation was given to the Earl of Suffolk as Lord Chamberlain, since it fell to his office to see that the Parliament-house was in order and ready in time.

On Monday after lunch – this was 4 November, and the day before parliament was due to sit – Suffolk had a look at the cellar on the pretext of a final check-up on the adjoining rooms. As he was going through the house, he saw none other than Mr Guy standing about in one of the chambers. The Earl asked the official in charge of the house who he was. Reply was returned that he was a servant belonging to Mr Thomas Percy, who had rented those particular rooms. Suffolk passed on without further remark. He made them take him through the ground-floor rooms and the cellar. There he saw such a quantity of wood laid up that he could not but express surprise. They told him that it was the supply which Mr Percy had laid in for himself and his family for the coming winter. The earl left the cellar, and after making a careful inspection of the rest of the premises, he went back to the palace to report on what he had seen. He made particular note of the store of wood in the cellar, and that he had seen one of Thomas Percy's servants. By the look of him, he seemed to be a man shrewd enough but up to no good. So they decided to send someone the following night on the pretext of looking for certain items which had been stolen from the palace. This man could take away the wood, and look carefully for what was underneath. It was desirable that the man who did it should be someone in authority, or a magistrate, for two reasons. Firstly, it was important that suspicion should not be communicated to others so that if, in the event, it proved to be unfounded, they would not look too credulous or over-sensitive about meaningless trifles. Secondly, they did not wish to antagonize the Earl of Northumberland, who was a very important man and a power in the land; for Thomas Percy was related to him, and, indeed, carried the family name. Northumberland might have been ready to believe that all this was done merely to diminish his reputation and standing with the king.

Before we proceed further with this story, I think it high time to say something about the way in which the plot was discovered. Various accounts have been related by those who had to do with it. They are probably more to be believed who are less inclined to accept what has been printed and published in the official book. It is likely that this was only issued to conceal the truth, and keep the secret of the man who really uncovered the treason. The identity of this man, as far as I know, has never been revealed even to this day.★ In the first place, it is difficult to believe that Mr Guy saw the Earl of Suffolk come into the cellar where the powder was, and yet the earl gave no sign of misgiving or annoyance. The very obvious thought occurs to us that when the earl visited a place which no other member of the Privy Council had entered before, least of all a man of his position and authority, it was extremely unlikely that Fawkes would have failed to warn his friends, and save both himself and them by flight. It must have been evident that the earl had either definite information, or else a very strong suspicion, as to what was going on. Moreover, since Guy had the keys to the cellar, how did the earl get in without his means? If the original owner of the house had other keys, how could they ever have supposed that the plot would not have been discovered long before? For myself I see no kind of likelihood in this incident.

To return to the letter: who can really believe that the Earl of Salisbury and his friends, men who showed the utmost astuteness in everything else, would have proved so dense when it came to interpreting a letter that was clear enough? They read in it of invisible enemies, of a terrible blow at the time when parliament was sitting, and that one of the nobles should absent himself, and this if he valued his life. They read further that God and men were bound by solemn obligation to punish the parliament. How could they fail to discover the true sense, which even a schoolboy would have found it easy enough to guess at, without taking it to the king as if he were some prophet. How could they arrive at a

★ If the plot was largely a contrivance of government, there would have been no such individual, of course. The writer of the narrative could not assume this, however, on the scantier evidence that was available to him than to us.

meaning so far from its sense and grammatical construction? Davus himself could have solved an enigma so obvious.* Personally, I cannot believe that this kind of thing called for the wisdom of Solomon . . .

It is also worthy of reflection that on the night he received the letter, Baron Monteagle supped in a house of his about a mile outside London. This was something he did very rarely. In fact, he had neither dined nor supped there for more than a month previously. Whoever took the letter to him was, therefore, someone who knew the baron very intimately, and consequently was well known to his household. How was it, then, that the page did not know the man to whom he spoke and gave the letter? One could add to this the incredible foolishness of anyone who entrusted a letter of this kind, being of such importance, to the hands of a page. It also showed monumental carelessness on the part of the baron to have such a letter read out in the presence of all who were at supper. This letter had been sent to him confidentially, and as something of the utmost significance. The secretary was at least right when he said that whoever wrote it showed great stupidity, if only for having written so openly of a secret so enormous. If it was, indeed, Francis Tresham who wrote that letter, opportunity would not have been lacking to him to deal with the man personally to get him to stay away from Parliament; Monteagle, after all, was his friend and intimate. The baron could have pretended that he was staying outside London that day on account of illness. Or he could have got them to believe that his wife was seriously ill, or in fact made almost any excuse of important business that would not brook delay.

Furthermore, Mr Tresham either believed that this letter would have the effect of persuading the baron to do what he advised, or else he did not believe it. If he did not believe it, it was the height of folly to have written it at all. If he did believe that he could persuade Monteagle, why did he not make sure of it by telling him by word of mouth, and using words more calculated to persuade? He could have done it on the very morning that he had to attend parliament,

* Davus: 'D. sum non Oedipus. I, D., am a plain simple fellow, and no solver of riddles, like Oedipus. The words are from Terence's *Andria*, i. 2, 23, and are often quoted by one who has been set a difficult question' (*Brewers' Dictionary of Phrase and Fable*).

so that, for the shortness of notice, he would either be obliged to follow his friend's advice, or else expose himself to manifest danger; or finally reveal what he had heard. When it comes to the point, no one who ever had dealings with Francis Tresham will believe that a man of his clear understanding, who acted cautiously and judiciously in everything he did, would have acted in this way. It would not have occurred to him to attempt to save his relative by writing a letter so foolish. This was simply to put himself and all that was his at risk, to say nothing of the lives of those who had entrusted such a secret to him. This letter had no signature, and it was in a hand unknown.* Its contents were such that the baron could reasonably have concluded that it had been written by an enemy. The writer's object might have been to conceal some great evil which he was trying to bring upon Monteagle. It was not obviously by a friend who was trying to free him from any such thing. He could justly conclude that it was all trickery and invention.

Moved by the above consideration, many have concluded that Francis Tresham would have failed in loyalty to his friends rather than in knowing how to reveal the plot and his part in it. The obvious thing for him was to reveal the plot to the baron before the letter was written. The baron in turn would have told the council. Tresham might even have revealed it immediately to the council himself, with the hope of receiving from the state the honour and acclaim that a service of such magnitude would have merited. In this way, the letter was only devised to cover up his own betrayal. It was further calculated to lead the world to believe that the king had shown enormous wisdom in knowing how to penetrate and interpret a mystery so hidden and obscure. They were confirmed in their view when they saw that all the plotters were either killed in the country, or else at the hands of justice, without any of them having given the least sign or cause for suspicion of having betrayed the secret. In the second place, when all the conspirators fled after discovery of the plot, Francis Tresham alone failed to join them.

* There is good reason to think that Cecil wrote this letter himself. Certainly, he told Sir Charles Cornwallis in his letter of 9 November 1605 that the letter was 'in a hand disguised'. How could he have known this without knowing the writer? For a graphological examination of the original handwriting carried out by Miss Joan Cambridge, see Appendix 2 at p. 247.

Indeed, acting as a man very sure of himself, he stayed behind in London. Thirdly, it was a strong argument that when he, too, was taken some days later,★ it was published throughout the City of London that he had confessed all he knew. Nevertheless, his confession was never published. Nor did they speak of him, except in general terms, and without bitterness or exaggeration. Very differently did they speak of the others.

It is believed with good reason that if the plotters had never revealed their intention to Tresham, thanks to the suspicion which they had of him, they would never have suffered. In the end, Tresham died in the Tower without ever having been publicly examined.† It is not known if he died of some mental affliction, due to the melancholy which, for many causes, could well have afflicted him. It could be that he was helped on to his death by the hand of those who, after forcing him to do what he did for them, did not wish that he should say anything more, or to reward him as he deserved. This much is certain, and I have it from a good source. He brought considerable pressure to bear on Mr Catesby so that the execution of the plot should be put off until the end of parliament. He claimed that he had to sell some of his possessions to the value of £16,000 sterling. Mr Catesby, the better to make sure of him after he had fallen under suspicion, made a show of agreeing. One could well believe that it was not Tresham who betrayed his accomplices. Certainly, all these gentlemen were continually together in London. The leaders only left the City the day preceeding and the day after the plot was discovered. The first edict published was directed solely against Thomas Percy. He it was who had hired the house containing the gunpowder. Of the others no word was said until it was known in London that they were all together and up in arms. But it is high time to return to our story.

Parliament was due to begin on Tuesday, 5 November. On the Monday night preceding, Sir Thomas Knyvett, a gentleman of the

★ Tresham was arrested on 12 November. He wrote a long, five-page statement in his own hand of his relations with the conspirators (SP 14, vol. 16, No. 63). Coke gave it the date 13 November. Only Thomas Wintour, Fawkes and Tresham were allowed to write statements or confessions in their own hand. Tresham was transferred to the Tower on 15 November (cf HRW, p. 192).
† See Appendix 1 at pp. 231–46.

king's household, was sent to search the lower rooms and cellars beneath the actual chamber where parliament met. He was to make his search as if he were concerned with other matters. But notice that at the entrance of the outer chambers he meets a man fully dressed, booted and spurred! Since it was already past midnight, this seemed to him rather strange. Knyvett therefore had him seized by some of his officials. Next he went to the cellar and asked for the keys. He found that the man they had already arrested had them. They made him open the cellar, and immediately began to move the bundles of wood. Their first find was a small barrel of gunpowder, and after that a number of barrels arranged in order to the number of thirty-six, large and small.* Nearby was a dark lantern with the candle lit inside. From this they immediately concluded what it was. They had the man searched whom they had just seized. Three fuses, or matches were found on him, one shorter than the others, and three tubes through which to pass them. These would serve to ignite the powder on the following morning.

The man whom they captured – none other than Guy Fawkes – showed not the least dismay.† He merely remarked to Knyvett, and the others who were holding him, that they had been lucky to find

---

* The quantity of gunpowder allegedly involved is impossible to ascertain. A missing 'confession' of Guy Fawkes, dated 20 January 1606, claimed that he went to Flanders to tell Hugh Owen that the plotters had laid 'twenty whole barrels of powder' in the cellar (EGF, op. cit., p. 195). Dudley Carleton told John Chamberlain on 13 November 1605, 'it is now confidently reported there was no such matter, nor anything near it more than a barrel of powder found near the court' (ibid., p. 138). The fact is, no one, apparently, apart from the trusted officials immediately involved, ever saw the barrels, or knew if there was, indeed, gunpowder inside. Cecil in his letter to Cornwallis of 9 November, referred to 'two Hogsheads and some 32 small barrels' (Win, II, p. 170). S. R. Gardiner was doubtless correct in claiming that the officially accepted number was 36 (op. cit., p. 113). Not only are gunpowder records now missing, but the government of the day showed a remarkable unwillingness to allow William Brouncker to inspect the records going beyond 1604 (see HRW, pp. 251–3).
† There are three different accounts as to where Fawkes was actually taken: outside the cellar, inside the cellar or in his own lodging. See JG, pp. 123–31. S. R. Gardiner tried to answer the difficulties (op. cit., pp. 132–6). This was a point that government officials should have known clearly from their own experience, needing no contribution from the plotters or later revision.

him outside the cellar, where he was putting the finishing touches to his preparations: otherwise, they would none of them be talking about it now, because they would all have been blown sky-high. Had he succeeded in this, he would have caused most serious damage to an ancient and most elegant pile. He would have destroyed the archives and records of the court. What is more, the king himself might have been in danger, and others of the royal household, although they were some distance away. It was still some four hours before daybreak, but already some were on their way who were going to sit in parliament. Without doubt, they would have lost their lives. News of the above incident reached the court quickly. The prisoner was taken there, and brought in. Some of the Council were called together to examine him, and the king himself was informed of the fact, although it was still some hours before full day. There was a considerable uproar in the palace, and the royal guard was commanded to keep watch not only on the palace itself but also on the neighbouring streets.

At the beginning of his examination before the Lords of the Council, the prisoner confessed without hesitation his intention to blow up the Parliament-house and all present in it on the following morning. He was asked who were his accomplices. For a whole day he refused to admit even that he had any. He said that he alone was the author of the deed, and that he had been moved to it out of his great zeal for the catholic faith. He even refused to recognize formally that the king was his legitimate sovereign. He knew him rather for a heretic and spiritual tyrant. Only one thing caused him sorrow, and that was that he had failed to carry out what he originally intended. Nor for that day did he wish to be known by any other name than Johnson, a servant of Thomas Percy. The Councillors were overcome with astonishment to discern in him a mind so fearless and resolute. They were amazed to see that although he had been taken red-handed, and examined in the presence of the king himself, to say nothing of many another august and important gentleman, he did not lose his composure or show even the least surprise. On the contrary, he replied to everything with great presence of mind, readiness and self-assuredness. So much so that one might think the deed were not his. They all said that the man did not seem to know the meaning of fear. Indeed, from his courage

LORD MONTEAGLE

and fearlessness one might conclude that another Mucius Scaevola⋆ had appeared on the scene. In fact, he showed himself for the whole of that day while he was held in the palace, so alien to every kind of fear, whether in his replies or his bearing, that at times he seemed to mock the people about him. These were often considerable personages and leading men at court, even when they had no precisely defined authority. When they asked him about the plot, he referred them to the reply which he had already made to the Lords of the Council. But apart from his easy bearing, and the freedom he allowed himself in his replies, it was noted that he did not, for all that, lack a certain modesty and discretion. It was reported that he had certain pious objects on his person, and wore a hair-shirt.

When they had finished examining him, he was led off, a prisoner, to the Tower. Here there can be no doubt that he was tortured with excruciating and most refined torments, whatever the little book has to say, which they published about this plot and the confessions of Guy, Thomas Wintour and other prisoners. Signs of torture were evident at the time of his execution, for he was scarcely able to move.† While he was being tortured, he admitted his true name and, as they say, put a name to some of his accomplices. But these were men already up in arms. They had revealed themselves on the very first day so completely that nothing new about them could have been learnt from Fawkes. To the very last moment, Fawkes did not fail in courage.

The lords of the council lost no time in sending to the Earl of Northumberland's house to find out if he could have received any

⋆ Fawkes's alleged sang-froid is scarcely plausible and suggests a man playing a part. Caius Mucius Scaevola was the legendary hero who, as a spy, entered the camp of Lars Porsenna, then besieging Rome. Mutius was taken before the king, but deliberately held his hand over a sacrificial fire to show the Etruscans that he did not fear torture. He was released (*Brewer's Dictionary* . . ., *v. supra*).

† The torture of Guy Fawkes seems problematic, as of the other central conspirators. According to the contemporary account, 'In the time of their imprisonment, they rather feasted with their sins, than fasted with sorrow for them; were richly apparelled, fared deliciously, and took tobacco out of measure, with a seeming carelessness of their crime, as if it were daring the law to pass upon them' (Lord Somers, . . . *Tracts* . . ., vol. II, London, 1809, p. 113). All of which fits their more probable rôle of agents-provocateurs rather than obstinate criminals who needed to be proceeded against by torture.

news of Mr Thomas Percy. This also was some four hours before daybreak. At the self-same hour, Christopher Wright was going through the street where the earl's house stood. He was on his way to the Parliament-house to see how matters proceeded. Wright knew nothing at that time of what had happened. He saw that the door of the house was open, and noticed a gentleman on horseback by the name of Mr Lepton. Wright stopped some little way off in order to hear what they were talking about. He heard Lepton say, 'So then, your lordships command nothing more of me.' It seemed to Wright that he had been speaking with some of the council. With these words, Lepton spurred his horse, and went off at a gallop towards the City. Christopher assumed from this that he had been sent off to find Thomas Percy's lodging, and that the plot was discovered. Wright therefore made his way quickly to Thomas Wintour's chamber and related all he had seen. Wright then went off without delay to Thomas Percy to inform him also. That night Percy had carefully chosen to lodge in a room which was not his usual one. Thomas Wintour, however, anxious to find out more about the situation at first hand, decided to make his own way to parliament. He found the guard lined up across the street before the court. They were forbidding anyone to pass further. Wintour enquired into the cause of this unusual watch, and so came to know the recent course of events. He next returned to find his companions. At this precise moment they had left on horseback to join the others in Warwickshire and Worcestershire, to let them know likewise what had happened. They rode all that day at a furious pace covering little less than a hundred miles. They found the rest of the gentlemen at the hunt. The huntsmen were eager for news.

Thomas Wintour's horse was not as strong and swift as the others, so that he did not reach the country before Wednesday dinner-time. He then found the company assembled at his brother's house in Huddington, some 110 miles from London. On the Wednesday night, they had taken war-horses from a stable near the City of Warwick.* Many of the gentlemen who had been at the hunt had already seen certain signs which pleased them little, for which

* Horses were taken from Warwick Castle, as it was later reported, at 3 a.m. on Wednesday, 6 November. (See EGF, p. 160: see also chapter 6 of this work, n.* p. 101.)

reason they had asked leave to depart, and had obtained it easily. They had noticed the sudden departure of Sir Everard Digby from their number after the arrival of Mr Catesby. They had seen them consult together, and later observed the arrival of Mr Thomas Percy and his friends. Already they began to suspect that some disaster would overtake them if they delayed too long in the company of those gentlemen. The others, for their part, did not want them to run the risk that they were running unless their heart was in it.

There were others who, although they had known nothing in the beginning about this design, when they saw these gentlemen reduced to the terms in which they were, decided to stay with them. They would help them as far as they could, at least by their presence. Some say that in addition to the arms with which they had already provided themselves, they had also seized the arms of Lord Windsor. This was in the course of their journeying through the counties of Warwick, Worcester and Stafford. These arms were notable both for quantity and quality. But though it is altogether certain that this had been their intention before the plot was discovered, I would not go so far as to say that they actually took them. Admittedly, they could easily have taken them if they had desired to do so. The truth is, they had ample equipment to arm considerably more men than those who were with them. These in fact never exceeded eighty in number.*

The seizure of the stable and horses gave Warwickshire plenty to talk about. When the sheriff of that county was advised of the fact, he took immediate measures to follow up those who had committed this act of violence. He wondered not a little at the cause which could have persuaded those gentlemen to commit such an outrage. It was at this point that the edict against Thomas Percy was sent posthaste to every part of the kingdom.† News was given of the plot, but no mention was made of anyone else connected with it. This was a clear enough sign that, up to that time, they had

* This figure is most revealing. Even allowing for a considerable reduction in the party from its number when it first set out, there could never have been enough present to constitute, or even begin, a serious rebellion. This was only the remnant of a company going over to reinforce the English regiment then re-forming in Flanders.

† Given in Rymer, *Foedera* (*v. supra*), VII, pars Ia, p. 143. Dated from the Palace of Westminster, 5 November.

received no particular information about the persons involved. But the messengers, sent out one after the other posthaste, went through the same counties through which those gentlemen were making their own way. So the court soon came to know the names of the principals. Without more ado, new edicts were sent out against Catesby and two or three others, and finally against them all. Great was the commotion caused by this deed throughout the kingdom, and enormously did rumour grow, as usually happens. The number of the plotters and their company, which we have already given, was soon said to be more than a thousand! Indeed, it was to be feared that many more might join them. For this reason, the king gave order to enlist soldiers. Already the general command had been given to the Earl of Devonshire. But in a short time the real truth arrived; that is, the 'rebel host' was extremely small, and the overall state of the country was still entirely satisfactory. Indeed, the country as a whole had opposed them so strenuously that there was no reason to fear that their numbers might grow. The trepidations of the court grew still. But it was providential that things fell out as they did.

Very fortunate was it that the band of conspirators was broken up in a few days. Otherwise a more widespread disturbance might not have been so easily pacified. If the insurgents had succeeded at any time in putting the Sheriff of Warwick to rout, it is believed certain that many others would have joined the conspirators. These would have had ample time to organize themselves at their leisure before the royal forces arrived on the scene. In fact, the sheriff clung to their flanks continually with 700 soldiers, although he had never received any order to attack them. That same day, the plotters resolved instead to attack their pursuers. No doubt it was because they were men of such great courage that they decided to risk their lives in this way. In any case, they were on horseback and well disciplined. Success might well have been theirs in putting the rest to rout.

The conspirators finally decided to await the sheriff's arrival in Mr Stephen Lyttelton's house in Staffordshire. Lyttelton was one of those who had stayed on with them after the hunt.* Next day, the

* George Lyttleton, second son of Sir John Lyttleton of Frankley (d. 1591), 'married Margaret daughter and heir to Rich. Smith of Shirford, Warwick-

Friday after the discovery of the plot, 8 November, they decided to try their luck. Shortly before dawn, they sent some of their number outside, to reconnoitre. The rest stayed inside to prepare their weapons for action. It was at this moment they discovered that their gunpowder, thanks to the weather, had become too damp to ignite. They therefore spread it out to dry at the fire; an operation which they conducted very carefully. However, while one of them was bringing hot coals to put on the brazier over which the powder was being dried, it so happened that while he was passing, the fire-shovel knocked against the foot of one of his companions. In consequence, a glowing coal fell on the pans containing the powder. The resulting explosion not only wrecked the room but some of those in it received severe injuries. Indeed those who were outside at the time thought they must all be dead.* The news spread quickly, that Mr Catesby, Mr Rookwood, Grant and others had lost their lives. The rest of the company were completely dismayed by this accident. Many of them lost no time in mounting their horses, thinking now only to escape. Indeed, they were advised by other gentlemen of their party, who were distributed through the house, that they would be well advised to escape by the best way open to them. While some of these gentlemen were making their getaway, they stumbled on Mr Thomas Wintour and Mr Stephen Lyttelton, who by now were returning from their reconnoitre. They brought back word of the sheriff's arrival. They in turn were told of the powder incident, and that some of the gentlemen had died. Mr Stephen pointed out to his companion that they could no longer hope to prevail by force of

* This is one of the strangest incidents in the whole story. There is no extant MS source for what happened although Sir Edward Coke described it at the plotters' trial. Gunpowder spread out on a pan will not explode, only ignite with a flash. It seems that the pan of drying powder was standing on at least two other bags in front of the fire, one of which exploded. It is incredible that gentlemen of the presumed sophistication of those involved should have acted so foolishly, not to say negligently. A reconstruction is offered in EGF, pp. 165–8.

shire; his eldest son, Stephen settled at Holbeach House, in King's Swinford, Staffordshire; was executed on account of the gunpowder plot, and left no issue. His 8th brother, Humphrey, was likewise executed for harbouring the powder conspirators at Hagley': T. Nash, *Worcestershire*, vol. I, pedigree at p. 493. Thus Humphrey and Stephen were uncle and nephew.

arms. If he liked, they could flee together. 'This I will not do,' replied Thomas Wintour, 'even now! I owe my friend Robert Catesby the last services that one man can do for another in this world. That is, I must bury him. In any case, I must first make sure that he is dead! Whatever happens, I have decided never to leave him dead or alive!'

By this time they had reached the house. They found everything upside down and in confusion, but the gentlemen in question still alive; indeed, still in a position to offer some kind of resistance apart from a few who could scarcely move. Among these was Mr Grant who had been so badly burnt by the powder that he appeared to have lost his sight. Meanwhile, the sheriff had drawn up with his posse. He saw the wreckage about the house, and that they were few indeed who could dare to come forth. He already had news that some had fled, and he suspected that some disaster had overtaken the remaining conspirators. He decided to lay siege to the house from closer at hand. When the plotters saw his intention, they made up their minds without more ado to die in that place rather than let themselves be taken. To prepare themselves better for death, they took to their prayers. They began with the litanies and other vocal prayers. After that, they kept silence for nearly an hour while everyone recommended himself to God.

A few of those in the house had the good fortune to escape since it was not entirely surrounded by the besiegers. When the besieged had finished their prayers, they opened the door, and went out into the courtyard. Thomas Wintour led the way, and some of the others followed him. He was wounded almost immediately by a shot from a crossbow, or carbine, in the shoulder, whereby he lost the use of his right arm. He was also wounded in the stomach by a pike thrust, but not very seriously. After this, he was no longer able to defend himself, and so withdrew to Mr Catesby's side. At this moment the two Wright brothers were killed by musket-shots, John first and Christopher after him. When the sheriff's men saw the first defenders die, they began to approach the house more closely. Mr Catesby and Mr Thomas Percy, putting themselves shoulder to shoulder, prepared to defend themselves. Mr Catesby took a golden crucifix from about his neck, which he always wore, and crossed himself with it. He uttered a cry at the same time which made it appear that he had been the author of the plot. It was to the effect that the Lord who had died on the Cross knew that his only purpose and intent had been to restore the honour of the Cross throughout the land; also to restore the only faith whereby souls could be saved . . . He could now see that it was not the Lord's will that the catholic faith should be restored in England by that means, and he willingly accepted the Divine decree. But he had no desire to be taken, or to fall alive into the hands of his enemies, while he could still use arms to defend himself. It is rather remarkable that among all the men in the place at that time no one wished or dared to approach those two gentlemen. The same man who had killed the two brothers still remained hidden behind a tree. After waiting a little while, he now shot the other two gentlemen with his musket. Although they were mortally wounded, they did not die at once. Catesby did not live very long, but Thomas Percy lived for quite some time. After being wounded, Catesby crawled into the house where he found an image of the Madonna, to whom he had always been very devoted. He hugged it to him, kissed it, and died with it in his hands.★

I understand that John Wright lived for a whole day, if not longer. It was a priest who told me this who happened to be in Mr Robert Wintour's house when news first arrived of what was going on. The gentlemen came to the house, and the priest administered to them the Sacraments of Penance and Holy Communion the following day. They showed so much devotion, as he said, and so little fear that he would remember it as long as he lived. The priest whom I mentioned above said of him to me that he had made up his mind not to be taken alive while he could continue to defend himself. He once asked the priest if it was morally permissible to neglect wounds received, and let them mortify, rather than bind them up, so placing oneself in peril of falling alive into enemy hands. From the latter one could expect not only death but torture and humiliation. Such was

★ More probably authentic eye-witness accounts of the end of the conspirators were supplied by Sir Richard Walsh, High Sheriff of Worcestershire, Thomas Lawley and others who were present (see GPB, 55; and especially several accounts of eye-witnesses in PRO, E.134, James I, 4 Trinity, No. 6). Some of these suggest more than plausibly that Walsh, in general charge of the operation, stood aside while competent marksmen picked off the plotters. In this way, Percy and Catesby, for example, died on one bullet (cf. EGF, pp. 178–82; HRW, pp. 179–82).

the resolution of these gentlemen. From it we can conclude what kind of account they would have given of themselves if they had been able to make a common stand against the sheriff. But with some dead and others fled, the rest still in the house were soon taken. They were either wounded, or else so injured by the gunpowder explosion that they could put up no defence. Among these were John Grant, Thomas Wintour and Ambrose Rookwood. The latter gentleman, in fact, did put himself on the defence, and received four or five wounds.

While the last scene was being enacted, Sir Everard Digby and some of his companions took to horse. He had with him a page and another servant who refused to be parted from him. Digby had previously urged them to fly, giving them horses and money, as he had already done to his other servants, so that they could fly to safety. Digby and the servants, being well mounted, now broke through a section of the enemy line, and rode on boldly. But the roads round about were crowded with people. He himself was already well known, and his costume and the horses they were riding showed clearly that they belonged to the conspirators. Seeing no other possible way of escape, he decided to turn off into the wood from which he would be able to slip out at his ease after nightfall. He found a dry ditch in the wood, and this he entered with his horses. He had not been there long, however, when the hue and cry, following the horses' hoof-marks, came to that very place. When they found him, they sent up a great cry, 'They are here! They are here!' Hearing the noise, Digby came out fearlessly. He cried in turn, 'It is true they are here! What are you going to do about it?' He then put spur to his horse with the intention of passing through their midst. But such was the throng about him, and so many people stood in his path, that he was obliged to choose between two alternatives. Either he could die fighting on the spot, or else he could surrender to his enemy. He chose the latter course for two reasons. Firstly, he wanted more time to prepare for death. Secondly, he wished to give the world that satisfaction regarding himself which in the event he gave. He was able to show the true cause which had brought him and his companions to this pass. This was nothing less than their desire to free the land from the tyranny of heresy and infidelity, and the Catholics from most cruel persecution by their enemies. It cannot be denied that the courage he showed when he came to die at least proved how little regard he had for his own life.

When he arrived in London, Digby tried hard for the favour of being allowed to speak with the king. He wished to tell him how great was the danger to which His Majesty exposed himself in persecuting his own subjects with so much ferocity. So much so that it was inevitable that from being friends and faithful subjects, they should become capital enemies. Digby received no such permission. Instead, he was sent immediately to the Tower where the other conspirators were held, apart from the four who had been killed in the country, and Robert Wintour who had escaped with Stephen Lyttelton. After two months, these two were also captured in the house of Mrs Lyttelton, widow, and relative of Humphrey Lyttelton. The latter hid them secretly in a room in a house. It was the cook who caused them to be arrested. He suspected their presence from the extraordinary provision of food sent up to his mistress and so approached the authorities. The two men were sent off to join the rest as prisoners. So it was that the total number of conspirators, dead or captured, amounted to thirteen: that is, the four who were killed, already mentioned, and the others imprisoned in the Tower of London. These were Sir Everard Digby, Ambrose Rookwood, Francis Tresham, Robert, and his brother Thomas Wintour, John Grant, Robert Keyes, Guy Fawkes and Mr Catesby's servant, Thomas Bates. They were all examined several times, but only the confessions of two of them were published and printed, that is, of Mr Guy and Thomas Wintour. These agreed in substance, but Thomas Wintour's confession was considerably longer, and mentioned many more details. I have made use of this for the most part in writing the narrative up to this point. In what follows I shall recount either what is of common knowledge to everybody, or else what I and many others have seen as eye-witnesses and know to be certain.*

* The narrator frankly admits the main source of his information to be the confession of Thomas Wintour, dated 23 November – altered apparently by Coke to 25–1605 (Salisbury MS, 113, No. 54: printed in S.R.G., *v. supra*; and in DC, pp. 116–23; see also Cal. Salisbury MSS, XVII, pp. 509–10). The standard account of the plot is usually taken to depend on the authenticity

To conclude this chapter, I only wish to say that, from the confessions of all the conspirators, it remained clear and self-evident that those of whom we have spoken so far had no other accomplices. Notwithstanding, some months later, when all the plotters were already dead, the heretics tried to besmirch the reputation of a number of others by various inventions. Their hatred against us was still unsatisfied by the blood of those who died. We shall say more of this anon. The king himself made it clear that the plot involved none beyond those who had already been discovered and taken prisoner, as we shall see in the next chapter.

of this confession. See HRW, pp. 247–50, for good reasons for rejecting it. Even if the confession were written by Wintour, however, it may not have been signed by him. Nor might it have corresponded to any reality, since, if Wintour were another agent-provocateur, he may only have told the story he was instructed to tell. Wintour is perhaps the most ambivalent of all the plotters. For a detailed discussion, see *The Month*: 1927, pp. 500–10; 1950, pp. 243–51; 1952, pp. 83–8, 162–76, 290–5, 295–305.

EIGHT

THE READER will easily imagine the very different reactions of people everywhere after the discovery and further unravelling of this plot. On the one hand, the protestants, and especially the puritans, used the occasion to exaggerate the tale. Not content with expressing their dislike of the cruelty of the plot, and the over-weaning insolence of those who had devised it, they attributed it to catholics in general as authors and sympathizers. They did this with so much noise and vehemence that there was scarcely anyone who dared to contradict them, or put up any defence of the catholics in the teeth of their rage. So much so, that many wondered whether the people would not suddenly resort to armed violence against the catholics. For the populace was much stirred by the clamorous anger of their enemies, and inflamed with a spirit of vengeance and hatred. On the other hand, the consternation and sorrow of the catholics was overwhelming. What must they have felt at this indiscreet zeal of a few which passed all bounds of reason? . . . Their enemies seemed now to be fully justified in stirring up the hatred of the ignorant populace against catholics and their religion. Now they could smear their reputation in foreign countries with impunity. Where access to the truth was not so easy, they could give out false and invidious information. They could thus overthrow the reputation that catholics had acquired by their indomitable patience through so many years of suffering. The catholics themselves greatly feared the overbearing and fanatical spirit of the calvinists who might use the occasion as an excuse for taking up arms against them. In this way, a general massacre might have been set on foot throughout the kingdom, even if it had not led to a final outcome all that happy for its authors.

The king and council, however, foresaw the danger arising in the first days of discovery. They put it about, and indeed it was the truth, that the plot was the work of only a few men, and the names of those few were already known. The king published an edict to this effect on 7 November 1605.* In this he professed to recognize by many proofs and much experience the undoubted loyalty and love which the catholics bore him. This was in spite of what a few of them had plotted against himself and the kingdom in deeds now all too evident. In this way, the fire was somewhat damped down which the puritans had done their best to kindle. People gradually began to distinguish between the malevolent and the innocent.

All the same, there were heretics who did not cease to blow the bellows at the fire, and keep the popular mind blazing with the memory of this outrage. Thy were able to do even more than the king himself against us, and this they did by adding new laws to the most cruel legislation enacted against us both in the queen's day and already in James I's reign . . . But this was done later than the time we are speaking about. It was done after they examined the plotters one by one, and established the fact that the catholics generally were completely innocent of their deed. They believed, none the less, that the more completely catholics were founded in their faith the more they were to be feared. So that the reader can better understand this, and form a clear and more complete judgement of what has passed, I wish to put on record here some of the words used by the king himself in the speech which he made to parliament some days after the plot was discovered:† 'If these conspirators', he said, 'had only been bankrupt persons, or discontented upon occasion of any disgrace done unto them, this might have

---

* This was the proclamation against Thomas Percy (PRO, SP 14, vol. 16, No. 20: reproduced in PS, pp. 86–9). It agrees 'to distinguish between all others, calling themselves catholics, and these detestable traitors'. Nevertheless, it refers to Percy in the beginning as being 'utterly corrupted with the superstition of the Romish religion', and 'seduced with the blindness thereof'. He is described as 'otherwise of lewd life, insolent disposition, and for the most part of desperate estate', which agrees with evidence from other quarters (see chapter 3, n.* p. 57).

† The King's speech is printed in the *Lords' Journal*, vol. II, p. 358, col. 2.

seemed to have been but a work of revenge. But for my own part, as I scarcely ever knew any of them, so cannot they allege so much as a pretended cause of grief. And the wretch himself in hands doth confess that there was no cause moving him or them, but merely and only religion.'

The above words of His Majesty are worthy of note, since they declare what the plotters always claimed right up to the moment of death. They were motivated by nothing else than zeal for religion when they undertook this plot, even if they did not know much about it. Later on in his speech, the King struck a note of wonder. He marvelled, 'that christian men, at least so-called, Englishmen, born within the country, and one of the specials of them my sworn servant, in an honourable place, should practise the destruction of their king, his posterity, their country and all: wherein their following obstinacy is so joined to their former malice, as the fellow himself that is in hand cannot be moved to discover any signs or notes of repentance, except only that he doth not yet stand to a vow that he repents for not being able to perform his intent.' These words bear clear testimony to the conspirator's sureness of conviction, however deceived, and also of his courage and perseverance. Even after severe and excruciating torture, he persisted in his first opinion. He continued to believe that it was morally permissible to do as much as he had intended. Vain are the calumnies of those who want us to believe that as soon as he saw himself shut up in the Tower, and the instruments of torment ranged before his eyes, he showed signs of wavering . . .

The king proceeded in this same speech to parliament to declare how it was owing to his own admirable interpretation of the letter that he and his had been freed from the general conflagration. Of this we have spoken above. The king went on to say that he did not wish to condemn the rest of his catholic subjects on account of this deed by a few individuals, and could not reasonably do so. He took some trouble with his words in order to remove from the minds of the puritans the idea which they favoured of making the conspirators' cause one common to all catholics. It is evident from the king's words that they were trying to persuade him and everyone else that this was indeed the case.

'It now remains for me,' said the king, 'to say what we must do for the future concerning this appalling and unheard of event. As far as you are concerned, my well-loved and faithful subjects, and of whatever rank, I know well that your hearts burn with indignation at this wayward deed. Your tongues are only too ready to express that very deep love which you bear me. Your hands and even your feet are in a constant readiness to carry out my will, and I well know you have no need of encouragement. I cannot fail on this occasion to praise your promptitude to serve me. But it could well be that zeal might force some of you to blame rashly those whose minds are far from this deed and wholly innocent of it. In truth, it would displease me no little if anyone who were guiltless or a stranger should come to be blamed for it. It cannot be denied that the sole cause which brought them to such a desperate plan was blind superstition arising from their religious errors. However, it does not follow that all those who profess the Roman religion have been knowing accomplices and abettors of the plot. It is true that no other heretical set or faction has ever defended as a foundation and principle of its religion that it was licit, or even meritorious, to assassinate princes and destroy peoples over differences and controversies of religion. But Romish catholics speak in these terms. Not even the Turks, jews, pagans, indeed, not even those of Calcutta who worship the devil, have ever done this . . . On the other hand it is true that there are many who are only blinded by some of the opinions and errors of popery. There are papists who either do not know or do not accept every foundation and principle of the papal religion, that religion which, in fact, is the mystery of iniquity . . . For this reason, we can reasonably admit that many papists, and especially those who were our ancestors and relatives, may quite possibly in many cases, and even often, have been saved . . . In this connection, we loath the doctrine of the puritans. We consider their cruelty worthy of the fire who are not prepared to admit that a papist of any kind can be saved. We will conclude on this point by saying that many good men seduced by some only of the errors of popery can be good and faithful subjects, while on the other hand not one of them who knows truly and believes fully all the principles and scholastic doctrines of that teaching could ever be a good christian or faithful subject.'*

* This latter part of the king's speech is omitted in the printed *Journal*.

Up to this point, we have given the king's speech to parliament [of 9 November 1605]. It was in such good and concise English that some believe it was written originally by Secretary Cecil. However that may be, we should certainly notice two principal points; the first was that the puritans and other mortal enemies of the catholics had given the king to understand that it was catholic teaching, and even fundamental to that religion, that it was licit or even meritorious to assassinate princes. In order to persuade the king more completely of their opinion, they printed two pestilent books full of lies and abominable calumnies. It would be truer to say that they wished to exploit His Majesty's convictions to push on success for their own desires and designs. Of one of the books, something has already been said above. Its subject and purpose was to prove that all the Catholics of this land are, by its laws, traitors and guilty of *lèse-majesté*.

The other book was even more impudent and malicious. It was entitled, *The Positions of the Papists*.★ A multitude of canons and pronouncements of pontiffs and doctors were artfully used to prove that it is lawful, according to the doctrine of the Catholic Church, to kill and destroy princes. Thrown in for good measure were a number of quite false allegations and sophistical inferences. For this reason, we should be hated and treated like traitors. There is no need for me to pause to explain the purpose and intention of these and similar works. I will only remark that, like all books which set out to stir up hatred and dislike of catholicism, they are often shameless in their lies . . . Who could be so foolish as to believe that christian princes, including the most potent in Christendom, would give their support to such a pernicious and diabolical opinion, and with so much prejudice and danger to themselves? How could they allow it to be preached and taught as a fundament or principle of catholic faith? . . .

One could here call on an infinite number of authors and catholic

★ Given in the Italian as *Le Positioni de' Papisti*: no book seems to have been issued in England with precisely this title in 1605 or 1606. Perhaps the narrator had in mind Thomas Morton's *An Exact Discoverie of Romish Doctrine in the Case of Conspiracie and Rebellion by pregnant observations* . . . London, 1605 (cf. *Catalogue of the McAlpin Collection of British History and Theology in the Union Theological Seminary, New York*, vol. I (1500–1640), New York, 1927, p. 189). A few other works published in 1606 might qualify (cf. ibid., pp. 200–1).

doctors to give evidence of what catholics really believe in this matter. But it will suffice to turn our attention to the doctrine which Father Henry Garnet revealed in his replies to Mr Catesby. The enquirer will find how far he was from the diabolical and infernal doctrine generated and brought to birth by the ministers of Calvin and Luther. He will find in Garnet's letters a spirit of true peace, gentleness and patience. He will discover in him, no less, the spirit of obedience, of not even wanting to know more than was comformable to the command of his superiors. He did not wish even to hear of anything that had to do with disturbing the peace of his country. The enquirer will observe that the pope, at that time Clement VIII, the General of the Jesuits, and Garnet's Superior, who was that holy priest Father Robert Persons, Superior of the English Mission, were all at one in obliging Garnet to this very thing . . .*

The same could be said of His Holiness, Pope Paul V,† who rules the universal church today. He likewise, by letter and embassy

* For Clement VIII's attitude in 1603, see EGF, p. 213. Spain at this time was still at war with England. In 1603 'Anthony Dutton' went to Spain, and a little after him Guy Fawkes. At Simancas there is 'a letter of the gentleman who came lately from our friends at Brussels, and sent Sergeant Fawkes to Spain, bearing date June 16, 1603'. This endorsement is in the hand of Joseph Creswell, S.J., an English jesuit, then at the English College in Valladolid. He enjoyed the confidence of Philip III, and seems to have favoured the plan to invade England even after James's accession. Philip was assured that 'the enterprise was never easier or safer'. Philip's invasion force would be assisted by 'more than 2,000 horse, including leading men and their adherents, and some 8,000 infantry' (Sim.E., 840, f. 134. Cf. ff. 125 and 126). No one who knew the English scene would have volunteered information so misleading. One is reminded of the Ridolphi invasion scheme of 1571 (see Edwards, *The Dangerous Queen*, London, 1964, especially pp. 297–356). Probable purposes of this scheme were to lure the Spaniards to exhaust themselves still further, or to discredit Catholicism in England as being generally Hispanophile. Whatever Creswell and some of his friends at the Spanish court thought of the plan, there is no reason to suppose that the Roman authorities, whether Jesuit or papal, were favourable even in 1603. For one thing, resources to carry it out were lacking. (See A. Loomie, *Guy Fawkes in Spain* . . ., especially pp. 30–46).

† D. H. Willson (op. cit., p. 228) claimed that Paul V 'was far less inclined to moderation' than Clement VIII in his relations with James I. In fact, Paul seems to have been anxious to establish good relations, if he could, from the very beginning of his pontificate in 1605. The violent wave of aggression against catholics in general after the plot, manifested in new penal laws and the

recommended peace and patience to the catholics – something of which His Majesty and his council are not ignorant. The pope would not have been able to do this if it had been a foundation of our religion, I will not say to kill princes, but even to be behind-hand or disobedient in dealing with civil magistrates. I will say nothing of those gentlemen who, when they were invited and even implored by the plotters to help them at that time, nevertheless remained firm in their obedience to the prince. They did this even when they were bound by close friendship and even relationship of blood to those unhappy gentlemen. Garnet and his fellow Jesuits had won over the minds of these men, as Garnet made clear in his letters. So at that time, as indeed before and afterwards, those who took their teachings from the jesuits remained loyal to their prince and peaceful members of the state . . .

It is not perhaps remarkable if, among all the catholics of England, and in the course of so many years, and in the midst of so much persecution, there have been a few to produce the bitter fruits of impatience and revenge . . . But it would be better for princes to be on their guard against the doctrines of the calvinists. These they should fear, and against these they should arm themselves and their subjects. This doctrine of rebellion can be read in the books of Luther, Calvin, Zwingli and others like them. The practice is found frequently among their followers, as anyone knows who has read the history of their times in Germany, France and elsewhere . . . But it is not my intention to enlarge on this matter in which I see that I have already delayed too much . . . Let the reader content himself with reading up on the apostle of Calvinism in Scotland . . . Let him read the words of John Knox. He will find in him not merely vague insinuation of this most seditious doctrine, but very clear arguments for it. He has whole chapters, in fact, and very long dis-courses to prove, explain and declare it, and to make it understood by the people.★

Let him also read Buchanan, one of the principal assistants and

★ For the inflammatory ideas and influence of some at least of the reformers,

imposition of a new oath of allegiance, made it impossible for Paul V to achieve anything through conciliation. The new oath seems to have been devised by Sir Christopher Perkins, a former jesuit, who knew well how to trip the consciences of his former co-religionists.

adherents of Knox. He was His Majesty's tutor in boyhood and youth. The reader will find that these two writers give the people full power over princes, putting in their hands whatever is needed to limit princely authority according to their own wishes. They can oblige them to do whatever they please. They can punish them at will and even condemn them to death after public trial. They can depose them, send them into exile, and deprive them of life like robbers and criminals . . . Their ministers can call them to account, and by excommunication cast them into the pit, making them unfit to live anywhere on earth. These are the very words they use . . .

I will not pass over what the present King of England concluded in this matter. Putting all passion aside, let him judge according to what he knows, not only from having read their books, but also from having experienced as King of Scotland how violent is their fanatical spirit, and how intolerable to prince and people it is when they find themselves with sufficient power and influence to give their principles practical effect. Let His Majesty remember the long and perilous servitude in which this race of men held him while he was in Scotland. When he thinks of the trials and perils through which he then passed with them he may be better able to say which of the two parties could be more aptly compared with the Turks, jews, pagans and the inhabitants of Calcutta . . . He himself was often wont to say that he had two kinds of donkey in his kingdom, that is the old donkey and the young donkey. The old donkey was the papist who willingly allowed himself to be loaded, and carried his burden patiently, even when it was heavy and weighed him down. But the young ass, by which His Majesty understood the puritan, was so intractable that it could scarcely be led at

see e.g., Owen Chadwick, *The Reformation*, London, 1964, especially chapter 6. The present narrative has a marginal note: 'Knox, Apel. fol. 28, 30, 35 [*The Appellation of John Knoxe from the cruell and most unjust Sentence pronounced against him by the false Bishop of Scotland* . . ., Geneva, 1558: see WTL, vol. III, London, 1834, p. 1081]. *The History of the Church of Scotland* [this is, presumably, *The Historie of the Reformation of Religion within the Realm of Scotland* . . ., 4th and best edition, according to WTL (ibid), Edinburgh, 1584], pp. 1807-3702]. Et a Anglia e Scotia [this seems to be *A Faithfull Admonition unto the Professours of God's Truthe in England*, Kalykow, 1554], fol. 77, 78: [George] Buchanan, [*De Jure Regni apud Scotos Dialogus*, Edinburgh, 1579], pag. 13, 23, 40, 58, 61, 70. [The numbers given are all as in Greenway.]

all, let alone have a load put on it. And even if by chance they did get a load on it, even a load that was small and weighed little, the beast did not cease to jib, kick and buck until he had thrown it off. Sometimes he would aim not a few kicks at the bystanders . . . Not long before the plot was discovered, some of the more intelligent of the king's council coined a phrase to the effect that the catholics were God's lunatics, and there was nothing to fear or suspect from them . . .

NINE

NEWS HAD BY NOW spread through the kingdom that the participants in the plot were no other than those who had been taken, and whose names had been published. After the plotters' examinations, it was generally held to be evident that no priest of any kind had had a hand in it. The catholics were decidedly glad at this. It was not only because they were glad to see declared innocent those who had the cure of their souls, and guided their consciences. They also knew very well that, since the priests were not guilty, everyone would have good reason to see not only that the deed could not be ascribed to the whole community, but that it could not even be ascribed to many individuals. It was clear enough to all that the catholics were accustomed to accept guidance in serious matters which could effect their spiritual well-being. This being so, few enough of them would have been prepared, on their own initiative, to undertake a negotiation of such significance, and so much concerning conscience. Anyone who erred in such a matter ran the risk of eternal damnation. They would scarcely proceed, therefore, without consulting their spiritual advisers.

The protestants were astonished that even a handful of men should entertain no kind of scruple as to whether the plot were permissible or no; indeed, that they should be entirely persuaded that it was licit, without asking so much as a word of advice from their priests, even at the beginning of the enterprise. They were all the more astounded when they saw that all the time they were in prison, and even when they were on the threshold of death itself, scarcely one of them repented of the deed, and none was willing to confess that it had been a crime even to attempt their cruel and bloody design. Many of the heretics, especially the Puritans, were left considerably chagrined, and even enraged, by the fact that the examinations and confessions of the plotters declared all the priests innocent. Of these there were at that time, and there still are at this present, more than 400 in the land.* It seemed to their enemies that the finest opportunity conceivable to make them hateful throughout the country had been lost. Surely they could have implicated a few in this foolhardy and odious plot, or at least among all of them surely one must have been guilty? With this object in view, they subjected the conspirators to every kind of interrogation carried out with the utmost diligence. In spite of it all, they could never get out of them more than has been said. That is, they had never even once consulted a priest about their undertaking. They continued to protest, both during their frequent examinations in prison and also when they stood up to be done to death on the place of execution, that all the priests in the country were, without exception, completely ignorant of the plot. In particular, they took trouble to declare the complete innocence of the Fathers of the Society of Jesus. They were well aware that three of these had been named by the protestants as knowing about the deed and consenting to it. The conspirators constantly maintained that this was false.

It has long been a common device with our enemies to calumniate the catholic clergy on every possible occasion . . . In protestant pulpits the congregations heard scarcely anything but hate-filled ranting against catholic ecclesiastics . . . During the whole of Queen Elizabeth's reign, priests were killed on various pretexts and excuses, but chiefly under colour of the crime of *lèse-majesté.* They

---

* This is a fairly common estimate for the time. Cf. Rev. T. E. Gibson, *Lydiate Hall and its Associations* . . ., London, 1876, p. 267, 'From the Douai Diary, it appears that up to the last year of Queen Elizabeth, 400 priests had been dispatched from that seminary on the mission in England, and of these 93 had suffered martyrdom.' Sir Henry Neville, writing to Secretary Cecil from Paris on 27 June 1599 (old style), reported the opinion of one English papist in France, 'that there are great numbers of Jesuits and priests now in England, and one of them sayeth at the least 600' (Win, I, p. 51). This seems much exaggerated. The jesuit catalogues are defective. That for 1593 shows fifty English Jesuits in the whole Society, but only eight in England, including two in prison (Mount Street Transcript).

passed, among others, a law whereby anyone who was reconciled through a catholic priest to the Roman church should be quartered alive as a traitor. This also applied to those in whose houses priests were found. The present king confirmed this penalty for the cases already mentioned in the first parliament at the beginning of his reign. What is more, he saw to it that the laws were observed. He had some killed simply for persuading others to embrace the catholic faith and to become reconciled to the Latin church.* They also used a great deal of industry to obscure the reputation of the many martyr-priests whom they killed solely because they came to England to restore the faith of their fathers in that land . . . Above all, they sought to destroy the reputation of the jesuits who worked on that mission, and of whom they had already martyred not a few. These men had been outstanding for doctrine and goodness of life . . .

They now resolved to make a new beginning with the Fathers of the Society, since these were men looked up to by everyone. Moreover, they had worked with great success in that field of labour. The task was, in the first place, to make them odious to catholics at home by connecting them with this plot. Secondly, they would besmirch their reputation abroad so that none would have any further sympathy with them. They could then deal with them at their convenience, killing some, and sending the others into exile. They hoped that by issuing most severe decrees against them, no one would receive or keep them in their houses. Indeed, the catholics themselves would feel obliged to give them up. Even if less than this were achieved, they did not doubt that the infamy of this slander would stick. This would put at a considerable discount for the future those who died in defence of their faith. It would remove all element of improbability from the pretext for the per-

* Sir Henry Neville wrote to Winwood on 21 June 1605, 'The king sent for all the judges lately, and gave them a very strict charge to be diligent and severe in their circuits against recusants, and to execute the laws in that behalf made, and namely those which concern their banishing or confining. Yet it is generally feared that there will be none of the priests executed, without which I doubt all the other provision will be fruitless' (Win, II, pp. 77–8; cf. Sal. Cal., XVII, p. 254). Three were executed in 1604, one a priest, for religion, and two in 1605 (*v. supra*: see also Catholic Truth Society pamphlet, H. 163, London, 1960, p. 29).

secution which they were now determined to unleash against all catholics . . . But it fell out otherwise when, putting into execution the beginnings of this devilish stratagem, they published that slanderous and false proclamation against the Jesuits, and more especially against three of them. The catholics were left in a state of wonder at the novelty of the suggestion, even if they were appalled by the cruelty of the decree.

When they began to reflect on the business, the papists succeeded in penetrating the intention of their enemies. They paid no further heed after that either to threats or calumnies. They saw quite clearly that if they surrendered the Fathers into the king's hands, as they were commanded to on pain of death, they would themselves be numbered among the accomplices of the plot. They would be treated as such, and deprived of all hope of mercy. Moreover, it would only open the way to an indefinite number of similar proclamations for the future. They would be obliged to do as much whenever the king, on a like pretext, was looking for third parties to betray them. In this way, they would in a short time be deprived either of their best priests, or even of all the priests there were. They saw through these calumnies well enough because they had seen those Fathers living among them for so many years. There was not a catholic living in England who could say that he had ever heard one of them, either in public or private, approve of such a thing. Still less did they ever hear them teach that such things were good and lawful. Nor did they ever give the least sign of it. They never taught that, even to free themselves from savage persecution, they should have recourse to means so bloody and cruel. Indeed, they should always avoid violence and recourse to arms.

Mr Taylor of Worcestershire gave this reply to the magistrates when they came to search his house. He told them that he marvelled that they could affirm such things in the edict against those Fathers, because those who had most dealings with them knew the opposite to be true. Here we must notice the colossal effrontery of the man who wrote that edict. This claimed, in His Majesty's name, that it was evident from the confessions and examinations of many of the principal conspirators that the three Jesuits were the authors and instigators of this plot. It names them as John Gerard,* Henry

* John Gerard: second son of Sir Thomas G. of Bryn, Lancs.: educated at

Garnet, and Oswald Tesimond. Providence permitted the blessed martyr, Henry Garnet, to fall into their hands. Even some time after he was taken, they were still unable to prove, not merely that he was the author and instigator, but even that he had any knowledge of the deed. They were unable to prove anything against him, and not merely from the confessions of many of the principals, although they claimed the contrary. They could prove nothing from the confession of anyone at all. From this we can judge how great has been the injustice they have inflicted on those three priests. We can estimate also how little we should believe the rest of those innumerable slanders which they have spread throughout the world against the jesuits, and more especially against Father Henry Garnet . . .

I am anxious that the reader should see that it is no part of my intention to conceal anything which belongs to this story. I would not wish to hide anything which our adversaries have produced or could produce, against those Fathers from that day to this. I will set down faithfully the reasons which moved them to print, publish and distribute throughout Christendom the claim that those three Fathers were willing accomplices and authors of the plot. It is not my purpose to hide or dissimulate anything. The king's representatives had the plotters examined again and again with the utmost care, and more especially on the subject of their accomplices. They were present at their separate examinations, and heard their exact denial that any other had been aware of what they were doing, apart from those who were already dead or taken prisoner. The majority of the examiners, if not all, were persuaded at the end of it that this was the truth. And indeed it was. They were not the only ones to believe it. It was held for certain in the court, the City of London, and throughout the land that the conspirators alone and no others were the participants of this plot.

After two months, however, they induced Thomas Bates, Mr

Oxford, Douai, Paris and Rome. Joined the Society of Jesus, and also returned to England in 1588. Finally escaped from England on 3 May 1606. First rector of the English College at Liège, 1614. 1627 went to Rome, and resided in the English College till his death on 27 July 1637. Gerard's autobiography was first published by John Morris, S.J., in 1881: new edition by P. Caraman, S.J., London 1951.

Robert Catesby's servant, to confess that his master and another gentleman had been together in the house of a certain nobleman some fifteen days before the plot was discovered in the company of those three Fathers. This confession was obtained partly by threats and partly by promises, especially of life and liberty. Bates himself bears witness to this in a letter of his written a few days before his death. I have seen this letter in his own handwriting in which he expresses his sorrow for his confession, and begs pardon from God. He also confessed that after the plot was discovered, his master sent him to a house in Warwickshire with a letter intended for Father Garnet. He found Father Oswald Tesimond at this house, and took him along to Mr Robert Wintour's house to speak with his master. But he left the house almost immediately, scarcely staying there for any time at all. Finally, he added that he thought that Father Oswald Tesimond knew something about this plot, but he could not be certain. He expresses great sorrow in his letter for having uttered even no more than this. He says also that he hopes the Lord will pardon him for the mistake which he committed out of the considerable hope of life which they held before him. He no longer cared very much for life. Indeed, he took it for certain that they would make him die along with the rest. But of the other two priests, that is of Father Garnet and Father Gerard, he had uttered not a word.

All this was the foundation on which our adversaries built their flimsy and unstable edifice of malicious calumnies and falsehoods. These are the so-called 'confessions of many of the plotters' from which, according to them, it is clear as daylight that these three priests were the authors and originators of the plot. These are the 'very certain proofs' which caused them to issue that barbarous edict against the Fathers. Would any man of sense say, or even think, that the confession of someone without social rank, and overwhelmed by threats and promises, should suffice as proof of anything against religious persons of known life and goodness? Still less should such a statement be used to secure their condemnation. But what am I calling a confession? Did Bates not subsequently deny what he said previously, goaded as he was later by fear of God and prick of conscience? And even if he had continued to affirm up to the moment of death what he had confessed previously, what more could be inferred from it than that he merely thought that one of them knew about the business? We cannot but contrast what was said in the proclamation about the clear confessions of many of the principals with the fact that one man merely said something he thought. He was only one individual, after all, and not of notable importance. Even this bare surmise of his only touched one of the three priests. Bates did not claim that this priest approved of, or consented to, the plot, but only that he knew of it. How many things do priests know of which they do not approve . . . !

For the rest, who cannot discern the irrelevance of everything else in his confession as regards the plot, even if it be supposed that what Bates said was true? What did Mr Catesby's writing to Father Garnet after the plot have to do with the case? Or the fact that Father Oswald went together with the servant to Mr Robert Wintour's house? Or the fact that the Fathers in question were found in Mr Catesby's company fifteen days previously in Baron Vaux's house? The truth is that this letter was written by Sir Everard Digby to put his wife in the picture. She was then staying at that house or in one nearby. He wished to warn her of the danger in which he found himself. As for Father Oswald, he went, in the first place, to bring those gentlemen the assistance of the sacraments, knowing full well their danger and need. This he did with evident risk to his own life and person. All these gentlemen could give testimony of what he said publicly in the presence of them all. He was sorry for them; not only for their wretchedness, disgrace, and the extreme danger in which they found themselves, but also because their foolhardiness had given the protestants a good excuse to blame every catholic in the land. The same gentleman could also testify how clearly he refused to accompany them lest he give the protestants a pretext to calumniate him and his fellow jesuits.

That those three Fathers found themselves in Baron Vaux's house was a mere surmise on the part of Thomas Bates.★ Later on, Bates regretted saying it at all. I myself heard Father John Gerard protest solemnly that he had not seen Thomas Bates for more than a year before he was taken prisoner. True, he was not without a reason for suspecting as much as he said. For at that time, the

★ Since the relationship of the Vauxes mentioned in the text is somewhat complicated, a table is given opposite.

baron's aunts had come to visit Lord Vaux and his mother. They had not been in that house for many years previously. Because Thomas Bates knew that Father Garnet was ordinarily to be found in the company of those two sisters, he assumed that he was also with them at that time. The same assumption could be made about Father Oswald. He enjoyed a very close friendship with his patron, Mr Catesby. He, too, went at that time to meet the two sisters, who were the baron's aunts and Catesby's cousins. It could be conjectured that Tesimond would not have failed to meet his superior, that is Father Garnet, when the latter came with those ladies. Indeed, all the Fathers of the Society owed them a great deal.

In the same fashion, one could suppose that Father Gerard would not have been missing on that occasion. Thomas Bates believed that he stayed continually in Baron Vaux's house both in order to receive his superior, in case he should decide to come, and also to offer some comfort by way of spiritual exhortation to the whole company, as was customary among catholics. But what had all this to do with the plot? Was this the first time that a number of catholics met together in this way? Or even the first time that these individuals so met? Would it have been the last time? It was not considered sufficient proof against Baron Vaux and his mother, who, after the first accusation, were set at liberty. Not only did it prove impossible to hang upon them the least suspicion of this plot, but

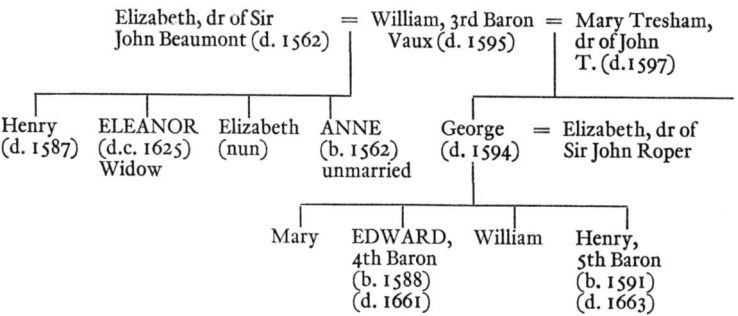

From Vaux, p. 110. The characters of principal interest in the present context are in capitals. The family seat was at Harrowden. The baron's house referred to as being some three miles from the first was doubtless at Irthlingborough (cf. ibid., p. 381).

they could not even be saddled with Thomas Bates's imaginative thought that those Fathers had, as he supposed, been there. If it had been possible to prove this, the baron and his mother would doubtless have been touched in life and property. It was a crime of *lèse-majesté* to receive jesuits or other priests from colleges and seminaries overseas into one's house. Finally, when Father Henry Garnet was captured, it was never proved against him that he had been in that house, or that any of the conspirators had spoken to him of the plot. He was not condemned in the absence of all 'proof' either against him or the other Fathers. But it merely consisted in his having heard the confession of someone who was never accused of the plot, and for not having revealed this confession.

Was anything ever proved against Father Gerard in connection with the plot? Or has anyone come forward up to this present time to accuse him? I ask the same about Father Oswald. Although he was the confessor for a long time of Mr Catesby and Thomas Wintour, he was, nevertheless, completely exonerated by the latter as altogether innocent of the deed. Likewise innocent was every other priest in the land. Catesby had already died in the country, but Wintour admitted this just before his execution. So all the reasoning of our enemies in composing and publishing that most false proclamation reduces to this. It leans completely on Thomas Bates's imagination; and he repented of what he had said shortly before he died, as anyone who reads his own letter word for word will clearly see.

The publication of the edict against the priests stirred up a great hue and cry in many parts of the country. Great was the trouble taken to find them. Without making our tale too long, however, I would like to say a few words here about the troubles suffered by that very fine gentleman Baron Vaux, and Lady Vaux, his mother. A special commission was sent down without delay so that a most diligent and painstaking search could be made of the house where the baron and his mother were then staying. Search was made at the same time of another house belonging to the baron some three miles from the first. They were hoping to find Father John Gerard. The commission was addressed to one of the most fervent puritans of the county. He had orders not only to go through the house thoroughly, but also, in the event of not finding the Father, to confiscate all the keys of the house. He should maintain most careful watch on the building until further orders from the king's court and council. All this and more was carried out with a care for detail that could scarcely be described. The baron and his mother were both well loved and very much looked up to throughout the region and county. The baron himself was the foremost nobleman of that area, and by consanguinity or affinity joined in blood to practically every leading and noble family in the county. He was also connected with them in very close friendship. In spite of this, the inquisition of his house was carried out with the utmost harshness. Some who were actually present at the time told me all about it. First of all, they besieged the house with more than one hundred men, and these heavily armed. The baron knew that his conscience was clear with regard to the plot, and so had nothing to fear from them. He therefore offered no kind of resistance, and immediately conducted the leader of the commission into the house. He introduced him and some of his company to the lady, his mother.

Lady Vaux handed over keys to all the rooms so that they could make the search at their own convenience. For two or three days on end, they examined the house with great thoroughness. They made their way with lanterns through all the cellars and dark places. They did not neglect to open chests and trunks, and even the caskets and desks belonging to the workroom of the lady of the house. They thought they might find letters, notes or memoranda of Father Gerard's, or some other mark or proof of knowledge of the plot. They found nothing. The man to whom the king had committed this task was a puritan, and altogether hostile to catholics. Nevertheless, he wrote to the court that, even after making most careful search, he could find no trace of what was looked for. Furthermore, he had observed that the baron and his mother were completely sure of their innocence, and had readily allowed them to search the house without hindrance. He had found nothing to suggest warlike preparation, or anything else which could argue in them the least knowledge of the treason. Not content with this clear information and indication of their innocence, the king's councillors ordered both to come to court. Incidentally, the baron was only a youth some eighteen or nineteen years old. When they arrived, the baron was examined by the Earl of Salisbury, that is,

Secretary Cecil. Vaux gave such an account of himself that the earl was entirely persuaded of his innocence. All the same, he told him not to leave London without the king's further orders.

The baron's mother was also examined, but her examination took place before the whole council.* She, too, purged herself before them of all suspicion in connection with the plot. She claimed that she detested it no less than did the king's councillors themselves. Indeed, she had been taught to do so as a catholic by those who had the care of her soul. The councillors insisted much that she knew Father Gerard, and had received him and lodged him in her house. She replied that it was her hope that no one would be able to accuse her justly of having received either him or any other priest in her house. For the rest, she was under no obligation to accuse herself, or confess without proof what they charged her with. 'You know well,' the councillors said to her, 'that he has been proclaimed a traitor as one of the principal participants in this conspiracy. For that reason, you are obliged in conscience to confess the truth in all this.' To this she replied bravely that, even if it were true that she knew Father Gerard, as they supposed, she still had not the slightest reason to believe what they said of him. On the contrary, she had always heard so much good said of that Father that she would be content to stake life and property on his complete innocence of that conspiracy. The lords of the council then showed her a letter which she had written to her cousin, the Sheriff of Warwickshire, to get him to release two priests who had been taken in that area not long after the disturbances connected with the plotters. Her cousin, who was a fervent puritan, had sent this letter to the Privy Council.

'Now what do you have to say to this letter?' asked the lords of the council. 'You wrote it with much insistence, and showed how anxious you were for liberty of those two priests. One of them is

* The Registers of the Privy Council, which must have contained many references to various personages involved at this time, are missing for the period from 1 January 1602 until 1 May 1613. It seems they were destroyed in a fire in 1619. (See HMSO, *Guide to the Contents of the PRO*, vol. II, London, 1963, p. 234. BM.Add.MS 11402 is a digest which includes the lost registers for 1550–1611, but does not fill the gap adequately.) For Elizabeth Vaux's story, including original documents, see Vaux, pp. 287–310. See also Cal. S.P. Dom. 1603–10, *passim*. (The original examination of Elizabeth Vaux is in GPB, No. 103.)

Thomas Strange,★ a jesuit' – Strange is at present in the Tower of London, where he has been many times most cruelly tortured. 'The other man is one of the Archpriest Blackwell's assistants.† By this letter, you have run into the crime of *lèse-majesté* as one who has given assistance to priests.' Lady Vaux replied, 'I do not deny having written for the freedom of those two. But I do not think that it can be proved against me that I knew them to be priests. It is not my way to enquire too closely into the quality of everyone who passes through my house, especially when they are gentlemen and catholics. This I certainly believed of these two.'

This reply gave little satisfaction to the lords of the council. They told her plainly that already her life and all she possessed stood at the King's Majesty's disposal. They did not see how she could find any quicker or better way of freeing herself from further entanglements than by revealing to them the whereabouts of Gerard the Jesuit. If she did this, they promised, on behalf of His Majesty, life, liberty, and possessions. She replied that she had no idea where that Father was to be found. But even if she knew, she would not have said anything else to save a thousand lives. 'Very well, madam,' said the Lords of the Council. 'It therefore remains that you die in conformity with the law!' 'And I will die,' she replied, 'rather than do what you want!' After this, they sent her away with the order that she should remain a prisoner in the house of one of the twelve who governed the City of London. Here she received the

★ Thomas Strange, S.J.: alias Anderton and Hungerford. Born Glos. 1577/8. Joined the S.J., 1600/1. Sent to England in 1603. Originally converted to catholicism by John Gerard, S.J., he was so cruelly tortured at the time of the plot 'that he was compelled, after his banishment on the death of Cecil, to drag on the remaining 33 years of his life in Belgium in extreme debility and severe suffering . . . totally incapable of any employment' (HFR, VII, p. 744: IV, pp. 3–16, which include several documents from the plot period).
† George Blackwell: Born Middlesex, c. 1545. Educated at Oxford. Converted to Catholicism, entered Douai College 1574, and ordained priest 1575. Returned to England 1576. Appointed Archpriest in 1599, since the Pope thought the appointment of a bishop inexpedient at that time. Much opposed by a minority group among catholic secular clergy – the 'Appellants', who appealed more than once against the Roman decision; but the pope insisted. The division in the ranks of the papists was fostered by the English government. Arrested in 1607, B. took the oath of allegiance, forbidden by Rome, and was deposed in 1608. He died in prison in 1613 (see Gil., I, pp. 225–31).

respect and treatment due to her rank. However, she was kept so closely guarded that not even the baron, her son, was allowed to visit her. Nor was she allowed anyone else from her own house to serve her, apart from one lady-in-waiting. Many of her servants were also seized and put in various prisons. Here they were many times examined, and threatened with terrible things if they would not confess that Father Gerard had stayed in the house of their mistress. But neither by threats nor promises were they ever able to get out of them what they desired.

All this took place in the space of nine or ten days while a strict guard was maintained, both outside and inside, on the house of Baron Vaux. By the end of this time, it was evident that if Father Gerard had been hidden there, either he would have died of hunger, or else he would already have revealed himself in order to save his life. Guards were also posted two or three miles round about. Wayfarers were subjected to examination to make sure the priest could not escape. But the watchers watched in vain. News got through to Father Gerard where he was hiding of this very severe search. Since they had put it about that he was one of the plotters in this conspiracy, it seemed to him essential for the defence of his innocence to write certain letters.* In these he takes care to give first of all the very pressing reasons which moved him to clear himself of this quite false imputation. After this, he protests solemnly on his soul, before God and all the court of heaven, not only that he was never an accomplice to the plot, but that he never heard even a word of it before it was cried publicly through the land. It had not previously come to his ears, even in confession. He called on God and

---

* Gerard wrote four letters in all, at least three of which were dated 23 January 1606, and are extant. One was to the Duke of Lennox, another to Salisbury, and the third to Sir Everard Digby. The fourth letter was lost, and the addressee unknown (see Cal. S.P. Dom. 1603, p. 282); this important reference was omitted from the index, at least under Gerard. The letters are given *in toto*, with other interesting letters vindicating Gerard, in chapter XXXI of John Morris's *Life of Fa. John Gerard*, London, 1881 (pp. 417–36). As late as 1631, a rumour was being circulated on the continent, 'the testimony of a priest being alleged', to the effect that Gerard had actually worked in the mine! (ibid., p. 426). A scholarly vindication of Gerard may be found in A. F. Allison, 'John Gerard & the Gunpowder Plot', *Recusant History*, vol. 5, no.2 (April 1959), pp. 43–63.

'A PLOT WITH POWDER 1605'

his conscience to bear witness that in all this he spoke without equivocation or amphibology of any kind.

Gerard urged a number of reasons to prove that he had no knowledge of the deed. In the first place, the attempt appeared to him unlawful, and displeased him as much as it might displease anyone else. Secondly, he was a religious and a priest, and for that reason very far from consenting to anything which would make him unfit to exercise the office of priesthood.* Thirdly, because he and his fellow-Jesuits had received strict order not to become involved in any kind of disturbance. Fourthly, the lords of the council in the queen's time had received from him all the satisfaction they could desire in matters of a similar nature. For he had been in their hands for three years on end. In this time, they had made every effort, by frequent and very cruel examinations, to determine whether he had ever taken part in matters of state. He could wish for no better witnesses than they themselves, who well knew his innocence through all that time. And this notwithstanding the fact that, whether through good treatment or bad, they had tried to compromise him. From which it seemed to him a good argument that, if he had not dabbled in such matters in the queen's time, and they well knew he had not, it was not very likely that he would involve himself now in a matter of the same kind but fraught with so much graver consequences. It was all the less likely since it was general knowledge how much his father had suffered and endured in the service of the king. His Majesty was pleased to remember this when he first came to the kingdom, and spoke of it in terms of respect to Gerard's brother. Gerard ends by saying that if Providence should see fit to let him fall into their hands at some time in the future, and if he

* A book campaign, often unscrupulous, against the Jesuits had been on foot for some years, not only in England but on the continent. The Appellants (see note on p. 159), encouraged by the English government, waged a ruthless war in print (see T. G. Law, *A Historical Sketch of the Conflicts between Jesuits and Seculars in the Reign of Queen Elizabeth* . . ., London, 1889, pp. cxxviii–cliii). One of the most scurrilous works of this kind was *Aphorisms, or certain selected points of the Doctrine of the Jesuits* . . ., a work published in 1609, with editions issued, seemingly in London, Paris and Geneva (see BM Catalogue under 'Jesuits: Appendix'). The Jesuits were accused, *inter alia*, of poisoning, transvestism, and using their churches as secret arsenals and torture-chambers!

were then convicted of knowing anything of this plot, he would not object to suffering every kind of torment conceivable. He would willingly allow, in that case, that everyone, of whatever religion or sect, should regard him as a perjured man of infamy. This letter was put about in London. I myself have read it. It fully satisfied not only the catholics but many also of the leading protestants, and even the king himself. It was shown to him by an earl who was a favourite of his.

In spite of all this good father could do, in the teeth of the general opinion that the priests were innocent, and in spite of the fact that they had no sort of proof against them, the councillors proposed to the king, and even persuaded him to issue an entirely false and unjust proclamation against the jesuits. Even one of the principal councillors said that he could see no reason why Father Gerard, who had fully exonerated himself of all suspicion of complicity, should be included in the edict. Nor could the councillors, surely, see why they should write in that fashion since they had no better proof against the other two. However, they decided on the necessity of publishing the proclamation in which, to make good Father Gerard more odious, they put his name in the first place. The second place was given to the name of Father Henry Garnet, his superior, and head of all the jesuits on the mission. The description of the Fathers was given regarding their height, age, colouring etc. [*sic*]. The object was to make them known to everyone, and ample rewards were promised to any who took them. On the other hand, as was said, very serious penalties were imposed on any who hid them. It was further promised that such people would be considered accomplices of the plot, and punished without pity.

This proclamation was first published in London. It was afterwards sent to every part of the kingdom to be put up in all the more important places. Special care was taken to see that it was posted up in all the market-places. In this way, the three priests could not stir, or dare to make a journey anywhere in the kingdom, without being recognized. It seemed impossible that in a short time all three would not fall into the hands of their persecutors. There were also spies who knew the Fathers by sight; and by order of the council, they prowled the streets of London by day and night in search of them hoping they might meet them or at least have news of them.

In the event, Providence allowed Father Henry to be betrayed as we shall describe in the following chapter . . . In this way, the labours of that holy Father were eventually crowned with martyrdom. However, the same Providence saw to it that the other two Fathers retained their liberty. One could describe the manner of it as miraculous, and this on more than one occasion.

More particularly, I have heard it said that Father Oswald got news of the proclamation one or two days after it was published in London. He thought it fitting to set out for London so that the people who were kind enough to shelter him in their house at that time would not run so much risk on his account. He made his journey by day, and through public streets. In almost every parish he found the proclamation posted up in which he was described to the life. All the same, he was never discovered or recognized although he dealt with all indifferently, and after walking more than a hundred miles, entered London in full daylight. In the past he had been very well known here. It is true that after he had stayed in London for some days, carrying on his business as usual, he was met by a certain spy. The lords of the council had made this man fulsome promises in the event of his capturing Tesimond. And now he arrested the priest. But Providence saw to it that he was freed from his hands. The pursuivant did not dare to call for help from the people on the street, and he had considerable difficulty in keeping up with the priest whom he followed for quite a way. Tesimond, meanwhile, argued with him, and urged him to be careful about what he was doing. He gradually led him away from the more frequented streets, and so he was able to shake him off and get away from him entirely. The spy went at once to the court and informed Secretary Cecil of what had happened. He told Cecil that he thought it might be possible to take him in London that very night. The earl realized that it would be impossible to find him, and he threatened to hang the spy himself instead. Next day, Cecil bitterly repeated the story in court to his own chagrin . . . Providence, however, allowed Father Henry Garnet to fall into their hands in order to demonstrate his own innocence and that of his companions; and not less the foxy, not to say diabolical, cunning which his enemies used to bring him into disrepute . . .

TEN

W E HAVE ALREADY described above how the two plotters, Robert Wintour and Stephen Lyttelton, were taken after being hidden for some time in the house of a lady related to Humphrey Lyttelton. Because he had assisted those gentlemen, and was found in their company, he was taken prisoner along with them. He had nothing to look forward to but death. Not many days previously, he had been staying in Mr Thomas Abington's house called Hinlip. Here he heard Mass and a sermon by Father Edward Old-corne, S.J., who normally resided there.* It was some two or three miles distant from Worcester. Oldcorne had won many converts to catholicism in the county, and was much esteemed by all the catholics. He was much loved for his great goodness and learning, and was well known to the gentlemen of the region, even to those who were not catholics. This was not primarily because he was a priest or a religious, but rather because he was a relative or friend of Mr Abington.

Mr Humphrey Lyttelton, who had no further hope of life but was desperately anxious to save it by any means possible, now got word of the cruel proclamation issued against the three priests. Apart from its threats against those who hid them, there were very generous promises of reward and recompense for those who betrayed them or helped in their capture. It seemed to Humphrey that here

* Edward Oldcorne: alias Hall. Son of a bricklayer. Born at York, 1561. Studied at Douai and Rome. Ordained priest in 1587. Went to England and joined the S.J. in the same year, 1587. Worked mainly in Worcestershire. Executed at Red Hill, Worcester, on 7 April 1606 (HFR, iv, pp. 202–44).

was a chance of saving his own life. It appeared to him altogether probable that in the same house where he had been himself, Father Edward Oldcorne and at least one other of the three priests posted up in the edict might also be found. He further believed it possible, by certain signs he had noticed, that such a one might be Henry Garnet. Furthermore, he knew very well that the owner of that house was very friendly to those Fathers. More than three or four of them at a time would sometimes stay at his house. Nor would that gentleman have failed to receive them into his home whatever the penalty to himself. This was especially true of Father Henry, with whom he had enjoyed close friendship for a long time. He reverenced the priest as a man of unusual goodness and holiness. He also knew that that house was among the safest that existed, not merely in the county but in the whole of England. It was a fine, large house and for that reason well suited to concealing secret places where, in time of need, church-equipment, books and even priests could be hidden. The occupants had had good experience of this in many searches. Not once in all of them had they ever been able to find a priest, although it was taken as almost certain that they were there all the time.

At this point, even if it does not otherwise appear to belong to our story, I will recount here briefly an experience which happened earlier to Father Oldcorne . . . It happened in this way. A number of Worcestershire gentlemen, puritans, and thus great enemies of catholics, particularly desired to bring about the ruin of Mr Thomas Abington. For one thing, he was well known as a zealous papist. For another, they were anxious to get possession of his house, which was an extraordinarily fine building. One of their number was called Sir Henry Bromley,* whose lands and possessions marched

* Sir Henry Bromley: son of Sir Thomas, Elizabeth's Lord Chancellor (1579: d. 1587), and Elizabeth, daughter of Sir Adrian Fortescue. Four times married, he died in 1615. He was the local magistrate, having his seat at Holt Castle, some four miles from Hinlip. He was known at court, at any rate, from April 1603. A rhyme was then current referring to him and Lord Thomas Howard, Lord Cobham and Dr Neville, Dean of Canterbury, and their attempts to influence the King: 'Neville for the Protestant, Lord Thomas for the Papist, Bromley for the Puritan, Lord Cobham for the atheist' (see G. B. Harrison, *A Jacobean Journal, 1603–6*, 1946 edition, p. 10). Evidently, Bromley found favour at court. On 8 February 1604 he received a grant in fee-farm of land

with Mr Thomas Abington's. It seemed to Bromley that all he needed to round off his property was Abington's house, together with certain properties adjoining. He did not doubt that he would be able to acquire these, either as a gift of Queen Elizabeth – she was living at that time – or else at a very cheap price indeed if he could ever have the luck to capture a priest, either in the house or in Mr Abington's company. It did not seem unlikely that one day he would succeed in this because he had intelligence that Abington ordinarily kept at least one priest in his house if not more. Bromley therefore procured from the Privy Council, with the utmost secrecy, a commission by which he could search Abington's house at any time when this seemed most opportune. With his main purpose always in view, he posted spies. Not many days afterwards, they warned him that he would now certainly find in Mr Abington's house what he was looking for. But he must act quickly and go there with a strong posse. The eager knight, who had been waiting for this moment, left his house immediately with a goodly and sufficient company. He arrived suddenly and in daylight. Avoiding noise or commotion, he put guards on the approaches to all doors so that no one could leave the house without a sentry being aware of it. He made his company scale the garden-wall, which was of considerable height and thickness.

The men who broke into the garden found Mr Abington walking in it in the company of another gentleman. They were quite unsuspecting of treachery and extremely surprised to see Sir Henry's men in the garden. Seeing them near the entrance to the house, they went to meet them, and asked them who they were and what they wanted. They heard them admit that they were Sir Henry

in the Duchy of Lancaster worth 100 marks a year (Cal. S.P. Dom. 1603–10, pp. 76, 98). In September, the same year, he received a further grant of lands in Essex and Suffolk worth £100 per annum (ibid., p. 147). It was Bromley who brought the surviving conspirators of Holbeach from Worcester gaol to London. His letter to Salisbury of 13 November 1605 (GPB, 89) makes it clear that he left London about 5 November, or soon after, 'to serve His Majesty in this county'. Salisbury had 'gone to the House', so he could not make his personal farewells. However, he did 'acquaint my Lord Duke [Lennox] who brought [him] His Majesty's pleasure thereof, as also my Lord President of Wales, with [Bromley's] departure'.

Bromley's men. He had come on the queen's orders to search the house, and now stood outside knocking at the gate. He had sent them in by that way to make sure no one escaped him. The gentleman replied, 'It seems to me that in behaving like this, Sir Henry has shown very little courtesy to Mr Abington, my cousin. One does not scale walls unless they belong to enemies in war-time, or unless they conceal those who evidently wish to harm the person of the prince. I do not know how the gentleman can defend himself on the charge of bad behaviour; but in order to save my cousin from the possibility of slander, let us go together to open the door.' Hastening forward, he entered the house by the garden-door, and immediately locked it behind him. Since the lock worked on the inside, this left the guard shut out in the garden.

It suddenly occurred to them that the man whom he was with was none other than the priest for whom Sir Henry Bromley was making the search. In fact, this was the case. They warned Bromley of it as quickly as they could. He entered the house and made most diligent search everywhere, but was unable to locate the man again. All they could establish was that this other man they had seen was one of Mr Abington's relatives, who did not wish that Sir Henry should see him because the latter, in his own presence, had entered his cousin's house in that way. All the same, Mr Abington had to put up with many hardships, and a long imprisonment in the Tower of London, before he could free himself from the vexations and accusations with which the knight pursued him. So in this way, Father Edward Oldcorne was freed for that time. He remained hidden in the same place in which, as we shall see, he was eventually taken along with Father Henry Garnet.

When Humphrey Lyttelton saw Father Edward in that house, as we saw above, he was convinced that there must be another of the three priests there, and perhaps Father Henry himself. In the hope of getting his own life and liberty, even by betraying innocent men, he passed on word to the neighbouring magistrates. In the event, he was deceived. They made him die along with Father Edward himself. Meanwhile, the magistrates passed on the information to the royal councillors. In order not to lose such a good opportunity, they commissioned Sir Henry Bromley with full powers. He had already been made Gentleman of the King's Privy Chamber some years previously. The councillors well knew that he would not be sluggish in a matter of this kind, and that he had more complete knowledge of that house than any other. Sir Henry arrived at Mr Abington's house on the Sunday morning some hours before daybreak. He was accompanied by a considerable band of well-armed men, the greater part of them on horse-back. I have heard from somebody who was there at the time that they numbered more than two hundred. Without delay, he laid siege to the house from every approach, and began to bang on the doors with the utmost force. It was his intention that they should either be opened quickly by those within, or else that they should be broken down. He was afraid that the priests would escape by some secret way, and he would be left looking, as on other occasions, rather a fool. The sound and fury of his attack was such that it woke up everyone in the house. As soon as they realized what was happening, they hurried about as quickly as they could to hide the church-equipment, priests and other persons who might fall under suspicion as belonging to the priests' company. In order to gain time, they began various parleys. But the knight had no difficulty in seeing through this contrivance. It only made him redouble his efforts to beat in the doors as quickly as he could. But those doors were strong and securely fastened from the inside. The time they lost sufficed for those within to make all ready, and hide whatever needed to be hidden. Eventually, Bromley forced an entrance and sent his guards through all the rooms, doorways and other places in the house so that no one could enter or leave, or even move about, without it becoming instantly known.

It so happened that Mr Abington was absent from home. So the knight went to the lady of the house, his wife, to show her his royal commission and prove the authority which he had to search her house for those who were named in the proclamation. She handed over the keys so that he could go everywhere freely. He went through all the rooms, which were numerous and large, accompanied by those whom he had brought with him for this purpose. They looked about them carefully, and inspected minutely every hole and corner in which one could suspect the presence of a hiding-hole for human beings. They went to it thoroughly for a long time, but without result. At last they began to grow weary and give up hope of finding what they had searched for with so much energy. Bromley, however, was determined not to leave the house behind him before he had in his hands those whom he knew for certain, as he said, were now hiding somewhere behind the walls . . .

Bromley searched night and day for the whole of that week. Then, on the Saturday, he had a stroke of good fortune. Two laymen, who acted as servants to the priests, were hidden in a place apart. They had had nothing more to eat than an apple, but had somehow managed to last out the whole of that week without other food. They now decided that, rather than die of hunger, it would be better to come out. They felt all the more persuaded to do this by the thought that the pursuivants would be completely satisfied by their capture. They would think that if there were others in hiding, they would also be forced to come out now with them, and for the same reason. When they left the house, this would give the priests who were still hidden a chance to escape. They also hoped that their pursuers would think that they were themselves priests. Content with their prey, they would be glad to leave the house. Without doubt, these two good men would have considered it a great gain to have saved, by giving their own lives, the lives of the two priests whom they loved more than themselves. It seemed to them that, by coming out now, they could harm none but themselves; even if, when it came to the inevitable test, it were found that they were not priests. It is believed that they acted as they did on the advice of one of them called Nicholas Owen, a man of great prudence.* He had always been regarded among the catholics as a man of singular goodness, and it is generally believed that he was a jesuit lay-brother. He suffered a long drawn-out martyrdom amidst most savage tortures. We shall speak of him more at length in his own place.

The two laymen soon became aware that the guards walked up and down continually by turns in the gallery where they lay hidden, and never left it. This gallery was situated right at the top of the house, and ran all round it, and over the other rooms in the same building. It was amply proportioned, square on plan, and well

---

* Nicholas Owen: 'We have no record of his parentage, birthplace, date of birth, or entrance to the Society'. He was admitted to the S.J. before 1580. The exact day of his subsequent death by torture is not recorded (HFR, VII, p. 561).

constructed. The two laymen waited for the moment when the guards were in the part of the gallery furthest away from them. They then came out so quietly that they were neither seen nor heard by the guards. They even stopped to lock up the hiding-place so that no one could tell where they had come from. After that, they made their way slowly and gradually towards the door, hoping to find it open. But at this moment they happened to meet the guards who were walking up to the same place. At first, the latter were taken by surprise at seeing strangers unknown to them, but they soon began to wonder who they were. The guards then quickened their steps to catch up with them. They asked the two men who they were, and how they had managed to get into that place since the doors were shut. They replied that they were part of the staff, and they wished to leave by the stairs if the guards would be good enough to open the doors for them. 'Not so fast!' said the guards. 'Perhaps you are the ones we are looking for! Are you priests?' 'We are catholics,' replied the others, 'and we have no more to say to you!' In fact, they wanted the guards to conclude that they were, indeed, the priests they were looking for. The guards asked them where they had been hidden all this time, and the reason for their concealment. They replied that it would not have suited them to be taken. For that reason they had hidden, but they were unwilling to tell them where. In this way, the guards now knew for certain that the place where they had lain concealed was in that gallery. They called for more men from those distributed through the other rooms of the house. Then they began to search again with all thoroughness. The gallery was panelled throughout in carved wood. They now smashed up the panelling, and even threw down the walls of the gallery in many places. With this kind of violence, they continued to search the whole house for another five or six days.

In the end, Providence allowed the searchers to find the place where the two priests lay hidden. It was worse than any prison. Indeed, in another few days they would have died there, thanks to the extreme confinement and discomfort of the place. They had, however, resolved to die rather than come out so as to save the owner of the house. It was his custom to shelter priests, showing in this great affection and charity towards them. Discovery meant that he would lose life and property . . . When the Fathers left the hole where they had hidden, the searchers found also a great quantity of books, church-vestments and other liturgical equipment. These things had made the place a good deal smaller and more uncomfortable than otherwise it would have been.

It was not difficult for them to recognize Father Edward Oldcorne. As was said above, they were used to his frequent comings and goings in those parts, and he was generally taken to be a relative of Mr Abington. Sir Henry Bromley and others of his train recognized him now as the man who had slipped through their fingers some years previously. They expended much further effort on trying to find out if the other were Father Henry Garnet. They felt certain that he was from the description of the person in the proclamation who corresponded to their prisoner in age and features. Not long afterwards, they found someone who knew him, and who told them who he was. This was a man who had been a prisoner in Worcester for many years. He made a show of rejoicing to hear that Garnet was taken. Perhaps he hoped to get his liberty, or else there was some other cause that one can only imagine. At all events, he resolved all Bromley's doubts, telling him that this was, indeed, Father Henry Garnet, superior of all the Jesuits in England. He added words of bitterness which I do not wish to record here, any more than the name of the person. I have no desire to rouse the reader's disgust, nor to render evil for evil: least of all to a man whom, I am sure, that holy Father has pardoned. Garnet, on that occasion, replied to him very gently, as he usually did, even when he had been very seriously affronted.

Two days after they began the search of Mr Abington's house, the gentleman himself returned home. He was detained by Sir Henry until such time as they could see the outcome of their present business. If the persons named in the edict, or any other priest for that matter, were found in his house, Abington also would be liable to the charge of *lèse-majesté*. So now this gentleman found himself arrested along with the priests. Bromley lost no time in despatching messengers to London to report on events to the Privy Council.*

---

* There is a good deal of obscurity in many points concerning Garnet's capture, and when the news of it was sent to London. 'Surely Bromley acquainted Salisbury with his good news of 27 or 28 January before the letter

Meanwhile, he conducted his prisoners to his own home until such time as he should receive a reply. This came from the court a few days later. He was ordered to conduct the two priests to London as quickly as possible. This he did, taking with him a very sufficient posse and a considerable number of mounted men.

It is noteworthy that the better acquainted Sir Henry Bromley became with the behaviour of Father Garnet, the more he came to regard him, and even reverence him. Bromley was a puritan of very deep conviction, but the more he dealt and talked with his captive, the more he liked him. He did not fail to notice that Garnet was self-effacing, patient and more than ordinarily magnanimous. So much so, that it became increasingly improbable that he could have had anything to do with the plot, or with any kind of revolution. They made their journey to London accompanied by the calvinist minister who was Bromley's chaplain and preacher. It is normal for puritan gentlemen to keep by them a minister of this kind, for they are more conscientious in the profession of their religion than many of the others. This man did not fail to notice Father Garnet's reticence and sparing use of words, especially in matters involving religious controversy . . . The minister began to imagine that Father Henry's silence arose from ignorance. For Garnet enjoyed many opportunities, if he had wished to use them, of showing his erudition and learning in matters of religion. Garnet, however, had shown no eagerness to enter into this kind of argument. The minister thought that he had here a tremendous opportunity for increasing his own credit with his co-religionists if he could success-

<hr/>

of 30 January which survives?' (EGF, p. 224). The latest writer on the plot noticed this point independently, and arrived at his own conclusion, reasonably enough, that Cecil ordered some back-dating (P.D., p. 232). Criticizing H. R. Williamson's work as 'primarily academic in tone, thereby limiting its appeal to the historian rather than to the casual lay-reader', Mr Durst, 'after three year's exhaustive research' (p. 2), attempts to tell the story in a more popular way. Unfortunately, the book tends to turn a field of study into a tilt-yard where other students are concerned. It has its own errors. Henry Percy, Earl of Northumberland, for example, could scarcely be described as 'a leading Catholic nobleman' (p. 20). Sir Robert Cecil's barony was of Essendon near Hatfield, not of Essendine in Rutlandshire (p. 32). For the rest, neither PD nor EGF can be regarded in any sense as final and definitive works on the subject.

fully dispute with a jesuit, and he the superior of all the jesuits in England. It would be a great advantage to worst him in debate, and convince the world that he, the minister, knew more than the jesuit. He felt all the more confident since he knew that everyone in Bromley's retinue would be on his side, and favour what he said.

The minister approached Father Henry and asked him if he were willing to debate some point of controversy between catholics and protestants. Father Henry calmly listened to what the minister had to say, but did not show much interest. He probably felt that the minister had been sent to him on purpose to get him to say something which could afterwards be brought up against him before the council. Or perhaps he believed that such a dispute would be fruitless, considering the disposition of his audience, who were all protestants. In any case, he was well aware that ministers of this kind had a habit of boasting of victory even when they were found out in falsehood and brought to a point where they could make no reply. But the less our good man showed himself disposed to debate, the more the minister insisted. In the end, he became so overbearing that he began to crow at Father Garnet's expense. In the presence of the others, he tried to provoke Garnet to defend his religion, that is, if he knew how to do it.

Father Henry now began to see that scandal might arise from his silence. The bystanders might attribute his attitude to fear of being worsted in dispute by the minister. This would only serve to confirm them in what Garnet took to be their errors. Without another word to the minister, Garnet now rode up to Sir Henry. He was riding a little ahead in the company of some other gentlemen. When Garnet caught up with him, he explained how his chaplain had challenged him many times to debate, and this in the presence of other people. Garnet had avoided the issue so as not to offend the men in whose custody he now found himself. He also knew how disputes of this kind fell out when there was no one present with authority to act as umpire for both sides. They were usually fruitless, and not infrequently harmful to the listeners. Instead of reasoning, the disputants would often resort to insult and mutual recrimination. They would be carried away by proud zeal, and an overbearing desire merely to prevail. But if his lordship wished to arrange such a thing, he should see to it that his minister observed decorum, and due moderation in his reasonings and arguments. Garnet hoped to do no less for his part. For the rest, he was willing to give the minister every satisfaction, and his lordship the best contentment he could. He sought nothing else but truth and the glory of God.

Bromley could only praise Father Henry's reticence and discreet way of proceeding. The knight called over his chaplain to put forward the subject of his choice, but he must use the utmost calm and moderation. The minister began a long discourse, as they usually do, which had no thread or method. He did not confine his arguments or language of debate to that used in the schools, but merely presented a riotous chaos of many things following no kind of order. All that appeared from it was an empty show of memory, without any foundation or reason that could persuade. There was nothing to lend even probability to the theme which he dealt with. Notwithstanding, Garnet did not interrupt him once, for all the time that his discourse lasted. He let him go on talking until he himself was tired of it, and his audience wearied with listening. The jesuit then began by repeating briefly and clearly the gist of what he believed the minister had objected against him. He then proceeded to refute it, and this not only in very erudite fashion, but showing learning of many kinds. He confirmed his arguments by the authority of the Scriptures together with the interpretations of the Church Fathers. In all this he proceeded with method and order. He revealed also his knowledge of Hebrew, Greek and Latin, and his acquaintance with general literature. The puritans make much of these things, and believe that in these studies no one can compare with them. Garnet was versed in every field of learning, and not only in theology and philosophy. He knew the sciences, mathematics, and music so well that he roused the admiration of all who listened to him.* Word of this dispute was spread by those who heard it throughout the City

---

* According to a journal-dictionary formerly belonging to Sir Thomas Tresham, Garnet possessed 'exquisite knowledge in the art of music, being skilful on divers instruments, especially the lute, and his knowledge therein such as ex tempore he was able to set any song of five parts or more to the same in most true concordance and musical harmony; and his voice was so rare and delightful that by report of such as knew it, it was supposed to be more than the natural voice of a man, so angelically had he the gift of delivery' (Bodleian Library, Oxford: MS. Bodl. Eng. Th. b. 2, p. 136).

of London. It made an impression not only for learning that was wide and deep, but also because the priest had given evidence of it in so short a time, and at such short notice. He had also used an excellent line of reasoning. At the same time, his modesty was such that everyone was left very much impressed.

Meanwhile, the poor minister drew off by himself. He was much embarrassed, and could only regret his unfortunate experience. Certainly, he was very sorry for having provoked the priest to dispute, and we can well believe that he took care to avoid similar encounters for the future. Sir Henry Bromley was more surprised than any, and could not restrain his admiration for Father Henry. So much so that, when he arrived in London, he told many of the leading gentlemen that he had never before met such a man, and scarcely believed that he had his like for modesty, prudence and learning. He added that if he had not been charged in connection with the plot, he would have thrown himself on his face before the king in order to beg for him every grace and favour possible.

The prisoners reached London, if I am not mistaken, on 3 or 4 February, old style.★ The two priests were kept separate from one another in the Gatehouse prison. The two laymen were put in a different gaol. I believe that Mr Thomas remained in Worcester. A huge crowd of prisoners stood waiting at the entrance to the prison in their eagerness to see Father Henry. He asked them in a loud voice if any of them were imprisoned for their catholic faith. Many replied that they were. 'God help you all!' said the priest, 'and myself as well who come to keep you company here for the same cause!' He was two days in that prison before being brought for examination. Meanwhile, the lords of the council made diligent enquiry from Bromley of what had happened in the course of searching the house where Father Henry was taken. They also wanted to know what he had done and said since his capture. But they learnt nothing from Bromley that did not turn to that good Father's considerable credit. Providence was pleased that our enemies should publish the truth of all that had happened since the first day of Garnet's capture up to his death. Certainly, we can learn nothing from others about what happened since they kept Garnet so strictly guarded in his prison

★ Garnet arrived in London probably about 6 February (Cal. S.P. Dom, 1603–10, p. 286).

that no one was ever able to see him who knew him. No one saw him whom he himself could trust. Still less was anyone ever able to speak to him.

I do not doubt that one could give many examples of Garnet's outstanding conduct, and enemies who were so anxious for his downfall could, no doubt, give the best of these. They kept him in a place where they could treat him according to their whim; and matter and occasion would not have been lacking to him for the fullest exercise of his celebrated patience. I can also say the same about Father Edward, and the two laymen who were held with him. They were all of them so closely shut up and guarded, and kept from any kind of contact with their friends, that we know nothing about them, except what their persecutors have been pleased to tell us, and from what could be judged at the time of their death, which was for all to see.

On the third or fourth day of his imprisonment Father Henry was examined by five or six members of the Privy Council.* I do not know exactly what happened at this examination. However, it is known in a general way that he gave them all so much satisfaction that, after his departure, they praised him as a man of considerable prudence. One of the lords said that, in his opinion, there was nothing in him that one could blame except his doctrine and the faith he taught. As to the plot, it seemed to him that they neither could nor should accuse him. But to end this chapter, I will relate one incident that in my view is worthy of note. It shows clearly how much this priest was to be esteemed for his rare good qualities. The fact is that they were among his worst enemies who examined him on this and other occasions. But they spoke of him in terms of reverence, respect and honour which were considerably more generous than these good lords usually adopted. This was true even when they were dealing with men of blood and quality, and while they were being examined on matters of much less importance than this.

The charge against Garnet was, of course, extremely serious, even if it was altogether false. In the ordinary way, priests and

* For Garnet's examinations, see P. Caraman, *Henry Garnet, 1555–1606*, London, 1964, chapter 37 (pp. 348–57). The first was on 13 February 1606. See also HFR, iv, pp. 80–6, 145–9.

Jesuits, even when they are being sifted by examiners of much lower rank, are badly treated, being held up to ridicule and generally insulted. On this occasion, however, they used Father Henry with so much respect that when they spoke to him they took off their hats. They addressed him in terms of courtesy, and always called him Mr Henry Garnet. Throughout his examination, they treated him in such a way that the influence of his goodness was clear to see; a goodness that was able to soften the hardness even of those who hated this saintly man right up to his death . . .* After this first examination, the priest was taken back to his prison. But a little while after this he was transferred to the Tower of London. Here Father Edward Oldcorne and the two laymen were also imprisoned. How these were treated, we shall read in the next chapter.

* It seems sufficiently unlikely that the Council would have been much affected by Garnet's goodness. They were doubtless aware, at least in his case, of the undesirability of making any signs of martyrdom appear externally before the moment seemed ripe.

ELEVEN

NOT ONLY THE CATHOLICS but the protestants as well had their hearts in their mouths to see how the Garnet affair would turn out. It was the general opinion of everyone that he was altogether innocent of charges in connection with the plot. For one thing, they could see that there was no mention of him in the confessions of the conspirators, which by now were printed. Nor for that matter, was there mention of any other priest. This was a clear enough sign that none of them had accused him, although the contrary was most forcibly declared in the proclamation. Certainly, if they had done so, the protestants would not have allowed so important a point to escape notice. For one thing, they were well aware that after Father Henry had been examined, word began to go round that he was altogether innocent. Although the public proclamation had claimed that he had been accused by some of the leading conspirators, now that they had captured and examined him, it seemed that they had nothing with which to charge him. Not a syllable could be produced in his accusation.

The protestants themselves were very dissatisfied with this proceeding, since they could not but see the grave injustice which had been inflicted on those Fathers in a cause of such importance by the authors of the proclamation. So it came about that an incredible number of slanders began to go the round while Garnet was shut up in the Tower in London. The bare-faced impudence of some of them was wellnigh incredible. All the same, even when they were put forward seriously and confirmed with the most solemn oaths, they were not all that easily believed. His enemies tried every way to spread these stories throughout the world. They even resorted to news-sheets and gazettes in Venice and Rome. In general, the only reaction they brought was ridicule and contempt. This is evident from what Father Henry himself said in the course of his trial. Indeed, his enemies never dared to charge him with them openly in case the world should think that they themselves had been the originators of such things. Not that men were lacking on that occasion to bring other false charges against him. The good man refuted these with so much evidence of right on his side that his opponents were finally obliged to condemn him for not having revealed a [sacramental] confession. As far as catholics are concerned, who well understand what the seal means, this only makes Garnet's martyrdom more illustrious. God himself has seen fit to honour this same martyrdom with manifest miracles . . .*

As we have seen, Father Henry was conducted from his first prison to the Tower of London. Here the guard is so strict that the prisoner must give up all hope of receiving help from his friends. Everyone shut up there must renounce all human consolations. The man who was then Lieutenant of the Tower, and for that matter still is, was renowned for his evil habits and dissolute life. He was well known for his hatred of catholics in general, and of Jesuits in particular. His name was Sir William Waad.† He made no secret of his considerable pleasure at having custody of Father Henry. At last he had in his hands the man whom he had sought for so many

---

* The most obvious of the 'manifest miracles' was that of Garnet's straw. An ear, seemingly of wheat, lay among the straw which was splashed with Garnet's blood at his execution. An image of his face was later claimed to be visibly formed from a speck of blood on one of the grains (see Caraman, ibid., pp. 443–7; EGF, pp. 247–9; PD, pp. 277–9). According to Sir Charles Cornwallis, when Joseph Creswell, S.J., was told of these wonders, 'he denied to have any privity; said they were fooleries, and the last Garnet's straw an occupation of certain blind men who out of such kind of stuff picked up some poor pence wherewith to buy them bread' (PRO, SP 94, vol. 14, part I, f. 120v.).
† Sir William Waad (1546–1623): son of Armagil, 'the English Columbus'; trained at Gray's Inn; foreign agent for Burghley in Paris, Italy and Strasbourg, and ambassador to Portugal before becoming a clerk of the Privy Council (1583–1613). Much trusted by the Cecils and deeply versed in 'plot' procedure. He was sworn as Lieutenant of the Tower on 15 August 1605 and so remained until 1613 (cf. DNB; HRW, p. 193; EGF, pp. 108–10).

years and with so much trouble. True enough, Providence had many times arranged that good Father's miraculous escape, as one could believe, from the snares and traps of this man. From a network of spies, Waad received information of the places where Garnet used to stay. It had always happened that although Garnet had no knowledge of these particular dangers hanging over him, he had always providentially changed his abode at the precise moment when this persecutor of his had made up his mind to take him. Sometimes Garnet had received word of impending betrayal, and so had kept out of the way.

Not content with showing his open satisfaction at Garnet's capture, Waad offered his prisoner many harsh words and insulting speech. Some of those present asked Garnet why he did not reply when he heard such opprobrious accusations made against him. The priest replied: 'I do not, as a matter of fact, feel much affected by what he said. In any case, I learned a long time ago to follow the Divine example in putting up with evil speech silently and patiently.' The usage of that prison is that prisoners have nothing in the way of bedding or clothing apart from what they themselves can get from friends who send these things in from outside. So it was that Father Garnet had only straw to lie on until such time as a certain number of devoted friends sent him a bed. It was considered a very special favour that he was allowed to take advantage of his friends' charity in this way. Perhaps it was directly ordered by the Privy Council. Certainly, the priest proceeded very cautiously, so that it would not be known from whom he had received this courtesy. He wrote to a well-known Catholic, who was also in prison for his faith at that time, as to a person in whose generosity he trusted. He asked him to provide him with certain items necessary as protection against winter cold. This person, having occasion to write to Father Henry's acquaintances, informed them secretly of his need. They sent him what he asked for so that he in turn could pass it on to Garnet.

The Privy Council went off to the Tower to examine Father Garnet. They claimed they had no wish to examine him on anything other than the plot. Certainly, they were anxious that people should believe that in some way or other he had had a hand in it. Notwithstanding, they put many questions to him which had nothing to do with the conspiracy, and had no other end in view than to find out from him who they were who had been helping Garnet and his fellow jesuits, and for so many years, in temporal matters. More particularly, they wanted to know whom he had visited in the course of his recent journey or pilgrimage. The good priest replied to all these enquiries with so much caution that nothing even to this day could be turned to the prejudice of any catholic in the country. Garnet also had many opportunities in the course of these visits and examinations to reveal his deep learning and erudition. More especially, he was able to deal with the question of equivocation; that is, if it were sometimes lawful to use it and return an answer of doubtful meaning. Later on, the Attorney-General retailed what he had said on the public occasion of Garnet's trial. He attacked Father Henry on that occasion as the inventor of doctrine new and unheard-of. In fact, the Attorney only succeeded in making clear in a few words this upstart theologian's own insolent arrogance and proud ignorance. Instead of replying in terms that were dubious and obscure, Coke used what came easily and naturally to him, namely shameless and bare-faced lying. But there is more to be said about this in its own place.

Even after the lords of the council had examined Garnet many times, they found nothing with which to charge him in connection with the plot. They therefore put his case in the hands of the Lord Chief Justice, John Popham, and the Attorney-General mentioned above [Sir Edward Coke]. The councillors well knew that these men were sworn enemies of the catholics and very anxious to bring the jesuits into disrepute. Popham and Coke accepted the task with so much alacrity that there was little doubt as to what might be expected of them in the matter of fair treatment for that most innocent of men. From the very beginning, Coke began to put about slanderous tales. Such was his assiduity, that soon the City of London was full of them. He even had it written to countries abroad that Father Henry Garnet had already confessed to all the charges against him. Not only that, but he augmented these fables with many other mendacious and extravagant inventions. Their very novelty, and the fact that the Jesuit himself was shut up all this time in the Tower, made it much easier for such stories to be believed, especially since many protestants listened to them only too willingly.

But they were not alone. Even the ambassadors of the catholic princes staying in London at the time reported these things back to their masters. When the priest had the opportunity of speaking for himself at his trial, and in full view as is the custom in that land, the charges against Garnet seemed vain and false enough. Indeed, all were amazed to witness the bare-faced audacity of those who had dared to publish such evident calumnies and lies to the world. They might be left in the end clearly convicted of their own plain falsehoods. The ambassadors were particular astonished by the gross injustice and deceitful methods practised on that good man Garnet, and lost no time in reporting to their princes . . .

On the other hand, our enemies took particular delight in the success of these calumnies. This was especially true of Secretary Cecil, the Attorney-General, Coke, and the Lord Chief Justice, Popham. They hoped that, using the same methods, they would be equally successful in deceiving the members of parliament. They likewise hoped to persuade them with the same lies, and bring it about that the jesuits, either all or as many as they saw fit, should be publicly condemned in parliament. This would have been to their own considerable prejudice, and would have greatly hindered the progress of catholicism in the land, thanks to the authority which the laws and statutes of parliament enjoy among that people. They particularly wanted the condemnation of those jesuits whom they wished to be regarded as accomplices of the plot, that is Father Henry Garnet, Edward Oldcorne, Oswald Tesimond, otherwise known as Greenway, John Gerard, Hammond and another going by the name of Westmorland. But nobody knows who was meant by this last, since there has never been a priest of this name, at least among the jesuits. Fathers [Joseph] Creswell and [William] Baldwin were also included.

Although parliament was willing enough that jesuits should be persecuted by all means possible, they did not think that it befitted the honour of that assembly to proceed against the Fathers without better and more evident proofs. The Attorney had offered nothing against them in the way of real evidence. They had heard nothing more than a long string of slanders, which he could confirm by nothing more than a few vain and airy conjectures. To these he could only add the exaggerations suggested by unlimited envy and endless tittle-tattle. Coke felt obliged to tell them that he himself had examined Father Garnet. From the admissions that he had wrung from him, he would draw up the formal proofs against him and the other jesuits under certain heads. He would present it to parliament next day. Coke went so far as to promise this. With the same kind of words which he had used to deceive the world on other occasions, he now assured the House, with as much gravity as effrontery, that their honours would hear a clear and open confession of Garnet's in which he admitted that he and the others named were instigators as well as accomplices of this plot.

The Attorney-General returned to the House the following day. The gentlemen present fully expected that Coke would now fulfil his promise. He launched instead into a long and prolix discourse. In this he quoted not a single word of Father Garnet which had anything to do with the plot, so far was it from being the confession he had promised. Not only did this speech along with its accusations make no impression on the minds of the members, but it left them all very much astonished. How, in a matter so grave and before an audience so large and important, could Coke have had the effrontery to promise what he well knew he could not fulfil? They marvelled that he could have proceeded thus in the presence of those who would be judges of his bare-faced impudence. One of the noble members, talking afterwards to a friend of his about the Attorney's discourse, made a remark apt enough. He said that those lawyers were so used to telling lies that there was nothing left in which they could tell the truth. It was providential that, although both houses of parliament were hostile to the jesuits, they left them unblemished with any mark of infamy. This, of course, was only in accord with their genuine innocence.

The unhappy outcome of this first attempt only increased the rage of the Lord Chief Justice, the Attorney, and their adherents, against Father Henry. Their failure merely served to fan the flame of their desire that the Jesuit should, by one means or another, be sentenced to death. It was not that they were simply driven by hate of him or his profession, though that was deep enough. They wished also to restore the image which it seemed to them that they had lost in the eyes of parliament by failing in their first stratagem. They therefore continued with their shameless calumnies, persuading themselves to believe that what they took from his own credit would somehow be added to theirs. They were not even ashamed to say that, whatever happened, he would be executed, whether the plot was proved against him or no. However, they did not lack sufficient cunning to give their decision some show of justice.

They now put Garnet in charge of a certain crafty character who began to watch his every movement to see if some word might not drop from his mouth, or some unguarded deed be committed, from which something might be drawn for their purpose. This man showed himself at first courteous, and even sympathetic, towards the priest. He made a show of becoming increasingly satisfied with the reticence, discretion and patience of the Father. From these things, he even conceived a leaning for the catholic religion which could embrace men of such goodness as Garnet. At length he told him that on account of the great regard which he now felt for him, he would be ready to do him any kind of service he could. His dissimulation was so skilful that he persuaded the good Father to believe that he really felt in his heart what he professed with his mouth. Garnet, in any case, as a charitable man, was ready to believe all things, and to hope all things. He now decided to make use of his new friend's services to write to his friends. He knew well enough how eager they were to have some news of him. Getting news out of that prison is considered one of the rarest favours imaginable, and, as a matter of fact, most difficult to achieve. The gaolers there are not prepared to run the risk involved in view of the heavy penalties. It incurs the Lieutenant's most serious displeasure to carry messages or notes without his knowledge to anyone outside.★

★ About the beginning of October, 1605, Waad appointed ten supplementary warders, men who presumably enjoyed special confidence and who could be trusted to keep the kind of secret arising in connection with the custody of the plotters. In a Docquet Book of the Signet Office (PRO, Index 6802) occurs the entry, 'A warrant to the Exchequer to pay to the Lieutenant of the Tower . . . the several allowances and fees of 14d per diem for every of the ten warders within the Tower of London above the number which by His Majesty's former warrant are paid. The said payment to begin from Michaelmeas last (1605) . . .' The precise day in November 1605, when this order was issued, is left blank. It is extremely unlikely in the circumstances that any letter was genuinely smuggled from the prisoners to the outside world without the knowledge of Waad and Salisbury (see F. Edwards 'The Stonyhurst narratives'; article in *JSA*, vol. 4, No. 2, pp. 106–7).

Father Garnet now wrote a letter to a priest. He was not only a man he trusted, but one of his own family who bore the same name, and was then in another of the London prisons. Garnet asked him for certain necessary items which he needed. In the margin of the letter, which was written with ordinary ink, he wrote with orange or lemon juice what had passed at his frequent examinations. He added that nothing could be proved against him in connection with the plot since he was completely innocent. But the gaoler did not take the letter to the good priest. Instead, he took it to the Lieutenant of the Tower. He warmed it at the fire and read all that was written in the margin. But the letter was now scorched and discoloured by the fire so that it could not be sent on. They therefore wrote it out again, counterfeiting the original hand, so that when Garnet received his reply he would be more convinced of the pretended fidelity of his gaoler. Everything succeeded as they hoped. Father Garnet knew how much his friends were anxious to keep up with his news. He therefore wrote a number of notes to various individuals. Among these was Mistress Anne Vaux, aunt of the baron who was mentioned above.★

For many years Anne Vaux had received and sheltered not only Henry Garnet, but all the other Fathers of the Society, and other priests as well. In this she showed great charity and perseverance, and ran considerable risk to life itself. Sometimes there might be more than twenty or thirty priests in her house at one time. This good and devoted lady refused to abandon our servant of God up to the very moment of his death. She was particularly anxious to serve and help him at a time like the present when he most needed

---

★ The man made use of in this way was probably John Locherson. With Edward Forset he eavesdropped on a colloquy between Garnet and Oldcorne (*v. infra*), and by himself on another occasion between Guy Fawkes and Robert Wintour. Waad wrote to Sir Thomas Lake on 6 July 1606, to ask that his brother John be 'next in reversion after my servant John Locherson to be a commissary of the musters in the Low Countries.' Waad further says of Locherson, he 'hath served me many years, and had the keeping of these books and accounts under me both for the Low Countries and Ireland'. He is 'a very honest, wise and discreet gent, and one that will be very fit for the place. The truth is, it will ask some pains at the first to understand the business, which I assure myself he will very easily conceive, being of so good understanding' (PRO, SP 14, vol. 22, no. 32).

her. She was therefore overjoyed at having found, as she supposed, someone whom she could trust to take messages to Father Henry, her spiritual director, and bring replies back again. The messenger showed such a winsome attitude to Garnet that it did not seem difficult to persuade him how worthy that good priest was to be loved by everyone. In the end, the poor lady was not only deluded in her trust, but as we shall see, thanks to this traitor, she herself was taken and held prisoner. Meanwhile, the messenger carried the letters to the lieutenant and the lords of the council. Proceeding afterwards on their way in the counterfeit hand, the same letters also managed to console Garnet's friends for a short time. In the long run, it was to cause him embarrassment a hundredfold.★

In the end, the only result of this correspondence was to establish Garnet's innocence. He wrote regularly that, even after so many examinations, they had not been able to establish anything against him in connection with the plot. At last his enemies despaired of making any further progress by this route. It was, of course, a most obvious sign of his innocence. They, therefore, turned their attention to another trick which was all the more dangerous for being more hidden. However, they continued to encourage the sending of letters and messages so that the Father would not begin to suspect

★ That forgery was used in this way, seems to be completely borne out by the fact that Garnet's apparently original letters to Anne Vaux, partly in revealed orange juice are now in the PRO (GPB, Nos. 241–6). The two-way correspondence has been printed, as far as it is now decipherable (HFR, iv, pp. 102–10; for photographs, see Vaux at p. 344; P. Caraman, op. cit., at p. 336). The correspondence seemingly began with Garnet's letter to Anne of 3 April 1606. Evidently, the fact that the government could forge in this way, probably by the hand of Thomas Phelippes or Arthur Gregory, must cast a good deal of doubt on the authenticity of many, if not all, of the confessions and signatures produced in the Tower at this time. Significantly, Phelippes was arrested about 4 February, on a charge that could be regarded as trumped-up, a day or two before the time when Garnet arrived in London (PRO, SP 14, vol. 18, Nos. 61–3). Waad himself seems to have offered Garnet this privilege (see below, p. 190). For the rest, it is difficult to imagine the Jesuit, who had successfully eluded the authorities for twenty years, allowing himself to believe in the possibility of an unintercepted correspondence of this kind. There is nothing in these letters to compromise Garnet or Anne Vaux, unless by adverse if not perverse interpretation. Nevertheless, it will be evident that the authorities had an instrument to hand to manufacture 'evidence' against either of them, if they so desired.

some kind of fraud. As we have seen, Father Edward Oldcorne was also a prisoner in the Tower – he had been taken with Father Henry in Mr Abington's house. This good priest was now lodged deliberately in a room next to Garnet's.

One day, Garnet's gaoler, after a few words of sympathy and encouragement, told the jesuit that he wished to tell him a secret which he was sure he would be glad to hear. But if the matter became known, it could do him a great deal of harm. He therefore begged the Father to promise that whatever happened he would keep his secret. Should he wish to profit by what he was going to tell him, he must make absolutely sure that no one ever found out. If this happened by his fault, he would be utterly ruined. The revelation was that, in the next cell resided that other good Father who was his friend. By the gaoler's means, Garnet and he might, at certain times, have the consolation of talking together and offering mutual support. But Garnet must also warn the other Father to be very careful about this business, and keep it secret. They must not underestimate the favour. Indeed, in this prison such a thing was unheard-of, and had never been conceded to anyone else whatever his rank. If they agreed, it would put the gaolers themselves in the greatest peril. Garnet accepted the favour, which he took to be considerable; and indeed it would have been had it been offered with sincerity.

The two priests conversed together a number of times. Their conversation, however, was never without witnesses; a circumstance which they themselves never dreamed of. As it happened, they never spoke together without someone being hidden in a place nearby to overhear them. The gaoler was there together with another person in a place which was made for this precise purpose, so that they could discover the secrets of any other parties who talked together in the vicinity.* Their words could be clearly and

---

* The other person who eavesdropped with Locherson (*v. supra*, p. 185) was Edward Forset (b. 1553?, d. 1630?): educated at Christ's Hospital and Trinity College, Cambridge: M.P. for Wells, Somerset, 1606–11: J.P. for Middlesex, 1620. Buried at Marylebone Church. (cf. DNB, and Venn and Venn, *Alumni Cantabrigienses*, part I, vol. II, Cambridge, 1922, p. 157.) Political writer: from 1583 he held the manor of Tyburn from Elizabeth: magistrate and surveyor in the office of works at the time of the plot. Not to be confused with Edward Forsett of Billesby, Lincs. (cf. Wood, *Athenae Oxonienses*, Bliss ed., ii, 5) who was

distinctly heard by those who were posted there to listen. Not very much time passed before the two priests, suspecting no kind of fraud, wished to make use of one another as confessors. Their confessions were soon finished. The eavesdroppers laughed to think that the priests confessed such trivialities, and matters which, among themselves, would have been considered praiseworthy rather than failings, or even imperfections! They then began to discuss various matters, and particularly their own case, and the replies which they had given in their examination. Father Edward asked Father Henry if they had ever saddled him with Mr Thomas Wintour's journey to Spain in the queen's time.★ Garnet replied that little importance should be attached to such accusations, not only because that business had nothing to do with him, but also because a general pardon had been given to everyone for anything that happened during the queen's lifetime. Oldcorne then asked Garnet if they had insisted much on connecting him with the plot. Garnet replied that they had, but that up to that time they had nothing against him but their own idle conjectures and vague suspicions. And the truth was that he was altogether innocent of the deed. There was no man living save one who could say that he had ever had the least knowledge of that conspiracy.

These words of Garnet spoken to Oldcorne were reported by the gaoler without delay to the Lieutenant of the Tower. He in turn reported them to the lords of council. They were delighted with this clue, slight as it was, and resolved to work it up into a cause sufficient to justify Garnet's death. What was worse than death, it was to be the foundation of unlimited slander aimed at his reputation. First of all, they decided to wring out of Garnet by torture, if they could do it no other way, the name of the man whom he could accuse of

★ See notes on pages 54–5, 63–4, 144.

a papist. The Tower was an uncomfortable place to be in, even for the gaoler. Waad reported to Salisbury on 21 November 1605, 'Mr Forcet has taken cold, and would be glad to go to his house to take some course for his health. I think if it shall seem good to you he may be spared, for Faulx is watched every night' (Sal. Cal., XVII, p. 502). In 1606, Forset was helping Waad to interview prisoners in the Tower (ibid., XVII, p. 210). By 1609, he was sufficiently trusted to stand in for Waad with one of two other gentlemen named, when the Lieutenant was absent (see BM Add. 14044, f. 3r.)

having knowledge of the plot. In the second place, they decided to imprison Mistress Anne Vaux. They now hoped to extract from her something which might have a bearing on the business. They might glean further details which would help to damage Garnet. With this in view, they ordered the gaoler to stop dissimulating with Father Henry, fetch the lady to the Tower, and keep her in custody. This the gaoler did in the following manner.

Anne Vaux was longing to see Father Garnet, and if possible, to speak with him. She had already acquainted the gaoler with this desire. He, in his turn, promised to do what she wished if she would wait for him at a day, hour and place appointed. He would bring her to see him in the Tower. The lady arrived at the pre-arranged place. But the gaoler failed to put in an appearance, and certain signs and indications led Mistress Anne to suspect treachery. It may be that she herself had arrived before the time. Perhaps the gaoler was busy with other matters. Or he may have kept out of the way deliberately so as to arrest her eventually in the manner which seemed most apt to him. At all events, she now decided to make her departure. But she was followed by certain men who had been posted there by the gaoler on purpose to await her coming. The good lady soon became aware that they were following her. She thought they might be pursuing her so that they could ascertain the house where she usually resided. If she made her way to another catholic house, they might arrest the others as well as herself. The pursuivants often use tricks of this kind to find out the houses of catholics so that they can search them later at their own convenience, particularly when there is the greatest prospect of finding priests there. So Anne Vaux in that predicament went to the prison at Newgate where a number of catholic prisoners were already lodged at that time. When the spies saw the lady stop there and themselves deceived in their hopes, they arrested her without more ado. Treating her discourteously, and in way which little befitted her rank, they took her back to the Tower from which she had come. At that time, ladies were not often imprisoned in the Tower, so that all London soon began to buzz on the subject of her imprisonment. The enemies of the papists lost no time in spreading any number of slanders about her through the City. Among other things, they claimed that Father Garnet was married to the lady, with similar suggestions no less ridiculous, or even mad, but full of poisoned spite . . .

Meanwhile, that dignified and most upright lady continued to confound her enemies by a display of admirable steadfastness, and a courage truly virile with which she bore her imprisonment. As for Garnet, when later he stood on public trial, he bore such testimony to his innocence that his enemies did not dare to bring up against him those appalling calumnies which they did not hesitate to spread in secret. They feared to be left in shame and confusion by a public outcry; out-shouted, as it were, by the voice of the whole kingdom . . .

About this time, that good priest and relative of Father Henry, Thomas Garnet, was taken from the prison, where he had been kept up to that time, to the Tower of London.* The transfer was made on the pretext of his having received letters from Father Henry, and written to him in reply. In fact, as has been said, the letters written by Garnet were written by leave of the lieutenant, signed by his hand, read by him, and rewritten in a counterfeit hand. But all this was done to sift Thomas as thoroughly as possible, so that they could find the kind of clue which they yearned for against Henry Garnet. For this purpose Thomas Garnet was subjected to most strict examination, with the certain threat of extreme torture, and even death, hanging over him.

After the principal lords of the Privy Council got knowledge of the clue mentioned above, they lost no time in bringing Father Henry to examination in their presence. Among them were the Earl of Salisbury, the Earl of Suffolk and the Earl of Northampton, that is, the Lords Thomas and Henry Howard. The first time that Garnet appeared before them, he was so troubled by thirst that he could scarcely open his mouth or wet his tongue. Indeed, it proved more than once necessary, in their presence, to give him something to drink. He was also heavy with sleep, so that he could scarcely hold up his head or keep his eyes open. Indeed, he complained then

* Thomas Garnet: b. London, 1574; executed at Tyburn, 23 June 1608. Henry's nephew, son of Richard G. Studied at Saint Omers and the English College, Valladolid. Came to England with Mark Barkworth, O.S.B. Admitted to S.J. in 1604, and seized at the port on his way to the jesuit novitiate in Flanders. Among the forty-six priests banished in 1606. Returned to England, 1607. Betrayed to the authorities by the apostate priest, Rouse (HFR, vii, p. 289).

and there that he had not slept at all for the five nights preceding. To this day, we do not know what was the cause of all this, but one suspects bad treatment somewhere. This was probably by way of some contrived trickery rather than by open, physical violence. Of this Garnet never complained. I do not claim anything, since proof is insufficient. In London many people were saying, and those people of understanding who had ways of finding out what went on in the Tower, that they had deliberately kept him without sleep. In this way, his head would have been so weakened that he could not hope to have the upper hand amid all the questionings and inter-rogations inflicted on him by his judges. In the end, he was so tired and confused that he compromised himself, and gave them much the sort of reply that they wanted. Others think that both his thirst and his lack of sleep were caused by means of some beverage or food given him to secure this precise effect. This was more probable in view of the fact that Garnet admitted that he had never been treated with extraordinary rigour in the whole time of his imprisonment. However this may be, it is certain that those lords found him in such a state that they were obliged to give him leave to withdraw and sleep for an hour before they examined him. This did not help much since, although he slept for the whole hour, he felt no better and his head was no clearer.

This latest examination was very different from all which had preceded it. It is true that, in the beginning, they tried to make him confess to having known something from somebody, or at least to have had a glimmering, about the plot. But when they saw him obstinate in his denial, they threatened him with torture. They as-sured him that they had witnesses who could bear testimony to his having had foreknowledge of the plot. In a way, they did torture him; for now they produced as witnesses the gaoler and the other man who was with him. I do not know whether there were more besides. At all events, they now, in his presence, reported all that had passed in the conversation which they had overheard between him and Father Edward. Garnet replied that the time had now come when, without offending God, he could declare the little that he knew, although they might consider it much. So now he admitted that it was true that there was one, and only one, man in this world who could say that he had known something of this plot. This had

happened without Garnet's wanting it or wishing it. Indeed, it had
been entirely against his will, and it had not been in his power to
refuse the hearing of it. He had only heard it in such a way that,
up to that moment, it could never have been lawful for him, without most grave offence to God, to breathe a word to a living soul.
He could reveal neither the person nor the matter since he had
heard it under the seal of the Sacrament of Penance. This, as catholics
and all those who understand the force and nature of this sacrament
will appreciate, is inviolable.

They now asked him who it was from whom he had heard this
in confession. Garnet named a priest who had likewise received news
of the forthcoming event in confession. This priest had himself come
to Garnet to confess and ask advice. He had received leave from his
own penitent to do this, although, before the plot was discovered,
he had never revealed, either to his penitent or to any other, the
fact that he had asked advice about it from Father Henry. This I
heard from that priest himself, who protested on his salvation that
it was true. Father Henry, foreseeing, as it seems, what was going
to happen, begged and commanded the priest never to let it be
known that he had confessed this matter to him or asked advice
about it. One of the lords of the council now asked him if he was
trying to tell them that, although the confessional seal was so secret
and inviolable, he was now about to reveal both the matter and the
person. But why had he not done so earlier, in order to save the life
of the king and the peers of the realm? To this Garnet replied that,
as far as the secrecy of the seal in the sacrament was concerned, this
depended entirely on the will of the penitent, and not on the priest.
Garnet foresaw the danger that the knowledge received in that confession could bring him; more particularly from those who thought
little of that sacrament, if they ever got to know that he had received
knowledge of this plot. He therefore begged leave from his penitent
that when the plot was discovered [he should have permission to
say what he knew of it (?)].*

* The Italian here is defective, and the phrase in square brackets is added to
complete what seems to be the obvious meaning of the sentence. The omission at such a crucial point is much to be regretted. The sense is supplied
from the Gerard Narrative (Morris edition, p. 175). This narrative claims
that Garnet was actually tortured.

We now turn our attention to that other good priest who was Father Henry's companion, Father Edward Oldcorne. In order to wring out of him anything that might have to do with the plot, they tortured him for five days on end. They used such inhuman cruelty that his very enemies were forced to commiserate with him. In spite of this, they wrung from him not the slightest shred of evidence which they could use against him. In the end, they felt obliged to condemn him to death and martyrdom solely because he had been in the company of his superior, Father Garnet. Five long days they tortured him, and every day for five hours. Those who have had a taste of these things say it would have been enough to kill anyone else. In fact, they did kill Garnet's servant, a man by name of Nicholas Owen. This occurred about the same time, and they used similar kinds of torment on him. We shall have more to say of this later. One can imagine how chagrined they were at not unearthing more material which could be used against Father Henry. But they spared no effort of cruel ingenuity in trying to find it in the confessions of others . . .

There was yet another man by name of Grissold. This was a man of good and upright life who had served the two Vaux sisters for many years, that is, Mistress Anne Vaux, and her sister [Eleanor], who was a widow. Grissold was captured some months before Father Henry was taken.★ He was kept in an underground cellar and treated with every conceivable harshness. From this man, too, they hoped to find out something in view of his many years' service in a house where Garnet often stayed. They hoped to find something to the discredit of the Jesuits, or at any rate of other catholics. With this in mind, they carted off Grissold to the Tower of London from his former prison. This was after they succeeded in capturing Father Henry. For quite some time, they subjected Grissold to daily torture in that place. It was done so cruelly that word got round that he died in the midst of his sufferings. In fact, he did not die, but he remained for a long time afterwards so crippled by his

★ John Grissold: of Rowington, Yorks. Fr. G. Anstruther, O.P., persuasively penetrated the alias of James Johnson (*Vaux* . . ., p. 384 and also pp. 255, 282–5, 345). Grissold – alias Johnson – was cruelly tortured before being released by the government to act, probably unconsciously, as a decoy (ibid., p. 384).

experience that he was not expected to survive. His patience and endurance underlined quite clearly the innocence of Henry Garnet and the other Fathers. All this would have been sufficient to satisfy the cruelty, and quench the hatred of any others, but not theirs. Not content with this, they turned their eyes elsewhere . . .

One of the two laymen taken with Father Garnet and Oldcorne was called Nicholas Owen. His nickname was 'Little John' both because he was short of stature and also because he had changed his name so as not to be recognized by his persecutors. He had been in their hands on several occasions. This good man was known up and down England among catholics of every kind. The leading papists knew him well. Indeed, one could say that none was better known than he, even among the priests. He was so much esteemed, and his trustworthiness so well known, that matters of considerable importance were entrusted to him all over the land. No one knew more than he about catholic affairs. He had been with Father Henry Garnet some seventeen or eighteen years, whether as a servant, or a lay-brother or coadjutor. Garnet made use of his services on every possible occasion since he knew him so well, and also the depths of his goodness and unbounded loyalty. But Father Henry used him chiefly, as did others, for making those secret places in which priests and church-stuff could be hidden in times of crisis. One could say that this good man was among the most important at work in the kingdom. And he went on working faithfully to the end. There can be no doubt that the lives and safety of many priests and laymen must be attributed to him and to his enormous industry and skill. For years on end, such fugitives have managed to elude the searches of the pursuivants, both in the late queen's time and in the reign of the present king. I myself can bear witness to that. I well remember one occasion, one among many, when I was hidden with six other priests, in a place prepared by Owen in order to evade imminent risk of capture.* So great was this good man's zeal, and so devoted was he to the work of the Church that he never refused an undertaking, however arduous. Nor, if it would serve the cause, did he ever flinch from any peril, although his work constantly demanded not only great toil but endless risks. For this reason, he usually worked alone. In this way, it was easier to keep his labours secret,

* See Introduction, n. (†) p. 91.

and in any case the danger from spies was always very great. He was under no illusions that if he were ever captured, he would be obliged to undergo the most frightful kinds of torture to make him give up the secrets of his many clients. This, in fact, happened to him.

The last time he was captured was not the only occasion when he was tortured. This had happened some ten years previously, when he was taken in the company of Father John Gerard. But they did not know for certain at that time that he was the man whose services were employed in making hiding-holes. All the same, acting only on suspicion, they tortured him with extreme ferocity. They tried him not only by torment, however, but also by flattery and trickery, hoping in this way to undermine his fidelity. All in vain. He refused to be worn down by one or the other. After a long imprisonment, and a very considerable sum of money paid over by the catholics, his liberty was restored. Certainly, the catholics had great need of his services. It is also noteworthy that, although he had a rare genius for devising ways of making his hiding-holes, this was not the principal reason why the catholics made such willing use of his labours. What they chiefly prized was his capacity to keep his mouth shut. True, he needed a great deal of ingenuity in constructing his hiding-places in view of the great trouble which our enemies took to find them. It was essential, however, that such places should remain hidden even from catholic members of the same family, and hidden also the identity of the house where they were.

It was noticed that Owen never spoke of any hiding-place which he had constructed, in any house whatsoever, although very often he might have had occasion to do so, and even a certain kind of necessity. Thus when he was discussing various methods of construction, he was obliged in some measure to give actual examples of places which he had made in different houses. He also took care to vary, as far as he could, ways and means of constructing these hides, so that if one were discovered in one place it would not lead automatically to the discovery of others. Providence itself seems to have blessed the places which he constructed. We need not marvel at this since he always began work in the most devout way possible. He invariably made his confession, and received Holy Communion, before he started a new job. Normally, he did two or three a week. Furthermore, as far as was practicable, he prayed all the time while he was working. He was a man of more than ordinarie blameless life; and nothing, perhaps, gave clearer indication of his goodness than the fact that in all the seventeen or eighteen years of his labours, no one ever heard him use a swear-word, although there were plenty of occasions, in the midst of so much work, when he might have used them. Indeed, I do not think that anyone even saw him angry in all that time. This is extremely unusual in a man untied to a master, up to his eyes in work, and mixing with people of every kind.

Owen took as his own example, and revered as a saint, Father Henry Garnet himself. If we can accept the testimony of those who knew him intimately, I heard his spiritual Father once say that he was a virgin, and for the eighteen years he knew him, had never heard him, either in confession or outside it, give evidence of anything which could be taken as mortal sin. This was the view of more than one, indeed of all who dealt with him in spiritual matters. It is also the common opinion of the jesuits on the English Mission that Owen was received into the Society by Father Henry some years before his martyrdom. For good reasons, however, he was not generally known as a jesuit. For one thing, they did not wish his example to be the cause of many another making an importunate demand to be admitted to the Society. Certainly, there were quite a number who wanted this. One could not have put them off, especially in view of their real merits, if it had been possible to allege an example of this being done. I well remember being asked about this by a man who was a good friend of his. If he had known that Nicholas was a jesuit, he could have used the fact as a considerable argument to facilitate his own entry into the Society. The second reason was that the jesuits did not think it expedient to receive lay-brothers on that Mission, so they kept Owen's admission very secret. Certainly, he himself behaved in such a way that no one could discern any difference between him and any other servant in the house. This was a good example of the humility which he showed in everything and on every occasion, and of his scorn for his own interests. On the other hand, one could well understand that he had a greater obligation to perfection than the others. So he was always most obedient to the will of his superiors, most discreet in his conversation, and at all times exemplary, being most observant of religious poverty and chastity. He was, after all, not merely imitating, but actually professing, the virtues which belonged to the religious state. These demand continual self-denial in all things. Apart from his considerable modesty and unobtrusive way of proceeding in all things, he could show a patience in adversity that was almost unbelievable . . . He had plenty of opportunities for its exercise, but there was one occasion especially when he showed the ultimate depths of this quality. This was when his horse fell over and Owen, in consequence, broke a leg. He accepted this with heroic endurance. In fact, thanks to the incompetence of the surgeon, the bones knit together badly, so badly that they had to be rebroken. He put up with the medico's error, and this new anguish, which was much worse than the first, with so much stoical acceptance that the people in the house where he was staying were astounded . . . These earlier and already unusual signs of a perfect life proved to be the premise and preamble of a rare and glorious death.

The capture of this good man caused the enemies of our religion no little rejoicing. One of our principal persecutors, the Earl of Salisbury,* exclaimed when he heard the news of his capture, 'So

* The fact that papists were well aware that Salisbury was the king's chief confidant, and one of their 'principal persecutors', is another argument against the authenticity of the traditional plot-story. Why did the conspirators not arrange an ambush for king and secretary, which would have been much more plausible and likely of success than the grotesque contrivance which passed into history? Salisbury himself was an enigmatic figure, but of supreme intelligence and knowledge of statecraft. He had few friends but some faithful servants. Appropriately, Sir Walter Cope wrote 'An Apology for the late Lord Treasurer . . .' on 24 May 1612 (printed in J. Gutch, *Collectanea Curiosa*, I, Oxford, 1781, pp. 119–33). The best appreciative modern study is Miss P. M. Handover's *The Second Cecil, 1563–1604*, London, 1959. There were darker sides to his nature. John Chamberlain told Sir Dudley Carleton on 27 May 1612, 'I never knew so great a man so soon and so generally censured, for men's tongues talk very liberally and freely, but how truly I cannot judge' (T. Birch, *The Court and Times of James I*, vol. I, London, 1849, p. 169). Cecil died of a 'long languishing sickness', which popular opinion did not hesitate to identify as syphilis (see Bodleian Library, MS. Tanner 299, ff. 11r–13r, for a collection of thirteen pieces of doggerel; Aubrey, op. cit., p. 138).

the fellow has been taken who knows all the secrets of the papists! We shall have to devise some new ways of dealing with him!' And in truth, as we shall describe, they were very successful in finding new ways. Indeed, they were still trying them out when they killed him. Even after his death, they did not cease to ill-treat him. They pursued him with slander and infamy, albeit in vain. Not only the tortures that he endured in life, but the calumnies which dogged him after his death, turned to his greater glory.

Events turned out thus. In the first days of his imprisonment, Nicholas Owen was put in the Marshalsea. He was deliberately left almost unguarded to roam at will through the prison. In this way, they hoped that his friends would come to visit him, and so make themselves known. When Owen realized this, he broke off relations with everyone he knew. So it was that, although catholics were being rounded up and imprisoned throughout London, no one was ever captured in the whole time of his imprisonment, nor even after his death, by the fault of this man. When his persecutors saw that they were wasting time in this way, they had him transferred to the Tower of London. There they tried hard to find out by using torture whatever he knew that could be used to harm the catholics. They tormented him with hideous cruelty. Every day, news arrived of freshly devised tortures which he had to suffer, and this went on for many days continually; but the truth is, we do not know the details, even to this day. All we know is that, sometimes for several hours on end, he was subjected to torture. The only sound to be heard from him was one which had long been familiar with him at all hours and times, 'Sweet Jesus!' and 'Lord, give me your holy grace and patience!'

The result of all this brutal, indeed bestial, torture was that, in the course of it, Owen's belly burst open, his bowels gushed out, and in a short while he died. This happened all the more inevitably since, for some considerable time past, he had been suffering from a rupture. But his heartless gaolers were not even content with that. Perhaps even they were ashamed of the relentless cruelty which they had used towards him. At all events, they began, after his death, to tear his reputation to shreds. They put it about that he had ripped up his own stomach. The deed was even represented in printed pictures and rhymes. Part of their object was to detract from the glory of a martyrdom which remained like an aura in the catholic world long after his heroic contest was over. Owen's enemies were also motivated by a desire to cover up their own cruelty. This had been inflicted on him in violation of their own laws, which forbid that anyone should be killed by torture. But their stupid and wicked inventions were all in vain. No one, not even our enemies, allowed them probability or gave them credence. Still less did the catholics. By public repute or their own experience, these well knew Owen's complete innocence, invincible patience and unwearying fidelity . . . Some of them did not hesitate to scoff at this calumny as false and ridiculous. They spoke of it with the liberty of the sons of God, rejecting it as unjust and impious. They were arrested and put in prison so that, seeing their example, others would not dare to contradict the lies and slander spread about by public authority.

It seems permissible at this point to discuss briefly the probability of this devilish calumny. I would like to put a question to the slanderers themselves, and in particular to the Lieutenant of the Tower, William Waad, who supervised the torture, and invented this fable. Waad is a man utterly corrupt. His word is worth little. But I would like to ask him if, during all the time he was torturing Owen, or on some other occasion during his imprisonment, he ever saw in him impatience of a kind to lead one to believe that even in desperation he could kill himself . . . Does William Waad seriously expect us to believe that, even after many days' torture, a man like Owen would abandon his hope of salvation by inflicting death on himself – and such a death? In any case, he could in a short time expect this kind of death from Butcher Waad himself! . . . Had Owen revealed the least part of the secrets locked within him, which his enemies so much desired to know, he would have received honour and riches, to say nothing of liberation from torture and prison. If conscience would never allow him to betray his friends and harm his neighbours, we cannot believe that he would have been ready to do that worse thing which would have led to eternal destruction . . . There are people ready to commit suicide, but they are not of our persuasion. It would be easy to prove that such things can happen and in a short space of time. Indeed, I could give quite a few examples without straying far from the City of London itself! But let us return to the subject. Waad knew well that, by torturing Owen, even to death, he might discover secrets which could enrich himself and his friends. This wealth would be derived from the goods of the first and foremost catholics in the land. Moreover, it would be impossible for any priest in future to escape their hands. In fact, they might have taken the greater and better part of all priests living in England at that time. This would have included the seminary priests as well as the jesuits . . .

By way of conclusion, we will show how vain was the slander of a man as brazen as Waad. We will mention here what amounted to an open confession by the gaoler who had custody of the martyr during his imprisonment and torture. This man told one of Owen's relatives in Owen's name, that he had need of certain things. But the good lady suspected that this might be the gaoler's crafty way of getting goods or money out of her for himself. To set her mind at rest, she asked for a note in the prisoner's own hand. 'What note?' asked the warder. 'How do you expect him to write notes when he cannot even hold a pen in his hand, or put his hat on? Don't you know that I have to feed him by hand and put his food in his mouth for him?' So, then, the man whom we are asked to believe drove a knife into himself with sufficient force to cut up his own stomach, did not even have the strength to move a finger or lift an arm! Furthermore, this relative of his was anxious to know where Nicholas was, and how he was getting on. She therefore went to the Tower and enquired about him from the same gaoler. He replied: 'You needn't bother to ask any more questions about him because he is dead. He died in our hands.' He did not have the impudence or hardihood to claim that Owen had done violence to himself. If this had been the case, not only he but a hundred others would have said the same thing. The credit for that fable would not have been William Waad's alone. One could mention any number of lies invented by this man and put about to harm and dishonour catholics, even if they were not usually on the scale of this one. But this slander almost reveals itself to be such, and calls for no great effort of refutation. Everyone knows that those undergoing torture are not allowed to have knives or anything else with which they can harm themselves. When they eat, they use a knife without a point, with its cutting edge in the middle of the blade. This is well over an inch from the point, if point one can call it.

Finally, William Waad cannot deny that he was well aware of

Owen's rupture. He knew that it was against all the laws of humanity to put a man to the torture who suffered from such an infirmity. Notwithstanding, he decided to torture him. But he took precautions to see that what in fact happened to him should not happen. That is, he tried to prevent his stomach from bursting and letting out his intestines. To obviate this possibility, as I say, Waad had Owen's stomach bound in with a circular plate of iron. But in the course of torture of that kind, the stomach is apt to swell, and suffers more severe pain and distention than other parts of the body. This was why Owen's stomach eventually burst, the wound opening as if it had been cut. All this is as much as we have been able to find out about Nicholas Owen's martyrdom. Time, no doubt, will reveal the rest, since Providence does not allow the heroic deeds of its martyrs to remain hidden . . .

TWELVE

ABOUT THIS TIME, it came to the knowledge of the lords of the Privy Council that Father Garnet was to be found in the house of a certain gentleman in Worcestershire. They lost no time in sending to have him arrested. But the operation was not carried out quite as quickly as they hoped, as we shall describe in the next chapter. Meanwhile, they decided to execute justice immediately on the conspirators already in hand. Perhaps the authorities also wanted to step up pressure on them, for they well knew that in all their examinations so far, they had only succeeded in establishing the innocence of Garnet and his fellow jesuits. They were afraid that when the plotters got to know of Garnet's capture, they would insist even more on his innocence. They therefore decided to kill them as soon as possible.* The manner of their condemnation was as follows.

On 27 January 1606 the conspirators were taken by barge from the Tower of London along the Thames to Westminster. Here civil as well as criminal courts had their sessions. There were nine of the

* The speed with which the plotters were executed was almost certainly a political contrivance. (See chapter 12, note (*) below.) While the date of the trial, corresponding almost exactly with the time of Garnet's capture may have been coincidence, it is difficult to believe in the double coincidence of the plotters' death before news of Garnet's capture arrived at Whitehall. It is also a fact that, even in the official accounts, the surviving plotters always vindicated the jesuits of complicity. Was this because they retained some adherence to their nominal faith and its pastors, or simply because it would have seemed artless if they had attacked directly the men whom the government had principally in its sights?

plotters altogether, namely, Sir Everard Digby, Knight of the Golden Spur, the brothers Robert, Thomas and John Wintour, Ambrose Rookwood, John Grant, Guy Fawkes, Robert Keyes, and Mr Robert Catesby's servant, Thomas Bates. We have spoken in sufficient detail of all these men. On reaching Westminster Hall, they waited about half an hour in the Star Chamber for the arrival of the other judges and lords who were to be present. The accused carried themselves all this time with notable self-assurance, showing not the least sign of fear, or anything that could remotely suggest agitation. On the contrary, their attitudes suggested determination and intrepidity. This gave rise to plenty of talk and even writing. Proof of this can be seen in the pamphlet which was published immediately after their death, bearing the title, 'The True Relation of the Imprisonment, Condemnation and Death of the Rebels'.* In this production all their words and actions that tended to their credit are carefully omitted. On the other hand, false inventions are multiplied to bring them and their religion into contempt, and to increase popular hatred. Notwithstanding, the pamphlet makes it clear that they were quite convinced in their own minds that they began and developed their business with the best of intentions, convinced that they offered no offence to God or conscience. For this reason, they showed no great fear of death, judging their cause to be right. The author of this little work says that they spoke little save in defence of their religion; that they never asked pardon, whether of God or His Majesty, for the offence committed. On the

* The book, or rather pamphlet, which the writer seems to have in mind was *The Arraignment and Execution of the late Traytors . . . with a relation of the other Traytors, which were executed at Worcester, the 27 of January last past.* By 'T.W.', published in London, 1606; BMC.114.b.14; reprinted in 'Somers' Tracts (*v. supra*), II, pp. 111–17). The initials were most probably those of Thomas Wilson, who at the time of the plot was Salisbury's surveyor. He supervised the descent on White Webbs, a house occupied by Garnet since 1600, on 11 November 1605 (cf. *Vaux . . .*, p. 282). Educated at Saint John's College, Cambridge, Wilson acted as foreign intelligencer in Italy in 1601–2, and as consul in Spain in 1604–5. He became keeper of records at Whitehall 1606–29. During this time occurred the disastrous fire which was supposed to have destroyed many vital records of this period (see chapter 9, n. (*) p. 158). He was clerk of imports, 1606–14: knighted in 1618, in which year he was 'employed to obtain admissions from Ralegh sufficient to condemn him' (DNB, *Index and Epitome*, London, 1903, p. 1421).

contrary, it still seemed to them that their deed was meritorious
and worthy of praise. In fact some of them apparently tried to put
the fear of death in death itself, for they did little else than recite
the rosary and multiply their Ave Marias. The pamphlet enlarges
on this, but proves no more than what we have already said, namely
that they thought little of death. Certainly, they had nothing else to
look forward to.

At last the judges entered the Great Hall. With the other lords
and gentlemen present, each took up his appointed place. The
accused were then brought in and made to stand on a dais. Here they
replied to the accusations, and did whatever else was required of
them according to the normal usage of the court. The indictments
were read first of all, in which the nature of their plot was declared,
together with the number and names of the plotters, in accordance
with their examinations and confessions. As we mentioned above,
they added to the indictments many calumnies and falsehoods invented by themselves, and directed principally against the Fathers
of the Society of Jesus. They accused them without producing any
proof, witness, or other circumstances of time and place. In this way,
they named in particular the three priests whose names had already
been published in the proclamation. They enlarged on this statement, and named other jesuits to make it clear for all to see how
great was the hatred with which they pursued the fame and name of
these Fathers, and how small was the foundation of truth on which
it was based. Here one must observe how they made those Fathers
accomplices and authors of the plot in a place so public and authori-
tative. Everyone can judge from their shamelessness in this how
much credence is to be given to those other calumnies of theirs which
go the rounds more secretly, when nothing like the same degree
of impudence is needed to spread such tales.

After the indictments were read, they asked the conspirators if
they accepted the charges as true. All repudiated them, and even
rejected the indictments as false.* The audience was not a little
surprised at this since the deed was notorious and clear for all to see.
The indictments had been drawn up according to their confessions.

* The official account of the trial was published in *A Complete Collection of
State Trials* . . ., London, 1730, vol. I, pp. 224–39. For Henry Garnet's trial
on 28 March, see pp. 240–301.

Mr Guy Fawkes was asked in particular how he could reject the indictment since he had confessed to knowledge of the plot from its first beginnings, and had always been at hand even in its most secret phases. Furthermore, he had been taken in the very place where the gunpowder had been stowed away for their purpose, together with the matches and fuses all ready to fire the barrels. Up to that moment, he had not denied this. Hence the lords commissioners replied, 'We are quite astonished that you of all people should want to deny the truth of the indictment!' The prisoner replied that he never had denied, nor up to that moment thought to deny, whatever was contained in the indictment against him. But he now heard in the course of it so many new ideas of which he himself had never even dreamed, that it should not seem surprising to them or to anybody else if he denied the charge at least in the form in which it was worded. He roundly declared: 'We have never dealt with the jesuits in this business. Nor did they ever persuade or urge us to undertake it. This is as false as it is true that we alone began and ended the business. So I say that all reference in the indictment to our meetings with them, and the advice and consent they gave us in this, is something entirely new. We never heard of it, and I deny it here and now as completely false. For this reason, I reject the indictment, and in no wise admit it as true!'

The prisoner was given a reply in such fashion that, even if we had no means of finding out the truth in the teeth of their charges or establishing the falsity of their slander, this reply alone would suffice to make two things very clear . . . Firstly, we could deduce without difficulty the untruth of the slander against the jesuits, and also the truth of their innocence. For the reply was that everything that had been included in the indictment had been stated so as to observe a form of law. One should presuppose as true whatever was written in it. I sincerely hope that the reader who is not blinded by the kind of hatred that damages the judgement will swiftly discern the complete inanity of such a reply . . . He will, no doubt, be as ready to laugh at the folly of those who answered as to sympathize with the unhappy lot of those who, while they observed the heinousness of the deed, were also obliged to witness the malicious unwisdom of our enemies . . . But in fairness, let us examine this reply in case we find in it any appearance of justice or truth. In this way, we shall have a better idea of its absurdity, and the real intention of those who made it.

They claim that it accords with the form of law to mention accomplices in the indictment, and that these, no less than the principals, may be published in the indictments. Who denies it? But where are these accomplices? They say that we must presuppose that they are the jesuits as friends and acquaintances of the plotters. Can anyone attribute intelligence to someone who reasons like this? If by chance the Lord Chief Justice of England, John Popham, or the Attorney-General, Sir Edward Coke, had ever been friends or acquaintances of a guilty man, would these two think it good form of law if they themselves were numbered with the guilty as his accomplices on grounds of such acquaintance alone? As for the supposition in the actual indictment, it is not merely without proof or testimony but is clean contrary to the witness and examinations of all those found guilty, and of all others who were examined in connection with the plot. I am quite certain that, in the hypothetical case, both of them would have flung up their hands in the air, and cried to heaven in protest against any such form of law. However little they believe in God or fear the devil, they would nevertheless have called on divine justice, if not the assistance of hell, to punish such an openly tyrannical and abominable form of law. But we will return to our story.

So the indictment was read. The accused with one voice denied it because of the falsehoods it contained. They were then called on to make their defence, as is the custom of that court. The sergeant-at-law, one by name of Edward Phillips, then took pains to impress upon his audience the seriousness of the crime. He exaggerated in every way conceivable all that was contained in the indictment. He omitted nothing that could make the accused more odious; and not only them but whoever else they had included in the same indictment. After Phillips had finished his declaration, the Attorney-General began to amplify and expound with minute care all the details of the indictment. Coke was a man more experienced and better adapted for this task than Phillips. Sir Edward's speech was decidedly long, and instead of the usual introduction, began with an apology for the inordinate delay in proceeding to the trial of the guilty. He did not doubt that there were many who wondered at this in view of the gravity of the crime and the clarity and weight of the evidence, which included the confessions of the delinquents themselves.

Coke tried to satisfy all critics by giving a variety of reasons for the delay. He failed to mention the real reason, as we can judge from the hollowness of the two chief reasons he offered. The first of these was that Robert Wintour and Stephen Lyttelton were not yet captured. And what if these two were not yet taken? Or what if they had only been taken after a considerable time? Would the course of justice have been held up so long for this reason alone? In fact, their pursuers had abandoned all hope of taking them, and it was only by the merest chance that they were captured in the manner they were. Coke's second reason was that if they had proceeded to justice too swiftly, they might have executed Johnson for Guy Fawkes. What a mistake! How could this be so important since Johnson and Guy Fawkes were the same person? In fact, they had known long before that the man's true name was Guy Fawkes. This reason, like the other, was only intended to conceal the true reason. This was to see if, with the passage of time, they could establish the fact that the jesuits had had a hand in the business. They could then determine the best way of fastening this infamy on to the whole society. When they saw that things would not turn out as they wanted, they still did not hesitate to mention them openly in the indictment. The fact that they possessed no scrap of evidence did not deter them. Nor the other circumstance that the only people who could accuse them, that is, the plotters, publicly admitted their innocence in the way which we have described.

In the second place, the Attorney-General took the trouble to offer his excuses for something else he had been obliged to do: that is, make mention of certain princes and men in authority. He had only mentioned them, as he said, because he was obliged thereto by the necessity of telling the whole truth in the indictment. He claimed that the names of such rulers had been so woven into the texture of the plotters' confessions that it was impossible to leave their names out. I cannot but praise the Attorney's modesty in this particular, and the great care he took not to offend these princes. However, they were not in fact accused by the plotters. Yet Coke wished to name them only in so far as the truth of the indictment and the nature of the prisoners demanded! My only regret is that he was not guided by the same sense of fair-play in dealing with the jesuits. Not only did he mention them by name, but even went so far as to accuse them, without having procured any sort of charge against them either by the plotters or anyone else. What is more, he had actually heard from the mouth of the guilty men themselves a public protestation against his false accusations and slanders. But for all that, he did not cease even at that time and in that place to sustain his false accusation most brazenly and shamelessly against the Fathers.★

For the above reason, I feel obliged to occupy a few lines in making clear the falsity of another slanderous fable invented by the Attorney. He told a story, in most offensive and exaggerated language, at the expense of another of the Fathers, John Gerard. This could be taken as a sample of a thousand other falsehoods and stories of the kind. It will serve as an example to the reader when he hears similar tales told at the expense of the catholics with the same kind of bare-faced audacity. He will not after this be inclined to believe such stories without first seeing very clear proof. The story went like this. The Attorney, talking in the same place to the same audience of weighty and even noble personages, assured them that Father John Gerard knew about the plot. He it was who administered the oath of secrecy to the plotters, and saw to it that they persevered in their first intention until the project was carried through to its conclusion. After this, he heard their confessions, said Mass, and gave them Holy Communion. This was the slanderous fable which he laid before a public audience . . .†

In fact, the above tale had no other source but the idle and over-

---

★ There is, in fact, no evidence to suggest that the Jesuits, whether Garnet or anyone else, were implicated in the plot. Apart from any moral consideration, it was against both the declared and secret policy of Rome at this time to entertain such schemes against princes. Garnet and the other accused jesuits were too devoted to their order to contravene clear directions of the highest authority. Jardine thought otherwise where Garnet was concerned (DJ, pp. 275–322). But his argumentation must seem much less convincing since the discovery of the contemporary decipher of a letter of 24 July 1605, in the jesuit archives in Rome (*v. supra*, chapter 5, n. (★) p. 91).

† Coke's chicanery, presumably connived at by Cecil, is very evident at this point. Wintour's 'confession' of 25 November 1605 (Sal. MS. 113, No. 54)

imaginative head of the Attorney himself. If this were not so, perhaps he would care to prove what semblance of truth he had to make him believe it. Perhaps it is something one can find in the confessions of the conspirators. Certainly, I cannot conceive of any other source from which such an imaginative idea could come into his head. Speaking for myself, I have read these confessions more than once, and at the very time when I had before me these lines to which I refer. I could not find even the shadow of a foundation for such a falsehood. On the other hand, there are many things from which one could infer the contrary. Nor can there be any doubt that if one could have found a basis for the plausibility of such stories, in the confessions of the plotters or anywhere else, the Attorney would have given them, not merely as a possibility, but as a full demonstration of what he so much desired to prove.

I have often wondered that, although our enemies published in print many serious slanders against the jesuits after the plot, it

was published in the King's Book (see reprint in D. Carswell, *Trial of G.F.*, pp. 116–23), but without two important additions made subsequently. The phrase 'by the hands of Gerard' was added in Coke's hand, 'upon the same' (see Carswell, p. 118, line 18 from page-foot). A further passage written in the margin in the hand of the original writer of the confession, was marked to be added after the addition indicated above. This second addition was prefixed by another phrase in Coke's hand, 'the effect of the oath'; all to be added to the original confession, but not included in the King's Book. The actual addition ran, 'You shall swear by the Blessed Trinity and by the Sacrament you now purpose to receive never to disclose directly or indirectly by word or circumstance the matter that shall be proposed to you to keep secret, nor desist from the execution thereof until the rest shall give you leave.' Even with Coke's explanatory phrase, the form of the oath is an afterthought and does not fit into the narrative as it stands. Blacker Morgan noticed a further circumstance to exonerate Gerard. 'There was always the damning fact that he was present and ready after the first conspirators had taken their oath alone together, to give them the Sacrament upon it, which seemed quite unaccountable. The date of that meeting as given in the Act of Attainder is 20 May 1604. I am the first to notice that this date fell upon a *Sunday*, and as the house where they took the oath was a resort of priests where Mass was frequently said, Catesby had evidently arranged for them to take their oath and sacrament on that day, which explains it . . .' (Letter to Rector of Stonyhurst, 18 March 1918: MS E/III/18: microfilm also at Mount Street 15/2/4/1). The probability is that the whole story of the oath was mere fiction (cf. EGF, pp. 101–3).

never occurred to them to include this precise accusation. Certainly, they had an excellent opportunity for doing so in the little book which included the conspirators' confessions.* One can scarcely attribute this omission to forgetfulness. The hatred which makes it impossible for them to pass over any detail, or any occasion, which might do the jesuits injury is sufficient proof of this. However, I think I have found the solution to this problem. That little book is supposed to have been written, as some claim, by the king himself, since it is not only in English but in a clipped style. At least it was produced by his order. Therefore if anything had been written in it other than the strict truth, it could have done considerable injury to His Majesty's reputation. This is something very dear to princes, and he would not lightly have exposed it to risk by writing down a falsehood so evident and notoriously undeniable. That this little book was written by the king's order and revised by him is clearly to be understood from certain words of the Earl of Salisbury. These occur in his opusculum entitled, 'An Answer to Certain Scandalous Letters'.† In this the author calls to mind that little book, and says of it, intending to praise the author, that every line shows clearly where Apollo put his hand . . . In the event, the Attorney's invention seemed so improbable to the gentlemen who were present at the tribunal when the indictment was read, that he found it impossible to win belief. They offered him no applause for this. So much is evident from the discourses of the Earls of Northampton and Salisbury respectively.

The above-mentioned earls often had occasion to refer to the conspirators' oath. They dealt with it from every conceivable aspect, but never once did they attribute it to Father Gerard. They knew very well that they had not the slightest proof that he was its author, as the Attorney would have it, nor yet persuaded the plotters to it, nor even knew of it in any way whatsoever. And this notwithstanding the fact that both earls had been commissioners deputed to examine the plotters. One can see clearly in Thomas Wintour's confession, printed in the same little book, how the oath

* The so-called 'King's Book' (*v. supra*).
† Correct title: *An answere to certain scandalous papers*, London, 1606; published anonymously (see STC, under Robert Cecil).

was given and taken by the conspirators. I quote their words here as they were published in the book. The author says, 'First of all, Mr Thomas Percy spoke to Mr Catesby and me in this fashion, "Shall we always, gentlemen, talk, and never do anything?" Mr Catesby took him aside, and had speech about somewhat to be done.' They then decided to undertake the business but on the express condition that an oath of secrecy should be presented to, and taken by, all concerned. This they decided to do in two or three days. 'At that time, Messieurs Catesby, Percy, John Wright, Guy Fawkes and myself all met together, and we swore to observe secrecy on the Little Office of our Lady, in a chamber where we were alone with no other person present. After that we went in to a neighbouring room to hear Mass, and in confirmation of the oath, we received the Blessed Sacrament. Then did Mr Catesby reveal to Mr Percy what he intended to do. And I, together with Mr John Wright, told it to Mr Guy, and this was approved by everyone.'

A short while afterwards, Mr Percy was sent to rent the house where eventually the mine was constructed. How can anyone fail to understand the opposite by what the Attorney falsely claimed was contained in these words? Is it not clear that those men alone by themselves agreed to the business? Among themselves alone they took that oath. By themselves alone they concluded the bargain. They did not share it with any other living person because it was to this effect precisely that they took the oath. It is also clear from this passage that these gentlemen were not persuaded to their deed by others. Mr Catesby found them on their own, and in this way he made his decision with his companions. As for their hearing Mass and receiving Holy Communion from a priest, and even that they confessed themselves before Communion, from all this one can deduce no more than that they did not consider that their decision involved sin, or contained matter for confession. Rather was it something meritorious, or at least something which would not hold them back from the altar. But as for the identity of the priest from whom they received the Blessed Sacrament, I have heard Father Gerard himself say, and make a solemn oath on it, that he knew absolutely nothing about it.

This confession of Thomas Wintour received the approbation of Guy Fawkes, as one can see clearly in the little book, where he is mentioned many times. Nor was it ever denied by any of the conspirators. It is, therefore, quite clear that the Attorney's long and bitter harangue had only one end, namely to smear the jesuits and make them hateful to the people; this was easier than prove anything against the guilty. In any case, since he had their confessions, there was no need of further proof. Coke compared the jesuits with the Order of Templars in the hope of getting them driven not only from England but from the entire world . . . He also made the completely absurd charge against them that they publicly and openly taught heresy. In particular, he claimed that they taught the lawfulness of killing princes. Not only was it lawful but even meritorious, and Coke tried to make it seem that they were doing no more than follow the teaching of the popes themselves. He confirmed it with the example of Sixtus V who, in one of his speeches made in public consistory, praised and approved the deed of the Dominican friar who murdered Henry III, King of France.⋆ The good man then completely lost the control of his tongue proper in that place. Beside himself with fury, he threw in everything together, losing all thought of restraint or truth in his overwhelming desire to harm the innocent, and titillate the ears of those who, as he thought, would enjoy maladroit utterances of this kind. As for the slander against Father Gerard, we will say more below about the method which the latter adopted to purge himself of the charge as soon as he heard that this rumour was going round.

The Attorney went on to say how much damage would have been done the kingdom if the plotters' design had taken effect. He then proceeded to discuss the persons of the conspirators. He

---

⋆ For the murder of Henri III in 1589 by the Dominican friar, Jacques Clément, see H. Fouqueray, S.J., *Histoire de la Compagnie de Jésus en France* . . ., tome II (1575–1604), Paris, 1913, pp. 178–81: also under J.C. in Michaud, *Biographie Universelle*, Paris, 1811–53; but Ludwig von Pastor (*Geschichte der Päpste* . . ., vol. X, Freiburg-in-Breisgau, 1926, pp. 235–7) deals effectively with the rather inevitable attempt to connect the jesuits with the crime, and also the further idea that Pope Sixtus V gave his simple approval. In the Consistory of 11 September 1589, Sixtus V held up the event as a warning of the nemesis that overtakes tyrants, though without approving of the instrument of retribution. There were, however, several versions current of what he actually said, and as often happens with papal utterances, all parties heard and interpreted according to their own convictions.

claimed that, although there were some prepared to say that they were men of little worth in order to reduce their credit, the truth was that many of them were men of good family, and even connected with noble houses. They had excellent qualities, but they had been shamefully corrupted, seduced, and jesuited. These were his considered words. He claimed that their possessions and circumstances agreed with their social standing, and names were given to three among them as pre-eminent in these respects. The general trend of his entire discourse was directed, in one way or another, against the jesuits . . .

After the Attorney had finished his long, hate-filled harangue, it was now the turn of the accused to make their defence. Since their deed was evident, they used very few words to defend themselves but they denied, as was said above, many of the circumstances indicated in the indictment. They confessed to the plot, but showed no regret for having ever begun it; nor yet desire to beg for the king's mercy. We may say a brief word about each in turn. Mr Robert Wintour spoke very little. He did not seem to mind death, and was quite satisfied in his own mind about the intention which had moved him to agree with the plot. His brother, Thomas, although normally highly articulate, had on this occasion extremely little to say. At another time, he had described the whole course of events, setting them out with order and clarity. He showed so much candour in his first examinations that the lords of the council, especially the Earl of Salisbury, were very satisfied with him. Indeed, the earl said that if it had been about something else, he would have made every possible effort with His Majesty to secure his life. Wintour now had little enough to say. He simply appealed to the king to exercise mercy towards his elder brother, who had only been persuaded to enter the conspiracy by his means. Mr Rookwood spoke more at large. First of all he showed how from infancy and childhood he had been brought up in the fear of God. He had been educated and nurtured in the catholic faith. For this cause alone, he had been induced to join the conspiracy. He was convinced that in this way, catholicism could be restored throughout the land. He did not deny that Mr Catesby's friendship had made him much more ready to accept the plot. He, too, begged His Majesty for a favour: this time towards his wife and two sons.

Mr John Grant used few words, but showed great courage and self-assurance. John Wintour, the youngest of the three brothers, defended himself by saying that he knew nothing about the plot before it was discovered. It was only at his brother's persuasion that he joined the company, and that was after they had taken up arms. Mr Guy Fawkes replied as we have already described. He claimed that the indictment contained many falsehoods, and particularly false was everything written down there against the jesuits. For the rest, he freely confessed the deed, and he would willingly die for it. Mr Robert Keyes spoke little, but he showed plenty of spirit. He claimed that his motive had been to promote the common good. That is, he hoped that his native land would be turned back to Catholic faith. The violence of the present persecution had driven him also to take part in the conspiracy. He had tasted persecution himself, having lost his goods because of it. He thought it the lesser of two evils to die rather than live in the midst of so much tyranny, and the unending persecution of ruthless foes. Thomas Bates, Mr Catesby's servant, was the last of the eight. He uttered no word and gave no sign that was noteworthy. If anything, as a man of lower class, he showed a certain amount of fear. However, when later he came to die, he showed no notable dismay.

After the eight accused had replied to the indictment against them, another particular indictment was read against Sir Everard Digby separately. What it amounted to was that he, as a participant in the conspiracy, had promised Mr Robert Catesby his assistance for his enterprise by supplying horses, arms, and other military equipment. He also placed 6,000 crowns of ready money at his disposal. For proof of all this, they alleged his own confession. After the indictment was read, they asked him if he had anything to say for his defence. He would be allowed to speak in accordance with the usage of that Court.* The knight's reply amounted substantially

---

* What did Digby understand by 'conspiracy'? Blowing up parliament, or joining Catesby and the rest to go to fight in Flanders? Digby, like Rookwood, seems to have been a man manoeuvered into a false position. Somers recorded an apparently contemporary tradition, 'it is said that when the hangman tore the heart from Digby's body, and pronounced the words, "This is the heart of a traitor", the mangled criminal had life enough to answer, "Thou liest!" (Tracts, 1809 ed., II, p. 114, n. 1). If Digby had been genuinely involved in

to the following. He could not deny the deed, nor had he any desire to defend it as good. What he did wish to defend as good and innocent was his own intention when he became involved in the plot. He had not wished to do anything which might not redound to the glory of God and help of neighbour. He was clear in his own conscience that he was far removed from ambition. Nor was he moved by appetite for riches and honours. In any case, as people well knew, he already enjoyed these in the measure that was attainable for him and due to him. Neither was he affected by any thirst for revenge owing to injuries already received. Such a motive was altogether alien to his nature. The only reasons which prompted him to take part in this enterprise were those which could move any man to take pity on afflicted friends and brethren. Such he considered to be all the catholics in the land. His only purpose was to secure for his country the greatest good possible, that is, knowledge of God and true faith. At the same time, he wished to free the kingdom from the blindness of heresy. This he took to be the greatest affliction which could overtake any christian land. To bring this about, he had placed himself in that extreme peril. He had set at nought not only his own possessions and influence, but the very lives and reputation of his entire posterity. He had turned his back on the whole world and everything it contained.

No one could blame Digby, as he claimed, for having the hardihood to keep silence about the plot, or even for having consented to it. For one thing, it had been revealed to him by Mr Catesby. For the sake of his friendship he was ready to put at risk life itself, and everything less than that. It was also clear that there was no longer any ground for hope on the part of the suffering catholics. Their persecution grew daily. The king himself had more than once broken his promise to them that he would help them in their misery; such misery they had experienced for so many years in the late queen's reign. The king had promised to grant them at least liberty of conscience. These promises, as Digby claimed, the catholics had received from the king himself by various ways and means. But now the king had shown himself so much their enemy that,

the plot, it is difficult to see in what sense he could have said this truthfully, and at such a moment, surely he would not have lied?'

in order to bring about their final ruin, he had summoned a parliament of puritans with the express purpose of punishing them, and heaping up afflictions. He intended only to ruin them by new devices and freshly devised cruelties. So the catholics found themselves driven by necessity to their late decision to throw down the Parliament-house with all their enemies inside it. In this way, they would free themselves in an instant from the extreme cruelty of law and legislators.

Sir Everard uttered these words with so much feeling and enthusiasm that at least one could not mistake his courage, or suppose that he spoke except from the depths of his heart. Certainly, he showed himself to be a man who could make up his mind, and who had no fear of death. Still less did he think of his own safety. Those who were present at the trial could not restrain their wonder. Even his enemies had to admit, along with the generality, that he revealed magnanimity of a kind. Everyone had considerable sympathy for him, well knowing that he could have enjoyed considerable happiness and prosperity in this life; indeed, not inferior to what was enjoyed by anyone of his rank in the whole country. All that was required of him was that he should accommodate himself to the times, and swim with the tide.* After his defence, Digby begged certain favours of His Majesty and the Privy Council. In the first place, it should be taken into account that his offence and the blame attached to it were completely personal. They depended in nowise on others. He had not persuaded anyone himself to take part in the

* Again, it is difficult to believe that Digby would have met with so much sympathy if he had been simply proved a traitor. It must be remembered that the narrator was present neither at trial nor execution, but had to rely merely on the impression of others. There is also the letter written by Digby, still a free man, to Salisbury, probably in the summer of 1605. He says, *inter alia*, 'your lordship may judge me peremptory in meddling, and idle in propounding, yet the desire I have to establish the king in safety, will not suffer me to be silent'. (See JG, Appendix B, and SRG, pp. 167–72; original letter, signed holograph, is in SP 14, vol. 17, No. 10). Digby asks for permission to go to Rome to beg the pope to 'stop the effect that may proceed from any discontented or despairing catholic', and that he may bring back reassurance that the pope will not excommunicate James. Digby also begs Cecil to adopt 'a more mild and undoubted safe course so that papists will not be driven to despair'. The letter reveals intelligence, sincerity, a certain spirit of independence, and essential loyalty to the king.

conspiracy, nor had he caused anyone effective harm. He therefore asked the lords of the council to intercede with His Majesty so that the punishment of his error should not be extended to anyone apart from himself. Since the lady, his wife, and sons were innocent, they should suffer no harm. Lady Digby should enjoy her dowry, and his sons their inheritance, in conformity with the laws of the realm, and in accordance with an agreement which had been entered into prior to the plot. Secondly, his debts should be paid out of his income. Thirdly, that as far as he was concerned personally, he asked no other favour than that the king should allow him to die as befitted a person of his quality. That is, instead of being hanged, he should be beheaded. Lastly, he had observed that, in the indictment and the Attorney's speech, mention had been made of several Fathers of the Society of Jesus as accomplices and instigators of the plot. He now protested on his conscience that they were all completely innocent. In particular, he mentioned Father Gerard with whom he had enjoyed close friendship and intimacy. His conscience now obliged him to say that Gerard had never had the least inkling of the plot. 'Indeed,' Digby added, 'I never had the courage to tell him about it for fear that he would have dissuaded me from it.' These were Digby's own words in that place, and at the moment when he was about to receive sentence of death. He wanted to repeat them, and indeed began to do so when he came to be executed. But he was not allowed to proceed or finish.

On this last point, if it would not detain the reader and impose on him excessively, I could here set down a number of letters which Father Gerard wrote to various privy councillors at that very time. From these it is very easy to see that he knew nothing of the plot before it was everywhere divulged. However, I will not omit, in a few words, to describe how he tried to prove his innocence. I will say something on the subject of those letters, of which I have copies by me at present, and which I was thinking of reproducing *in extenso*.

I said above in chapter 9 that, before the proclamation was published, when Father Gerard saw that they were making every effort to represent him as an accomplice of the plot, he wrote a letter of some length protesting his innocence and giving proof sufficient. This letter was seen by many. The king himself read it, and was completely satisfied by it. In spite of this, some who loved him less brought it about that the proclamation was published against him and two other Jesuits, as was said above. When Gerard realized this, knowing very well that there could be no kind of proof of any such thing against him, he quickly wrote off four letters which he sent to London. Three of them were directed to three of the principal lords of the Privy Council. The fourth was sent to Sir Everard Digby, who was then a prisoner in the Tower.★ The three councillors were the Duke of Lennox, the Earl of Northampton and the Earl of Salisbury. In all these letters, Gerard humbly but insistently begged to be allowed to purge himself according to the forms of law of that most false imputation, and so establish his innocence. He had been accused of an enormous crime, and one of which he had never had any knowledge, let alone been a participant. He appealed to their lordships and to the zeal for equity and justice which they wanted everyone to believe was in them.

By way of proof, Gerard's letters offered two kinds, the one negative, the other affirmative. For affirmative, he asked that the letter sent to Sir Everard Digby, and which was enclosed in the letters for the privy councillors, should be given to Digby in their

★ Sir Everard Digby was supposed to have written several letters from the Tower himself, apparently to his wife and children. They were first published by Thomas Barlow, Bodley's librarian, and Bishop of Lincoln from 1675, in his book, *The Gunpowder Treason*, London, 1679, as an appendix on pp. (239) to (260). They were described on p. (239): 'The several Papers and Letters of Sir Everard Digby, which are (as we have been credibly informed) the original Papers and Letters written by him concerning the Gunpowder Treason, were found by us Sir Rice Rudd, Baronet, and William Wogan of Grays Inn, Esq., in the presence of Mrs Ursula Giles, and Mr Thomas Hughes, about the month of September 1675, at the House of Charles Cornwallis, Esq., who was Executor of Sir Kenelm Digby, (son and heir to the said Sir Everard), tied up in two silk bags, amongst the deeds, evidences and writings of the said Sir Kenelm Digby. Rice Rudd, William Wogan.' All the parties named may be presumed to have been in good faith in publishing the letters for what they were. Nevertheless, 1679 was the year of the Oates Plot scare, in which a great deal of spurious 'evidence' was produced against the papists. In the absence of the 'originals', which seem to be no longer extant, or so my own search, hitherto fruitless, suggests, it seems superfluous to comment further on the letters or to take them into account in assessing Digby's degree of guilt or innocence. They were accepted as evidence by T. Longueville in his study of Sir Everard, *The Life of a Conspirator*, London, 1895, published anonymously.

presence. Digby should be examined on the points contained in it. These agreed with a certain conversation which took place between Father Gerard and the cavalier some three days before the gunpowder plot was discovered. It was evident from this conversation that Father Gerard had never had the slightest inkling of the plot. This conversation was fully reported in the letter with all the circumstances of time and place, and giving the very words that passed between them. If Sir Everard should not confirm and accept as true all that was contained in this statement, Gerard would be willing to pass as guilty of this crime in any degree whatsoever.

And now for Father Gerard's negative proof. He besought their lordships that, when the conspirators came to die, their lordships should see to it that they were publicly examined as to whether Gerard himself had received any news at all of the plot from them. Or their consciences could be obliged in some other way to do this. There could scarcely be any question of his having been an accomplice. If they did not all admit to his innocence, he would accept their silence, or even an admission of guilt, as valid proof against himself. Gerard added the proviso, however, that the admissions of the accused should not be influenced by any hope held out to them of life. Furthermore, it should be clear that they died catholic and with hope of salvation. This and the other kind of proof seemed completely sufficient to Gerard, as indeed they were, to vindicate his innocence.★

Father Gerard's letters reached London, and were delivered to the privy councillors on the same day that the conspirators were put on public trial. If they had wished to do so, the commissioners could have done what Gerard asked. But it was never the intention of those gentlemen to clear that priest or any other in the eyes of the world. Rather were they concerned to make him and his companions more hateful, and to fasten upon them the infamy of this conspiracy . . . It was providential in this connection that, although Sir Everard knew nothing of the jesuit's request, nevertheless when he heard him falsely accused in this way at the public trial, he himself proclaimed the innocence of that Father. He cleared him not only on the score of this present plot, but further insisted how much

★ It is, perhaps, significant that Gerard felt it necessary to insist that the plotters should give clear signs of their real religion, if any, when they died.

he hated everything of the kind. This was rather more than Gerard had asked for in his letters. Since Father Gerard was not allowed to vindicate his innocence in this way, he published these letters just before he left England by leaving them with his friends to disseminate . . .

By this time, word had got round that Thomas Bates had accused Father Gerard, and that it was because of his accusation that Gerard had been mentioned in the proclamation. It is evident from a letter written by Bates a day or two before receiving sentence himself, that the story about Gerard was altogether false. The letter in question was written to a priest after Bates's first examinations. It also followed some display of weakness by Bates, after which he had received the sacraments. One can still see the original of this letter written in his own hand. I give here a copy of it verbatim.*

'Sir, I humbly thank you for your great comfort and pains taken for me. I praise God I find myself more stronger to resist and do hope shall more and more. Sir, when I was at Hobadge [Holbeach] House, where my master was slain, that morning at my going away from him, by reason of the misfortune that fell amongst us by powder, Mr Christopher Wright flung me out of a window an £100 and desired me, as I was a Catholic, to give unto his wife and his brother's wife £80, and take £20 myself. I took out by guess some £22, as I think, and left it with a friend of mine, and desired him, if I did miscarry in this action, he should bestow it amongst my children. Now, I would entreat you to give my fellow George instructions what to do in it. I refer it to you. Mr Wright had of me at times in money and kind, as much as came to some £28, but my master told me he would pay me, but he did not. Now whether my wife may take that money out of that I refer to you.

'Also, further, I have dealt with my keeper to deal with the Clerk of the Council for my pardon, and have promised an £100 if it may be had, which I made account that money should have served that turn; but I am out of all hope for that, unless it be God's will to deliver me. This morning I was sent for down, and there was a

---

* Bates's letter is given here from the English version in Gerard's narrative (Morris edition, p. 210). This letter, if genuine and allowed to leave the Tower, was probably intended to begin an interchange of letters on the lines of the Vaux-Garnet correspondence. The original letter has perished.

fellow ready with a new suit of fustian, and my keeper made me to essay it, and neither said it was for me nor anything, but I know it was provided for me. The meaning I know not. And before that my Lord of Salisbury asked me what I wanted, and caused the keeper to buy me a new gown, and bade him use me extraordinary well. All this makes me full of doubts, for I fear it is but to serve their own turns of me and then to hang me. Is it not best for me, if the clothes be offered me, to refuse them? I pray you resolve me in that, for I have a purpose to tell the keeper, "I have clothes good enough to serve me as long as I live, I fear, and therefore will none". I beseech you to send me word what your opinion is in these things being offered me.

'At my last being before them I told them I thought Mr Greenway knew of this business, but I did not charge the others with it, but that I saw them all together with my master at my Lord Vaux's, and that after I saw Mr Walley and Mr Greenway at Coughton, and it is true. For I was sent thither with a letter, and Mr Greenway rode with me to Mr Winter's to my master, and from thence he rode to Mr Abington's. This I told them and no more. For which I am heartily sorry for, and I trust God will forgive me, for I did not out of malice but in hope to gain my life by it, which I think now did me no good. Thus desiring your daily prayers I commit you to God.'

From this letter of Thomas Bates we can deduce first of all the superficiality of the writer. It is clear that, even if all our enemies said about him were true, we should not attach great weight to his evidence. It is also very clear from this letter that he described something which did not in fact fall out as he says. In the second place, it is clear that he never accused either Father Gerard or Father Garnet. In fact, he was not in a position to accuse either of them. Nor did he accuse the third priest. All he said was that he thought that priest knew something of the business. Later on he showed himself very sorry even for holding this as a mere opinion. It took the fear of death to make him say even this much. Or rather, the hope of life. When I say he described something which never happened, I refer to the incident when he says that he saw the three Fathers in Baron Vaux's house. In fact Father Gerard affirmed on oath that he did not see him for two or three years before his death. I have understood from others as quite certain that when he speaks of having seen them on that occasion, Bates did not, in fact, enter the house. Only his master went out in order to speak to him. So if the Fathers had been in that house, he certainly would not have seen them. But I have dealt with this particular above in chapter 9. There is no need to say more on this point.

Another notorious falsehood I must nail here. This concerns a false charge made against Garnet at his trial. It was to the effect that Thomas Bates confessed to having communicated this business to Father Greenway in confession. From this letter, one can see that the contrary is true. Father Greenway swears solemnly, without wishing to make use otherwise of any privilege connected with that sacrament, that he never heard any such thing from him in confession.* Bates, however, is the only man who accuses those Fathers. If his accusation has no better foundation than we have indicated here, the kind of justice meted out to those Fathers is all too clear . . . This is particularly true of Father Gerard and Father Garnet whom Bates, in his letter, expressly denies ever having accused.

Father Gerard himself attached a great deal of importance to this letter. He saw it shortly before he left England. It was written entirely in the hand of Thomas Bates. Gerard wrote out a copy for himself, and published it, together with the other letters which he wrote for his own defence. Of these letters many copies were to be found. I have one of them by me. In it I notice a clause which, in my opinion, should suffice to convince the world, and any man of reason, of his innocence. It is this. Gerard noticed a sentence in a little book by the Earl of Salisbury which had just then been printed.

---

* The meaning of the phrase, 'without wishing . . . sacrament' is obscure. It seems that the authorities at one point made Bates take over from the dead Catesby the rôle of having revealed the plot in confession to Greenway. Catesby was clearly indicted in 'Garnet's Declaration, 9 March 1606', as the man who revealed the plot to Greenway (see *English Historical Review*, vol. 3 (1888), p. 514). Tesimond was not so solemnly bound to silence as Garnet, having given only a 'promise of secrecy'. Nevertheless, he was bound by his word, by friendship and ordinary prudence. Perhaps he was afraid that if Garnet were only bound in the same way, he would go directly to the authorities. This does not mean that Tesimond approved of the plot even tacitly. Certainly, if he had had no qualms, he would scarcely have approached Garnet at all, but let events take their course (see pp. 188–9 *supra*).

In this the earl declares that he had no hankering after the blood of anyone apart from those who by this inhuman conspiracy had desired the death of so many others. He quotes the words: *necis artefices arte perire sua* – engineers of death die by their own contrivances. Gerard offers that if at any time they can lawfully prove against him that he had any kind of hand in this plot, he is ready to suffer the most cruel and infamous death that could possibly be devised. He goes on to beseech the lords of the council to make every possible effort to establish either his guilt or his innocence. But if their lordships will not do this, he says that he will accept it all patiently, being content to put everything in the hands of Providence. He thought in fact that they would not do it since he well knew his own innocence and the plain impossibility of proving anything against him.

Now to return to Sir Everard Digby. We left him at the point where he had finished protesting the innocence of all the jesuits, but more particularly that of Father Gerard . . . After this, the Earl of Northampton launched forth on a long discourse, directed principally against Sir Everard.* His main intention was to reply to the knight's references to the king's promise made to catholics before the queen's death. Northampton began by saying something about Digby himself. He described his unusual and excellent qualities, and how much the late queen thought of him. Indeed, the earl had often heard her talking about him in terms of compliment and honour. There had been other occasions when he found himself obliged to bewail the sad fortune of someone he had loved in the past. So now he could commiserate with Digby's sorry plight more than anyone else who knew him. Northampton then enlarged on the enormity of the crime, and proceeded by a devious path to prove what he had promised in the beginning; that is, that the king had made no promise to the catholics to alleviate their plight. He had never held out to them hope of toleration or liberty of conscience. In fact, all that Northampton said, or on this subject could say, was uttered in vain. Admittedly, it would scarcely have been appropriate at that moment to think of the king breaking his word

* Northampton's speech is given in *State Trials* (*v. supra*), pp. 237–9. Long-winded and largely irrelevant, the main object seems to have been to wear down the audience and jury.

to Catholics; indeed, the very thought could only do him dishonour. All the same, some of the persons who affirmed this are still alive, even if others are already dead. They insist that they received these promises from the king's own mouth. They are men, moreover, of such worth and quality that one cannot easily deny them credit.

No one could doubt that it suited the king at the time. It was an important factor in his situation that the catholics of England should consider him to be not so much an enemy as one inclined to favour them, and willing, if only in part, to make their load lighter. He well knew how much difficulty they could have made for him if they had made up their minds that he was their enemy and persecutor. There can be no doubt that the catholics were quite convinced that the king made those promises, and there was some better foundation for this belief than the general rumour which circulated at the time. The considerable joy and alacrity with which they received him is sufficient witness of their attitude. Even his favourites, not to mention many who were not, spread word everywhere not only of what has been said above, but even that he would put up no strong resistance to becoming a catholic himself. This last, no doubt, was a monumental fiction. He was always what he is now, a most convinced upholder of Calvinism. He has always declared himself to be such, and anyone who hoped that he might become a catholic, and dared to show it, could be sure of bringing a great deal of trouble on himself. The Earl of Salisbury made this quite clear in the same place at the same time.

When the Earl of Northampton had finished his speech, the Earl of Salisbury took up the thread to support the same argument. He took pains to free the king from every implication of having failed in any promise to catholics. The main point of his proof was that the king had always shown himself firm in his own religion, and quite inimical to the spread of catholicism. After coming to England, he could never bear with patience the least reference to toleration, or even connivance in that field. Although Sir Everard Digby was related to him by marriage, the earl felt obliged to point out that he had done His Majesty great wrong in making public something so false and prejudicial to him. In fact, it was completely repugnant to king and council that it should be believed of His Majesty that he had promised the catholics alleviation of their lot. They did not

Ein Spruchwort ist vō alters gstelt
Ein Krah sich zu der andern gsellt
Solchs sicht man hie auff diesem Blatt.
Da sich ein Rott versamblet hatt
Etlich Englischer Edelleut.
Zuthun das Gott höchlich verbeut.
Der Ruhrsinck Robert Catesby,
Der ander war Thomas Percy,
Allbeide von edlem geschlecht,
So man daselbst nennet Schilt knecht.
Diese brachten noch mehr ins Spiel
wiewol es war ihr eigen will,
Dann wer gern dantzt dē ist gar gut
Pfeiffen, das er bald sprungen thut
Robert winter wolte nicht seyn
Der letzst. brauchet mit sich vmb
Sein Bruder in solch hellisch verbund
Iahn vnd Christoffel wright zur Stu
ihrn willen theten auch ergeben.
welchs sie beud Kostet ihr leben.
Robert Bates sein Herrn getreuw
wolt seyn. Welchs ihn hernach geruw
Der beste Mann/meyns hinder sich
war Guido Faukes, welcher sich
Anzuzunden hat vnternommen
Das Fewr hernach, sein noch komm
In dieser Gsellschaft, Digby, Grant,
Rockwoud, Keyes, andr Vngenant.
Ihr

Robert
Winter

Christopher
wright

Iohn
wright

Bates

Conspiran Angli, moliti perede regem.
Et regnum, perdunt seqr caputq suum.
Supplicium specta, lector: mirabor, m vllum
Si pectus sceleris tanta libido cadat

Anno 1606.
Menæ. Feb.

Voicy (amy lect
ilz ont este traine
mis sur vn banc, et
en haulteur et les

THE CONSPIRATOR

Guido Fawkes   Robert Catesby   Thomas Winter

Ihr Anschlag war zu rotten auß
Den König sampt dem gantzen Rath
Des Parlaments durch eingelegt
Pulfer: der Rath übel ausschlegt.
Vnd Komt an Tag gar wunderbar
Durch einen Brief der anschlag gar:
Etlich seind in der Flucht erschlagen,
Die andre hat man bei dem Kragen
Genommen vnd in Gfangnuß gstellt,
Vnd nach dem das vrtheil gefellt,
Seind etliche auff Hurden glegt,
Vnd zum Galgen hinauß geschlept
Ein Strick ihn vmb den Halß gethan,
Ans Galgenholtz gehencket an
Doch von stundan abgesnitten:
Auff einer Banck bald in der muße
Der Büch eröffnet s'Ingeweid
Geworffen in ein Fewr bereit:
Das Gottloß Hertz ihn vmb den Mund
Geschlagen vnd darauff zur stund
Der Kopff abghauwen. vnd endlich
Der Leib getheilet in vier Stuck,
Welch hie vnd da seind auffgehangen
Die Köpff gesteckt auff eysern Stäge
Vnd offentlich der gantzen welt
Zu einem Schauspiel furgestelt.
Sich das ist der Verrähter Lohn:
So muß auch allen andren gehn

angellant von Leben zum tod hingerichtet worden

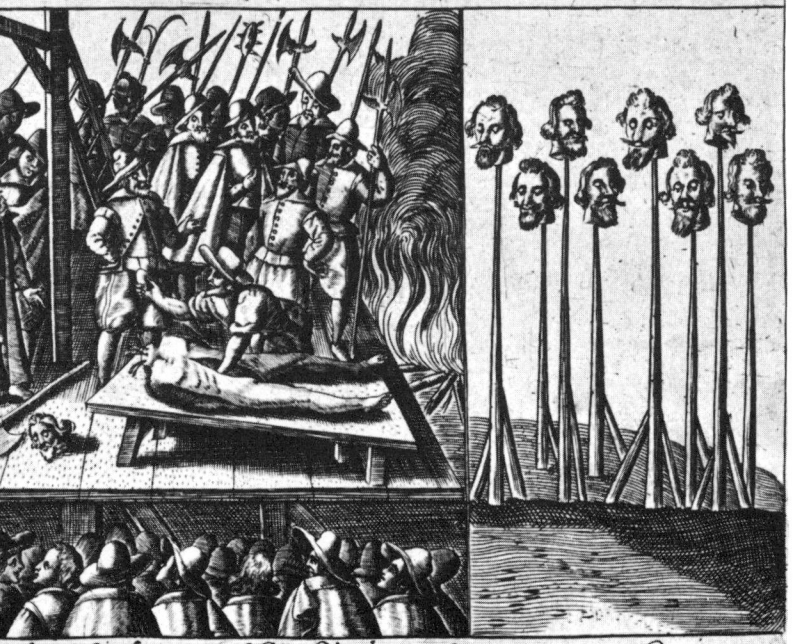

ne les conspirateurs contre le Roy D'angleterre sont executez a mort. Premierement
ras au lieu du supplice, et pendus a vne potence, mais incontinent oster, puis on les a
ventre, et leurs iettez le coeur a la face, en apres escartelez, les quartiers pendus
sur des perces de fer, et les entreilles brule.

THEIR EXECUTION

wish to be thought other than capital enemies of the papists' religion. In fact, it was believed that Sir Everard did not get the favour he asked for of being beheaded simply because he broadcast these hopes entertained by catholics; hopes conceived from the promises and fine words given them by the king while he was still in Scotland. This, of course, was before he was assured of succeeding in England. It was therefore concluded that the knight, no less than the others condemned to die, should suffer the usual death of those executed for treason. That is, he should be hanged, drawn and quartered. The sentence was carried out on Digby with more than ordinary cruelty, as we shall describe later.

After receiving sentence, all the accused were taken back to prison until the Thursday and Friday following. On those days they were led forth to die at the place of execution. Only Mr John Wintour was excluded, the youngest of the three brothers. He was executed later in Worcester, as we shall see. So on Thursday, 30 January, four of the conspirators were drawn on hurdles from the Tower of London to the piazza before Saint Paul's Cathedral. These were Sir Everard Digby, Mr Robert Wintour, John Grant and Thomas Bates. They made Sir Everard ascend the scaffold first for execution. After he had spent a little while in silent prayer, which he did devoutly, he was called on, as custom is, to acknowledge his fault and the treason for which he had to die. He admitted the deed, but declared at the same time that revenge had been no part of his intention, any more than the increase of his own wealth and renown. His one idea had been to free the catholics from their harsh persecution, and to plant catholicism anew in the kingdom . . . He did not recognize in what he had done any offence against God. However, he did admit to having offended the laws of the land, according to which he had been condemned to die. This did not cause him much sorrow. Indeed, he had too deep a faith, and too much regard for his religion, to think much of loss or injury in this life.★

★ There is no reliable, contemporary account of the executions. Everything was carried out as hurriedly as the trials. They also took place not at the accustomed Tyburn gallows, but those on Thursday, 30 January, at the west end of Saint Paul's Cathedral 'over against the Bishop of London's home' (Birch, op. cit., p. 48); and those on 31 January near Westminster Hall, 'in the old palace' (ibid.). To make even more certain that there would be few witnesses, the Lord Mayor instructed the alderman of every city ward to

The calvinist ministers who were present exhorted him to pray with them according to custom, and so to recommend his soul to God. This he unhesitatingly refused to do, saying that he wished none to share his praying save those who were one with him in faith. For that reason he called on the catholics present to help him with their devout prayers. He asked them to pray to God for him, and with him. When he had said this, he began to pray himself with such manifest devotion that many were moved by it. None who saw it failed to be impressed. When he had finished his prayers, he stood up, and bowed to all the gentlemen on the scaffold: first of all to the men of title, then to the other gentlemen and knights. His manner was extremely gracious, and he observed all customary and due courtesy. At the same time, he showed warmth of feeling, and even light-heartedness. So much so that when they recalled it afterwards, they could not remember seeing in him any sign of fear in the presence of death. He took his leave of them in much the same way as if he were departing from the court or city to go home. For all that, he showed so much devotion and fervour in his prayers that many of the bystanders, even those who were protestant, said openly that they considered him to be among the elect and on his way to heaven. They could only hope that when their own time came to die, they would find themselves equally well disposed for it.

The cruelty they used at Digby's execution was extraordinary. It was the usual practice, and in accordance with law, that those who were executed for treason were allowed to hang until they were half-dead. In his case, however, he was scarcely allowed to fall from the ladder before the rope was cut down. He was thus completely conscious and alive, save for the fact that in his fall from the gallows he hit his forehead, and was left somewhat stunned. But he offered no resistance while they cut up his stomach, and chopped him into

'cause one able and sufficient person, with a halberd in his hand, to stand at the door of every several dwelling-house in the open street in the way that the traitors were to be drawn towards the place of execution, from seven in the morning until the return of the Sheriff' (quoted HRW, p. 224, from Repertories in the Town Clerk's office: printed in D. Jardine, *Criminal Trials*, II, London, 1846, pp. 181–2). Presumably this precaution was taken on both days. There is a similar dearth of any impartial eye-witness account of the execution of the equally problematic traitor Edward Squire, involved in the plot of 1598–9 called after him.

four pieces. As usage was, his heart and entrails were thrown into the fire. After that, his head was hacked from the trunk and shown to the people. It was noticeable that there was no discernible alteration in his face and features. He seemed to have the same look and manly aspect that he had when alive. One incident I will mention here which was recounted by witnesses most worthy of belief. Sir Everard left behind him two sons who were but small children. The elder was not more than four years old. The younger was still a baby, some twenty-one months old. These innocents were then in the arms of their nurse, some sixty miles distant from London. At the very moment when their father died, the younger child smiled, and showing signs of unusual happiness, cried out 'Tata, Tata, Tata!' He had never said a word before this. Nor did he say another for a long time afterwards.

After Sir Everard was executed, Mr Robert Wintour, the elder of the Wintour brothers, went to his death with considerable firmness and outward calm. He was considered to be one of the best and wisest men in Worcestershire. The manner of his death was not much different from Sir Everard's, although before his execution he used very few words. He remained rather withdrawn into himself, and was obviously praying. The third to die was Mr John Grant. He also showed great courage and much devotion. He was asked if he was not very sorry for his mistake, since it was a crime of such enormous proportions. He replied that that was not the time or place to discuss cases of conscience. He had come there to die, not to dispute matters of that kind. In any case, he referred himself to those who knew more about such matters than he did, and in the last resort to the decision of the Catholic Church. For all his other faults and errors he asked pardon of God. The last of these four was Thomas Bates. He acknowledged that he had been guilty of an offence before God, his king and his country. At least, this is what he said if we are to believe the pamphlet which was published after the death of the conspirators under the name of a certain 'T.W.'* It is, in any case, full of lies and blasphemies.

Bates claimed that he was induced to do what he did by Mr Robert Catesby, his master. If this is true, one can see how heavily purely human motives and arguments weighed with him, and one

* See note * p. 203 above.

can therefore judge how much credence should be given him, if any at all, on other occasions when such motives operated very strongly. As for the rest, I have heard that he died with much more courage than some expected of him, and to the great edification of the catholics who were present. I myself came up to London the Saturday following, and I made a careful enquiry into details of this kind. This is how these four men came to end their lives that day. So great was the impression made on many by the first three, that they returned home full of wonder and even compassion. In particular they were much grieved at the fate of Sir Everard. Little else was spoken of for some days except the great courage and nobility of soul which he showed when he came to die.

The following day was a Friday. The second group of four were drawn like the first on hurdles from the Tower of London but this time to the Old Palace of Westminster, or more correctly to a piazza adjoining the Parliament-house. The names of these four were: Mr Thomas Wintour, second of the three Wintour brothers, Ambrose Rookwood, Robert Keyes and Guy Fawkes. As they passed down the Strand, the hurdle came opposite the house where Ambrose Rookwood's wife was lodging. One of them gave Mr Ambrose a reminder as he had promised to do. Rookwood now opened and raised his eyes which before this he had kept shut during the whole journey in order to be more recollected in his prayer. He raised himself up as far as he could on the hurdle. He then cried aloud to his wife, who stood waiting for him in a window, 'Pray for me! pray for me!' She likewise cried back at the top of her voice. 'I will do that! And you be of good heart, and offer yourself to God! He gave you to me, and I freely and willingly restore you to Him.'

When they arrived at the place of execution, the first to be led on to the scaffold was Mr Thomas Wintour, since he was one of the chief organizers of the plot from its first beginnings. He said that he died a catholic, and gave no sign of wishing to say more. Indeed, he seemed to be intent on his devotions. But many of the spectators knew that he was a man of sound judgement and a clear and fluent speaker. They made it clear that they wanted a speech from him. When he became aware of this, he told them that it was not the time or place to deliver discourses. Nor did he think it necessary seeing that he had already expounded the whole course, progress, and intention of the plot to the complete satisfaction of the Privy Council. He therefore asked all present to rest content that he should spend the little of life that still remained to him with God his Creator. To assist him in this, he called on the catholics present to help him with their prayers. One thing, however, he did wish to say. He understood that a number of jesuits in the kingdom had been defamed as accomplices of the plot. Among them was Father Tesimond. Wintour now felt himself obliged to speak the truth about this, which was that those Fathers were completely free of blame. Especially true was this of that priest with whom he had enjoyed more familiarity than the others. He had even more confidence in him than in his fellow priests, since he had been his own spiritual Father. This should not prejudice him in any way; especially since he wished to offer unequivocal testimony to his innocence of the deed now that he, the speaker, stood at the point of death.

After this gentleman came Mr Ambrose Rookwood. He spoke shortly about himself and his intentions. He said that he died a catholic. He begged the king to show favour to his wife and sons. He also called on God, with much devotion, to have mercy on the land and restore it to the true and ancient religion. He prayed that the king and queen and their progeny might also be converted. He was then put to death, giving evidence of the same kind of christian goodness that he had shown in his life. The onlookers could scarcely restrain their tears since he had been well known and loved for his exemplary behaviour while he lived. The third man to die was Mr Robert Keyes. Whoever wrote the little pamphlet spoke slanderously of him. He claimed that he threw himself off the ladder like a man in desperation; with so much violence, in fact, that he broke the rope. This was altogether false, as all those who were present knew too well. I myself enquired into this particular from those who actually saw and noted all that happened. I heard them say with my own ears that this gentleman died so devoutly and well that it aroused no little admiration on the part of many who were present. It is true that, when he was asked if he did not now regret the plot and recognize as grave sin ever having begun it, he still refused to see any wrong in it. All he would admit was that the conspiracy had its unfortunate aspects.

Mr Guy Fawkes, the man who was to have fired the powder,

was the last of the eight to complete this final act of the tragedy. His weakness was such that he could scarcely go up the ladder. He said little, but made it clear that he would die fearlessly and with much devotion and confidence in God. If it were not beside my purpose, I would like to note down here some evident and considerable lies which were printed in the little book of which we have spoken. It would have been useful to let the reader see how, without shame or scruple, our enemies are wont to lie even about matters witnessed by so many people. The execution at that time provided a very good example of it. But this chapter is already rather longer than the others. Moreover, I have taken it upon me to write up simply the history of those events as faithfully as I can. It is not really part of my task to refute the lies and ill-natured gossip of others. That little book is full of this kind of thing. I will finish my chapter here. I will then go on to describe events as they fell out after the death of these gentlemen.*

* At the end of the text as printed here, the MS has 'Cap. 13' – chapter thirteen. Evidently, the present work is incomplete. It is likely that the narrator intended to produce a work covering much the same ground as John Gerard's narrative. This had seventeen chapters in all, chapters 13 to 16 dealing with the trial and execution of the jesuits, and the last being 'a catalogue' of the penal laws against catholics in the time of Elizabeth I and James I (see John Morris, *The Condition of Catholics* . . ., pp. 224–331).

Appendix 1

Francis Tresham escapes from the Tower?

MOST STUDENTS of the subject agree that Tresham's death in the Tower is prominent among the lesser mysteries surrounding the great mystery. In the translator's view, the surviving evidence, such as it is, bears the interpretation that Tresham was in fact allowed to escape. The idea is not absurd on the face of it. Even without the connivance of the authorities, at least three people have achieved that feat, including the jesuit, John Gerard, Tresham's contemporary. The rôle of the latter in the plot seems to have resembled Monteagle's rather than Percy's or Catesby's. If so, it would have been reasonable to allow him, like Monteagle, to slip through the net. Certainly, the circumstances of his alleged demise suggest contrivance. We have only Salisbury's insufficient word that Tresham had 'been a long time subject' to the 'natural sickness' of which he died.* The rapidity of his death suggested nothing that was chronic. Some curiously cryptic utterances of Sir William Waad also become remarkably clear on the hypothesis of Tresham's escape. 'For my own opinion, if he escape, it must be by great care, and God's providence, that he may die of that kind of death he most deserves.'† And again, 'I find his friends were marvellous confident if he had escaped this sickness, and have delivered out words in this place that they feared not the course of justice.' Not only the manner

* Win. II, p. 189: though it is true that while he was in Newgate in 1601, he contracted 'a dangerous sickness by the loathsomeness of the place' (JRD, XXXI, p. 258).
† Sal. Cal., xvii, p. 553; and next quotation, Vaux, pp. 331–2. For a reconstruction, admittedly inadequate, of the possible sequence of events, see EGF, chapter 20.

of his death, but also of his burial was extremely obscure. Indeed, it adds up to the fact that we do not know precisely how, when or even where this event took place – if it did.

Tresham's flight would doubtless have been assisted by the fact that he already had a licence to travel which included facilities for taking horses and servants. It was issued on 2 November 1605, well inside the date when all would agree that the government had at least a fair idea of what was going on. That he intended to go abroad was confirmed by a note in Coke's hand, presumed to be of November 1605. 'About All Hallowtide last, Lewis and Francis Tresham offered to sell their chamber in the Temple, saying they would travel, and sold it.'* If Francis was allowed this privilege, what had he done to deserve it? Certainly, he had given only doubtful allegiance to the catholic cause for some years past, and had in fact been spying on his neighbours. Most recently, while in the Tower, Tresham made a statement to the effect that he had not seen Garnet in sixteen years, when in fact he had seen him in a matter of months before.† This was used very effectively at Garnet's trial to make both of them appear prevaricators, and men whose word could not be trusted. Garnet would doubtless have been convicted in any case, but skilfully used by Coke, Tresham's statement created a predicament which made the jesuit's condemnation seem more in accordance with reason and justice.

The best clue, though admittedly not sufficient to establish final certainty regarding Tresham's escape, occurred in a letter of Dudley Carleton to Sir Thomas Edmondes, bearing date 1 December, and written from Calais. Carleton was an able and observant man, and came to enjoy considerable success as a diplomat, being created the first Lord Dorchester. Carleton mentioned seeing at that time two Englishmen who evidently did not wish to be recognized, and had all the appearance of having 'stolen over'. They had almost no luggage, and avoided conversation. 'One of them looked like Francis Tresham.'‡

Before we attempt to follow Tresham's trail further into Europe, certain objections must first be met. The most serious is presented

* See chapter 4, n. (†) p. 77 above: and Sal. Cal., xvii, p. 528.
† See EGF, plate III, at p. 144 and pp. 232–3.
‡ ibid., p. 206.

by certain documents, apparently signed by Tresham, and certainly dated, though not by him, after the time when on this thesis he was supposed to be in Europe. The only lengthy document in Tresham's hand, however, is his 'voluntary declaration' of 13 November 1605. Written the day after his arrest, it falls well inside what all would agree to be the period of his imprisonment. But there are also clearly dated letters from Sir William Waad. The best known, perhaps, is that of 23 December, in which he tells Salisbury of Tresham's death at 2 a.m. that morning.* In the circumstances, however, it seems legitimate to appeal to forgery and misdating to explain documents which were intended to deceive posterity, perhaps, even more than contemporaries, very few of whom would see them. There is always a danger of appealing too freely to the *deus ex machina* of forgery to explain away unwanted evidence. Nevertheless, no one can deny the extensive resort to this expedient on the part of the authorities as shown by Garnet's letters to Anne Vaux. Nor need one suppose this was the only occasion on which it was used. Mr Ross-Williamson, following John Gerard, S.J., concluded reasonably enough that the Wintour confession at Hatfield on 23/25 November 1605 was a forgery throughout.† If so, there would have been very little difficulty in reproducing a few of Tresham's signatures, or adding misleading dates to letters by the hand of Coke, Waad, or other trusted servants of the government. The fact that Tresham was allowed access by his servant, his wife Anne, and her maid, Joan Sisor, was an extraordinary circumstance; something not allowed to any other prisoner. True, there was the pretext of Tresham's failing health. But it is highly coincidental that Tresham should have been the only conspirator afflicted in this way at this

---

* Given in extenso in HRW, p. 198, and Vaux, pp. 331–2.
† HRW, pp. 247–50: see also chapter 11 of this work, n. (*) p. 186. I am grateful to Miss P. Renold for bringing to my attention Arthur Gregory's letter to Salisbury seemingly of May 1606. After referring to his 'other secret services', Gregory says, 'Your Lordship hath had a present trial of that which none but myself hath done before, to write in another man's hand, and discovering the secret writing, being in blank, to abuse a most cunning villain in his own subtleties, leaving the same at last in blank again; wherein though there be difficulty, their answers show they have no suspicion' (SP14, vol. 24, No. 38). This document was first noticed seemingly, by J. H. Pollen, S.J., in *Father Henry Garnet and the Gunpowder Plot*, London, 1888, p. 29 and n.

time. Certainly, if he was allowed to escape from the Tower disguised as his wife or maid, or even as his servant, Vavasour, he merely anticipated what the Countess of Nithsdale achieved in far more difficult circumstances in 1716. Her husband, the earl, disguised as his wife, managed to slip past the guards and out of the Tower – and with no one's connivance.

There is the further curious fact that Tresham's 'dying note'* was held up, as Tresham's servant William Vavasour confessed, 'about three weeks and odd days', before it was delivered by Anne Tresham to Sir Walter Cope to deliver in his turn to the Earl of Salisbury. Francis probably escaped on 21 November, old style. Since the delay given is not precise, the difference between old and new style dating would still allow for a sufficiently good correspondence between the time when Tresham may have been actually seen by Carleton on the continent, and the alleged date of his death in the Tower. In any case, official dating on the documents seems to have been deliberately smudged. William Vavasour's examination† was dated 24 March, altered from 22 March, in Coke's hand, while the date 23 March appears in Waad's hand. No date is indicated by the examinee.

On the whole, the families of the conspirators received short shrift. Bates's wife was allowed to keep a modest sum of money, but the estates of the rest were ruthlessly parcelled out among courtiers and others in the next few years. Francis Tresham's family, however, seems to have escaped vicarious retribution. Lady Muriel, or Meryll, Tresham, Francis's mother, was made the administratrix of her husband's estate as if Francis had never inherited. Thus she 'retained the leasehold property for the discharge of the debt, and lands were held in jointure by both his [Lewis Tresham's] mother and his brother's [Francis] widow, Anne'.‡ With the disappearance

---

* EGF, plate III, at p. 144.

† GPB, 207: see EGF, plate II at p. 144. I am indebted to my colleague the Rev. W. K. L. Webb, S.J., for supplying, or reminding me of, evidence which makes it clear that the date of Carleton's letter mentioned above, was old style, that is 21 November 1605. This puts the date of Tresham's escape at about 20 November, perhaps earlier.

‡ M. E. Finch, 'Five Northamptonshire Families 1540–1640', article in *Northants Record Society*, vol. xix, Oxford, 1956, pp. 93–4. See also PRO, E. 124, vol. 3, ff. 63v–5r.

of Francis from the scene, 'the main part of the estate now passed to [his] younger brother Lewis. Since he was the second son and had not been bound with his father, he was not liable for the discharge of his debts. The burden was shouldered by Lady Tresham. Honour alone impelled her, for she was under no legal obligation to pay debts in excess of her husband's personal estate. Yet she spent the rest of her life on the task.' This task included 'vexatious lawsuits' which were presumably also expensive. According to one authority, 'Francis Tresham's reckless and unstable character must be reckoned a major cause of Sir Thomas's financial difficulties'. Lewis, no less, 'was impetuous and reckless, and incapable of . . . restraint', with the inevitable consequences for the family fortune.*

The second brother, Lewis, seems to have stayed in England, at all events at this time, and scarcely enters our story. The third brother, William, however, may have become very involved with Francis, with whom he seems to have maintained a relationship which possibly included genuine affection. William served in Sir William Stanley's regiment in Flanders. An entry in the register of soldiers in the Archdukes' forces, for 3 April (new style), 1598, records an order that William Tresham be paid 40 scudos or crowns a month, backdated as from 1 January 1596, which no doubt indicates when his service began.†

William Tresham's record of service was not distinguished. Certainly, by 1599 he had lost heart in the Spanish service. Henry Neville wrote to Cecil on 6 June (old style) to tell him that 'here are diverse English gentlemen that seem weary of their exile and evil entertainment among the Spaniards, who seek to have access unto me. Among the rest here is Charles Paget and one Mr Tresham, who was some time a Gentleman Pensioner.'‡ William Tresham did nothing to redeem his reputation in the eyes of either the Spanish or English authorities over the next few years. John Petit, one of Cecil's spies on the exiles, described him as 'a vain fellow, full of

* ibid., pp. 82 and 94.
† Archives du Royaume, Brussels; Secrétairerie d'Etat et de Guerre, 18, ff. 27v. and 62v. This is confirmed by Sim.E. 612, 'Tratado sobre los entretenidos ingleses a 10.iii.1596 a Bruselas'. This describes him as having served some months in the regiment of the Earl of Westmorland, but this seems to be an error (Loomie/Hicks transcripts, Mount Street).
‡ Win. I, p. 45. For what follows, see pp. 52, 71–2.

wind', and as a man who played 'with both hands . . . to be trusted by neither side'.* This, no doubt, explains why his attempts to get leave to return to England during this time met with no success.

The further details of William's undistinguished service in the Low Countries hardly concern us. It is, however, relevant to note that he wrote to his brother Francis on 29 September 1605, from Antwerp. The letter was addressed to 'Sir Thomas Tresham's house at Hoxton, near London', that is, the house of the Monteagle letter. It was annotated, 'This man is not at home'. William excused himself for not having written in a long time since there was no news worth sending. He described the attempt on Bergen op Zoom by Spinola's forces, with which he had been fighting. He referred to his captain as John Blount. Evidently Francis, for some reason, wanted William to learn Spanish, and that quickly. 'Sir', wrote William, 'you urged me much in your last letter for to be in a Spanish company, one reason was for to learn the language, the other for sooner preferment. For the language, I acknowledge it.' So he will spend three of four months in garrison at it 'under a Spaniard. For preferment there was never any of our nation that came to preferment under them.' Evidently, William is getting money from home. 'I pray you send my money to the same party as the last was. For he is one that here can show no kindness . . . ' William signed himself, 'Your brother in all service'.† It is possible that this letter was used, after its interception or surrender, as a basis for William Tresham's alleged examination alluded to above.

William must have been in the ranks, since he is not named in a list of men serving in Flanders seemingly of the late summer, or early autumn of 1605. 'The Lord Arundell's company' is mentioned, and Sir Thomas Studder as his sergeant-major, not having been replaced as yet by Sir Griffin Markham. Three Blounts were commissioned as captains, John, Thomas and James. 'Mr Faukes of Yorkshire' was mentioned along with 'Mr Whiting, ensign to Captain Orme', although there seems to be nothing else to suggest that Fawkes's connection with the English regiment in Flanders continued after the spring of 1603.‡ Of William, there is no further word,

* See Cal. S.P. Dom. 1598–1601, pp. 343, 358–9, 456.
† PRO, SP 77, vol. 7, part II, f. 235r. and v.
‡ PRO, SP 77, bundle 7, part I, ff. 329r.–32v.

apparently, whether in the Spanish army registers, or in the correspondence of the English ambassadors at Paris and Brussels including reports of spies and merchants. Perhaps this was due to the fact that Tresham was now indeed serving in a Spanish company under an assumed name. This would make him virtually untraceable in Spanish sources. While his alibi is thus not established, one can still doubt the veracity or authenticity of two documents which claim that William Tresham was in England at the time of the plot. Interrogatories in Coke's hand at Hatfield include the date in the endorsement, '1605', and the statement, 'Lewis Tresham, brother of Francis, hath a chamber in the Inner Temple. William Tresham, brother also of Francis. All three about the time in conference.'* An alleged examination of William Tresham follows one of Lewis Tresham, dated, 9 December 1605. William's examination, including the signature, is entirely in Popham's hand, though endorsed in Coke's hand. Popham's hideous scrawl cannot be mistaken for the rather careful and even elegant hand of William Tresham.† On the whole, these official documents may be designed to mislead us into thinking that William Tresham returned to England about this time, when in fact he did not. This deception may have had the further object of obscuring the trail of Francis if he were allowed to escape from England. According to William's above-mentioned examination, 'he went over to Ghent' – presumably from France. This was 'about midsummer last; and served under Mr John Blount, and was to have ten crowns a month, but received but a third part, and the residue came in the Archduke's debt. And so it is of other soldiers. And returned from thence about a fortnight after Michaelmas.'‡

Apart from the dubious fact of Tresham's return, all this has the ring of truth. Certainly, there are no other records to suggest that William Tresham was implicated in the plot, or that it was seen fit to implicate him. He may have been sent to England on the 'private word and passport' of the English ambassador at Paris or Brussels.

---

* Sal. Cal., xvii, p. 528.
† The Calendar (SP. Dom. p. 269) gives the date of this document as 9 December, but there is no indication of date on the original (SP 14, vol. 17, no. 23). Another example of William's genuine hand, with signature, is SP 12, vol. 282, f. 107r. (no. 45).
‡ SP 14, 17, no. 23.

The evidence has not survived. If he came to England, he was probably imprisoned in the Fleet. His brother, Francis, certainly was for some three months in 1591.* Was William the silent companion of Francis whom Carleton recognized near Calais? Tresham's licence of 2 November 1605 included permission to take with him 'two servants, three horses or geldings, and £50 in money with all other his necessaries' (*v. supra*). William might well have passed as a servant. It is also possible that William met Francis in Europe without ever having in fact returned home himself. On the other hand, a later reference suggests that this first stranger, whoever he was, arrived some little time before one of the Treshams, whom we may reasonably conclude was William. Meanwhile, some Englishman who wished to conceal his identity arrived at the English Embassy in Madrid in September 1606. The ambassador, Sir Charles Cornwallis, wrote of him to Salisbury in his dispatch of 17 September 1606. 'Such hath been the importunity of the gentleman named in the paper hereinclosed as I could have no rest with him till I promised to make his desires known unto your Lordship who, as he saith, doth also know himself by some late events. I am taught how to recommend any that hath given proof of evil affection either to religion or government of my country. I therefore refer him and what he would to your lordship's consideration.'†

Who was this man whose identity had to be kept secret? He may have been one of two men who lived at the embassy for a time, both of whom had a past to hide. At all events, neither could have been the Tresham of whom Cornwallis wrote more than two months later as if he had just arrived, and whom, without rashness, we may take to be William. For on 26 November (old style) 1606, Sir Charles Cornwallis reported to Salisbury, 'Hither is lately come one Mr Tresham, who continued so long a prisoner in the Fleet. In what condition he departed England I know not, but hither I suppose he cometh upon a begging errand. Men of his condition bring their mouths filled with complaints of the rigour there used against those of their religion, and serve to keep the hatred and mislike of this nation kindled. But this poor gentleman (having been now with

---

* See JRD, xxii (London, 1901), p. 103. Order to the Warden of the Fleet on 4 December 1591, to release Francis T., who has been there since September.
† BM Cotton MS, Vespasian C.IX, ff. 522v.–3r. Copy.

me) protests his faith and allegiance . . . [T]he consideration of what he has been, his years and lamentable complaints, do much affect me. He confesseth his departure without either taking of the oath, or licence of His Majesty. Doubt not to obtain leave, as he says, was the cause.' However, the next day, the ambassador found his heart much hardened by reading a Spanish translation of the laws against recusants passed by the English parliament.* In view of this circumstance, and what a man of Cornwallis's intelligence must have deduced from the mere presence and speech of such a gentleman as William, it is sufficiently unlikely that the latter came to enjoy any position of even modest responsibility in the ambassador's household. Still less that a series of letters coming from a man who could well have been a Tresham would have been sent to Thomas Wilson under an alias for William.

From May 1607, in fact, date a few letters written from the English embassy in Madrid by John Jude and Matthew Bruninge. The two were obviously close friends, and had been so for some time. Both names seem to have been pseudonyms. Bruninge is of more interest to us since he may well have been none other than Francis Tresham. It could be of interest to the reader to consider certain unpublished passages so that he may arrive at his own conclusions – or perhaps no conclusion! Certainly, the known examples of Tresham's writing resemble Bruninge's hand to a remarkable degree.† They resemble William Tresham's hardly at all. One cannot say that Bruninge and Francis Tresham wrote identically, but one could claim that the differences are those that a man might introduce who wished to disguise his own hand. There seems to be nothing to invalidate this conclusion from the little we know about an authentic Matthew Bruninge who lived near this time.‡ Bruninge and Jude corresponded mainly with Thomas Wilson, the

* This was presumably the pamphlet, 'Las leyes nuevamente hechas en el Parlamento de Inglaterra este año de 1606 contro los Catolicos Ingleses . . .' (Copy in Sim.E., 2512.)
† EGF, plate IV, at p. 145; see also the plate included in this work.
‡ See BM Add. 37130, a volume of pedigrees by C. A. Buckler: 'Illustrations and venerable proofs for the pedigree of Anthony Bruninge of Wemering in Hampshire'. On f. 7v. is a reference to 'Matthew B., eldest son of Thomas, living in Ireland in 1629'. There is no other Matthew Bruninge noted, at any rate until after 1750.

Earl of Salisbury's secretary. It is evident in Bruninge's letter to Wilson of 9 September 1607 that Bruninge owes a good deal to his mother; and that the lady is not over-friendly to Wilson. 'It doth not a little grieve me to hear that my mother should be so irrespective of you, from whom (in my behalf) she hath received so much good . . . My mother is a woman and may be overcome and persuaded to her own hurt; much more to mine. I beseech your worship, let not your care forsake me herein. I am fatherless, and have none to rely on but you, my good master, to whom I do wholly give myself to be ruled and commanded in all that I am or shall be . . . For the money, I am very sorry it hath caused you trouble so much. I was told to direct them to you, not for payment but for procurement of it from my mother, who I did little think would have been out of the town.

'The charges of the making of a suit, of my passage, and the company from which I could not square without some note of singularity of a more than six weeks expense in so dear a country did draw some money, though indeed I came well-furnished yet not for any want but rather seeing the conveniency with which I might take it without trouble to myself or friends, did indeed, presume of so much being but the moity of what remains due from my mother, with purpose not to expect more till I return into England, which I think will be within the compass of the year.'*

The point of Bruninge's return is important in attempting to identify him with Francis Tresham since the latter's passport, issued on 2 November 1605, was for two years only – an unusual arrangement since most travel licences were made out for three years. Tresham would thus have been obliged to return 'within the compass of the year'. Bruninge had written four such letters to Wilson since his departure, the latest being of 20 June. They were sent by Richard Cockes at Bayonne, an English merchant and government agent. Bruninge promised to send back worthwhile information but hitherto there had not been much 'by reason the king seldom comes hither, we few times to go abroad (whereby we should observe anything) but with my Lord [ambassador] in visits or suchlike'. The letters of Cockes make no mention of Bruninge, even by allusion, as it seems. Jude, writing to Wilson on 1 October

* PRO, SP 94, vol. 14, part I, f. 130r. and v. Signed holograph.

1607, old style, tells him, 'Mr Bruninge . . . carrieth great advantage over the rest that came with him both in my lord's favour, respect . . . and proficiency in the language.'*

Bruninge did not return to England, but by 16 April 1608 he had made no little progress in the ambassador's confidence. As Jude wrote to Wilson, Sir Charles Cornwallis told 'Mr Bruninge, who in his own modesty forbeareth to declare it . . . that now putting some order in his house, and having had both trial and liking of his vigilance and discretion, he would expect service and credit answerable to the place he was to hold, and therefore, willed him to provide and fashion himself accordingly. Mr Bruninge is so jealous of your opinion and timorous to be thought wasteful as he forbeareth to signify any want in a confident hope that his mother's blessing is on the way towards him.'† Jude puts in many good words for his friend: 'I assure you his care to live within his compass, his discreet and winning carriage towards all men hath been such as though his expenses hath been far less that that of those who came with him . . . His opinion and reputation hath been much more than either of theirs.' This was said not to disparage the other two, whoever they were, 'but that you undertaking the truth, being his commander and undertaker to his lordship, might be pleased to remember his mother of the chargeableness of this country, and the expectation we all have of her son's good proceedings, if by his withdrawing or delaying his maintenance it be not hindered. For the other I have not a little marvelled with myself that so dear and loving a mother as he esteems her to be hath given so little proof of her tenderness and care over him, so toward and so well-deserving a son, as in the space of one whole year not to have sent so much as one letter or tittle of her love and memory to him.' If Lady Muriel Tresham were, indeed, the mother in question, she would have been too preoccupied with paying family debts to have money over for making goodwill gestures even to a son in exile.

On 16 July 1608 Jude again approached Wilson on behalf of Bruninge – now spelt Browninge. 'His only fear is, having received lately £10, and now sending a bill for £5 more, lest your worship should conceive him to be wasteful and riotous of his money, and

* ibid., part II, f. 167r. From Madrid – signed holograph.
† ibid., vol 15, part I, 49r.–50v. Signed holograph.

not careful to spend it to such ends and uses as may be for his good.'★ Things often cost twice as much in Spain as in England, it was claimed. Wilson should consider that 'his fashion serving my Lord in stead of gentleman-usher, and chief waiter, cannot be main-tained without some change and charge. Besides, the making of new apparel, repairing old, washing and all other necessary besides diet for himself and chamber, are not to be had without money, whereof he hath not a penny but what he receives from thence.' This was, of course, an extremely curious arrangement for a normal member of the staff who would presumably have been paid, like the rest, from the ambassador's allowance. 'And therefore I doubt not but his mother, understanding so much from your report, will be content to allow with all readiness and willingness that money which he hath made bold to charge your worship with.' By way of conclusion, Bruninge's mother was to be urged to send him over a gold chain, or £20 with which to buy one, so that her son could keep up with the Jones's of Cornwallis's household. 'For the forthcoming of it, my Lord is content to undertake, and stand charged to his mother for the answering of it at his coming home.' Jude made it clear in a letter to Wilson of 18 January 1608/9, old style, that while he had no money himself, he relied for everything on Cornwallis. Jude, fond of a nautical metaphor, may well have thought that with his return to England, his own ship might well come home if he maintained friendship with a man such as Bruninge whose background sug-gested ease if not affluence.†

On 30 November 1608 Bruninge wrote himself to 'Mr Pyrkins', who represented 'his late father'. He offers him love and service. He also offers Pyrkins information on political affairs in Spain in a way which strongly suggests that Pyrkins may be none other than a name for Cecil. Bruninge sends messages to his mother and brother, and encloses a letter for the latter to Mr Wilson, by whose means he is where he is, and 'hopes to attain better fortunes'. He wants 'the scutcheon of his arms, with the crest fairly drawn'. The letter is partly in cipher and without address.‡

A letter of 30 November 1608 (old style) was apparently dictated to one of the embassy clerks. The writer thanks his cousin for a letter of 17 June 1608. He refers to his duty to respect his late

★ ibid., ff. 83r.–84v.   † ibid., vol. 16, part I, f. 5r.   ‡ Sal. Cal., xx, p. 273.

father's friends among which the addressee must be numbered; although, 'if you presumed he loved you not in the same kind as he did, these words of mine would be in vain to persuade a belief'. The writer refers to himself as his father's 'next succeeding heir'. Had the father's abilities . . . been correspondent to his desires, my fortunes might have sailed with a broader sail . . . In the behalf of my deceased father, I represent unto your good acceptance my love and careful endeavours to serve and wait upon you, for your kind care of my careful mother. I owe you very much, and will pay you for it the tribute of my love till death deprive me of the heart which will force me to neglect it.' Fulsome assurances follow of his readiness to serve his cousin. There is an apparent clue of identity in the mention of a specific name, but it does not take us far. 'I assure you that many times I have solemnized your remembrance in company of one Mr William Maund, who called you cousin, and (much to all griefs) was here unfortunately slain with his own sword.' No details are added.* He then proceeds to give, as he had apparently been told or encouraged to do, information on the scene in which he finds himself. With some reason, in view of the triviality of what he actually offers, he offers apology for his shortcomings as well as gratitude for an opportunity to have risen above them. 'I also thank you for employing me in a business of so much import though I am sorry I shall not be able to give you such satisfactory performance as I would, yet you shall always find in me the effect of diligence and care to supply the rest.' Further, 'I make no doubt but to better my former letters'. The writer could improve his performance with a little more instruction: 'if I did also know your purpose, and the end to what you would employ them, and to those whose view they should come, that I might address my methods to some serious style(?) not unbefitting the view of understanding censurers'. He is still 'in the infancy of experience', and bashful at offering anything to the 'eagle-witted judgment' of his recipient.

Later on, he returns to his own case. 'I am very glad that you are so near my mother, and am no less joyful to have received her blessing in such loving manner. And am also glad to hear of my

---

* Neither the Calendars of State Papers for the period nor the indices of persons in the HMC reports give any indication of a William Maund.

brother's health.' Returning to the subject of mother, 'I hope what she hath sowed in the ground of my preferment shall be increasingly reaped in the enlargement of my fortunes'. Love is also wished to the brother, and a letter enclosed to him by the hands of Mr Wilson. 'I think my present estate is not unknown to you, though my hopes may be some client to your understanding.' It is the 'loving favours' of Mr Wilson on whom the writer chiefly relies: 'by whom, indeed, I possess my present being here, and hope by his means to obtain better fortunes. Therefore I entreat you at your leisure to repair unto him, and take occasion (as my much well-willing friend) to thank him for his kindness . . . And so being yourself acquainted with so worthy a gentleman could do you no harm. He recommended me very dearly unto my lord and told him I was heir' – word originally in code – 'to £100 per annum . . . And truly I have been very much favoured of my honourable Lord: and Master Aight (?) wrote a very kind letter for me to my uncle Brunynge. Good cousin, I do beseech you to consider that now I am either rising or never. And my credit now to begin or never. It much imports me therefore that my mother at her house in London do so entertain any that come from here that I may be credited by it. For I doubt not but soon will I come.' He has maintained himself 'in very good fashion' since his first arrival. He is sorry if his mother finds it expensive, but hopes she will view such expenditure as a necessary step to his preferment. He wants a further £100 by the return of the messenger who will be going to England with this present letter, no doubt one among others. This sum would appear to be needed mainly for clothing and personal items: 'I must of force new apparel myself, which will not cost a little for here very shoemakers go in their velvet.' He had written on 25 October, but now apologized for not answering his 'cousin's' letter on that occasion, which was merely to ask his mother to pay a Mr Alexander Stafford the sum of £5. Like William Maund, this seems to be the unique entrance that Alexander Stafford makes on the stage of history.★

The general impression of this letter is, once again, that of a man who has something, or even a great deal, to conceal. It is difficult to know to what extent, if any, the names of persons may be taken

★ Salisbury MSS, vol. 195, no. 61: signed by Matthew Bruninge. No address, endorsed as 'to Mr Pyrkins'. Calendered in HMC 9, vol. XX (1608), p. 273.

literally. Evidently, it was not intended directly for the Earl of Salisbury, for the recipient is bidden to pay his own court to Thomas Wilson. The authentic Matthew Bruninge had only one cousin, according to the surviving genealogy. This was Richard Bruninge of Wemering, Esq., married to Eleanor or Ursula Vuedall, They were recusants, and in June 1608 the Lord Treasurer was directed by the Privy Council to grant John Person His Majesty's two parts of their land, as by law allowed and directed.* It is sufficiently unlikely that such a man would have been able to do any good in high places for Matthew, or if he had, that there would not have been some surviving record of the fact. Certainly, there is nothing to suggest that the authentic cousin of the bona fide Matthew Bruninge went by the name of 'Mr Pyrkins'.

'Matthew Bruninge', writing in the hand resembling Francis Tresham's, wrote to Thomas Wilson from Madrid on 24 March 1609. It was dated in new style, a useful reminder that we cannot presume without more ado that, even when they wrote from an English embassy abroad, English exiles necessarily wrote in the dating style of their own country. The letter contains a hint of anxiety, seemingly for the first time. Bruninge respectfully requests an answer to letters sent home by Adrian Tibault: 'I shall be glad to understand how you will be pleased to dispose of me if my lord stay another year'. A little later, apprehension breaks through. 'I do not a little fear that either you have forgotten me or are displeased with me, not having since July heard from you . . . but I hope you will not . . . leave to second your so good beginning of my fortunes which were they as high as hope may promise, or fortune perform, it should not be the least height of my happiness to offer them with myself at your command and service.' He ends somewhat lamely, 'If perchance my fortune prove blind and so keep me not worthy to be accounted other than in the number of the forgotten, I shall be sorry my fortunes corresponded not with my humble hopes that I might have approved my service and love by some performing thankfulness.'†

---

* PRO: Index 6803; Signet Office docquets for March 1608 to November 1610. Unfoliated.

† Salisbury MSS, vol. 195, no. 97; M. Bruninge to T. Wilson, from Madrid, 24 January 1609, new style. Signed holograph.

By March 1609 Jude seemed about to end his exile. On 5 April Bruninge was also contemplating return. 'And by Mr Grosley I wrote to my mother to send me £20 to the end I might come home not unprovided.'*

Jude seems to have made his way back to England in the entourage of the returning Cornwallis. He wrote from Dieppe on 17 October 1609, old style, to his future master, as we may presume, Thomas Wilson. Of Bruninge, there is, apparently, no further word. It is possible that he made his way to Rome, and was the 'Mr Tresham' mentioned by Persons in a letter of 22 July 1610.† Unfortunately, Persons, an old man now, and in fact on the brink of death, mentioned no christian name. With the end of the Dutch war against the Spanish domination, the soldier William Tresham could no longer look for employment in the army, and might well have made his way to Rome. On the whole, it was more likely to have been William than Francis who interviewed Persons. William eventually got back to England. 'In 1611, Lewis . . . leased a part of Rushton for 200 years to his brother-in-law, Sir Thomas Brudenell, and to his brother William Tresham, probably by way of mortgage. In November 1612, these lessees assigned the residue of the term to [William] Cokayne, providing that if £1,200 were paid to him at the end of two years, the assignment was to be void.'‡

Of Francis Tresham, or his problematic alias, nothing more is known to date. But there is no more absurd phrase in a historian's vocabulary than 'we shall never know'. Perhaps excavations at the Tower will one day unearth a hitherto unknown grave containing unimpeachable evidence that it once contained the body of Francis Tresham. Perhaps a continental record office, or a private archive in Britain, still holds the essential clues to Francis Tresham's survival long after 23 December 1605, the day he was supposed to have died.

---

* PRO, SP 94, vol. 16, part I, ff. 53r.–54v. To Wilson from Madrid.
† EGF, p. 209.
‡ M. Finch, op. cit., p. 95.

Appendix 2

The Monteagle Letter

A Handwriting Analysis by Joan Cambridge*

BEFORE CONSIDERING the possible authorship of this historic document, it is first necessary to assess whether, and if so to what degree, the script is disguised from the writer's normal graphic movement; then to determine the method of disguise adopted.

Examination of the original letter provides considerable evidence of deliberation and over-control, mainly in the form of abnormal increases in pressure, with marks where the pen momentarily rested.

It is also apparent that, contrary to his natural inclination, the writer was, in this document, doing his best to adhere to the basic structure of the contemporary formal script, so that the speed of its execution was artificially inhibited.

Perhaps the most interesting feature in respect of deliberation is the manner in which the 'd's are, with one exception, formed throughout.

The exception is the 'd' of 'frends' in line 1, and close inspection shows that initially this consisted of a fluent, slightly leftward movement. Then, as if aware that this personal gesture might disclose his identity, the writer amended the stroke so that it appears stilted and arhythmic, as also do the other 'd's in the document, indicating how self-consciously he penned them.

Furthermore, broken strokes, displaced movements and overall

* The publishers would like to thank the *Observer* newspaper for permission to reprint here the original of the report published by them in November 1967.

rigidity throughout the text, give adequate confirmation that the writing is disguised. However it is perhaps not without significance that Robert Cecil himself described the script as being so, for at that time knowledge of the principles and practice of Questioned Document Examination must certainly have been elementary.

Accepting that this anonymous letter is disguised, an attempt must then be made to break through the masked forms in order to obtain some indication of the writer's normal style.

Mention has already been made of the stilted 'd' forms which distort the naturally fluent movement in that specific letter, but in addition there is evidence of self-conscious control in respect of the lower loop of the 'g' form, suggesting an awareness of individuality in these extensions. Indeed in the enlarged sample of the last 2 lines of the text, it can be seen that 'god' was originally written as 'yod', as subconsciously he sought to avoid the use of the offending 'g'.

Also spontaneous writing habits occur throughout the text, of which the writer was unaware. Of these the serif-like stroke on the 'e' form is the most significant, since it appears throughout, although the habit of amplifying the 't'-bar stroke and the fluent 'h' and 's' forms must not be ignored in this respect.

Investigating the proposition that Robert Cecil himself penned the warning message, it is found from examination of original documents written and signed by him, that his natural graphic movement, normal pressure pattern and character of the stroke allow of this possibility.

Further to this, however, comparison of his spontaneous letter forms, particularly the 'h', 's' and 'e's, indicate definite similarities with those in the Monteagle letter.

In addition his naturally leftward flaring 'd' forms and highly individualistic 'g' movements are compatible with the restrictions exercised on those forms in disguise, while his habit of adding a stroke to his 'e's has a definite parallel in the anonymous note.

So on aggregate there is sufficient evidence to support an opinion that in all probability Cecil, himself, wrote the Monteagle warning.

HANDWRITING COMPARISON

The word 'frend 'in Cecil's ordinary writing, above the same word pluralled in the Monteagle letter.

1. Open serif.
2. Open serif-like stroke.
3. Fluent, slightly broad movement.
4. Fluent leftward-flaring stroke. No resting mark.
5. Resting marks (indicating writer not using his normal hand).
6. Heavy pressure, with awkwardly restricted movement.
7. Initial movement amended; result heavy and arhythmic.

Appendix 3

Francis Tresham, William Tresham and Matthew Bruninge
A comparative examination of handwriting by Joan Cambridge

IN INVESTIGATING the possibility of the common authorship of any two handwritten documents which purport to be executed by different individuals, there are certain factors which have to be taken into consideration.

Thus the dating of the documents is important, in order to establish the period of time which had elapsed between the execution of the one and the other. For at certain stages of life, marked changes in the quality of graphic expression are liable to occur, to the extent on occasions of giving the impression that two writers were involved, even when the authenticity of both specimens could be proved. While if, for example, marked stroke deterioration is seen to be present in one but not the other script executed only six months later, then it is unlikely that they share common authorship.

Also the effect on the stroke and on the letter forms of different writing materials can be considerable, again to the extent, on occasions, of giving an impression of dissimilarity even when it is admitted that two specimens were written by the same person.

While it can never be ignored that it is quite possible for a graphically fluent writer to so change his style over a period of months, that the initial impact is one of absolute difference between scripts executed before and after the change, especially as there will then be no evidence of deliberate disguise or conscious variation of the letter form.

In fact in such circumstances, similarity is generally found in the more subtle graphic indices and the script movements least accessible to conscious change.

Thus in making a comparative examination between the handwriting of Francis Tresham, when he wrote his Declaration on 13 November 1605, and that of the man known as Matthew Bruninge, who wrote from Madrid on 5 April 1609, it should not be ignored that in the three and a half years or so which had elapsed between these dates, Francis Tresham, if he had escaped from the Tower, would have sought to have lost his original identity.

In consequence he would also, most probably, have been aware of the need to adopt a somewhat different handwriting style. For it is evident from the records of their questioning, that both the Tresham brothers, William and Francis, were aware of the individuality of graphic expression, since both recognized that a particular book had been copied in the handwriting of one George Vavasour.

So it is not to be expected that obvious similarities of letter forms, of elaborated paraphs or of terminal strokes would be much in evidence. Rather must the proof of common identity be sought in such factors as the tension-release pattern of graphic movement shown in each script, the relative size ratios, the horizontal and vertical expansion, the degree and type of connectedness found in relation to the stroke quality and basic right or leftwardness.

In which respect it is found that Francis Tresham's acknowledged script of 1605 has, on the original document, a firm, coherent, lively stroke quality, with a slight tendency to flood the upper and lower loops, due to sudden increases in pressure. It is also right-slanted with a dominant angle of 50°, and large in its expansion with pronounced upper and lower extensions.

The overall graphic rhythm is good, and as well as there being a high degree of continuity, there are cleverly combined connecting movements throughout, such as those which frequently link the letter 't' with the following letter form.

Further to which, the script signed by Matthew Bruninge in Madrid, on 5 April 1609, also shows in the original document a firm, coherent, lively stroke quality, with a certain tendency to flood in the upper and lower extensions, due to irregularities in the pressure pattern. Indeed not only are these indices quite compatible with those assessed in respect of Francis Tresham's handwriting, but since only three and a half years would have elapsed in the life of the writer, if the documents do, in fact, show common authorship, it is not to be expected that marked changes would have occurred in his vital expressiveness, unless the earlier specimen showed symptoms of ataxia or stroke-disintegration, which it does not.

Thus because it can be shown that in addition to the stroke quality there is also a basis of similarity between the two scripts, by virtue of the right-slanted largeness of that signed Matthew Bruninge, with its predominant upper and lower expansions and underlying rhythm of tension and release, the next step is to examine closely the text of the latter, in order to ascertain whether there is any evidence of the cleverly combined connective movements, which mark Francis Tresham's hand.

For although there are definite dissimilarities of letter form and style throughout the two scripts, as has been explained, these are not necessarily of negative import in situations such as this, whereas the presence of unconsciously motivated movements of similar individuality, would be of positive significance.

In fact it is mainly in the variability of so many of the alphabetical forms of the script signed Matthew Bruninge, that the actual artificiality of that handwriting is disclosed. For it is found that such letter shapes as the 'f', the 'b' and the 'd' are rarely spontaneously executed, but rather are awkwardly drawn throughout, with increases of pressure which break the graphic rhythm, but which have not been caused by technical difficulties associated with the condition of pen or paper.

In which respect, when it is noted that in Francis Tresham's handwriting, it is these particular letter forms which are most individual in their execution, the significance of their stiltedness in Matthew Bruninge's script increases in import.

While when it is also found that definite similarities exist in respect of the 'L' movement, and that there are several occasions where the connected 'f' form continuity habitual to Francis Tresham, can be traced in the Bruninge script, so on aggregate there is sufficient evidence to support the opinion that the Francis Tresham who signed the Declaration in 1605, was the same man who wrote from Madrid in 1609, signing himself Matthew Bruninge.

S̃ Tho: windebank I pray you draw
another Bill signed to me for making
out two p̃ʳ seales, one to yᵉ Excheqwer
for 100ᵗʰ yearly in P̃sonad̃g̃s, another
for 100ᵗʰ in Chantrys to yᵉ Dutchy, in
such forme as yᵉ last was and let
yᵉ warrant to yᵉ Excheqⁿ be to one lea
uing a Blank and so yᵉ other/
More I haue not at this Tyme
but rest   yoʳ louing
                                         freind
you may send this   Salisbury
ingrossed for you
knoe if you haue alredy
a mowld, all must be
in Fee Farme/

THE WRITING OF ROBERT CECIL

Good Mr Lock, I receaued by your lettres dated in July and adressed vnto M^r freman, that you had made ouerture vnto the Honorable personage, Mr Secretary Cicill of my demaunde, and that his honor was well inclined to fauour my sute; to me news of much comfort) moreouer that his honors opinion was, that first the matter shuld be opened vnto her Matie by Mr Secretary herbert. vntill this present the truth is I haue not written vnto Mr Secretaire herbert concerning this matter. the reason was for that I did vnderstand that her Matie was in progresse, a tyme very vnfitt for negotiation: And now being aduertised that the spaniards are landed in Irland, both to make knowen that I haue not any intelligence with that Enemy, as also that I am most desirous to imploy my life in the service of her Matie and of my Cuntry; I haue desired Mr Winood her Maties Agent here to impart so much vnto Mr Secretary Cicill, & withall to signifie that I am most redy and willing to be disposed of conforme to the good pleasure of her Matie. And if you would do me the fauoure as to make knowen vnto his honor my sayd zeale, and that by your meanes I might know what shuld be her Maties & their honors pleasures concerning my demande; I should haue my self much beholding to yow, and withall will thankefully recognise your courtesy. for the more expedition and better assurance of that yow shall notifie to me, I haue sent my seruant the present bearer hereof, who shall attend vpon you, stay, and returne as yow shall aduice him. And this also I beseche you to signifie vnto Mr Secretaire Cicill, for I wold not send any thether, if I had any opinion that his honor shuld haue it otherwise than well. yow see how boldly I do importune yow with my particular busines, the which if it shall by your meanes haue the desired effect, assure your self, that your Courtesye shall not be employed vpon one, either ingratefull or vnthankfull, or in any wise inconsiderative of your frendly trauells. the assurance whereof shal giue end her vnto. with wishing vnto yow as vnto my self.
5th of 9^{ber} - 1601 - Paris -

your very louing friend

Wm Tresame

PART OF A LETTER BY WILLIAM TRESHAM

About some 10 dayes since here departed fro hence 2 brothers, sones to Mr
Yonsay of London Merchante, they came fro Sevill (where they had been
many monethes) to see this Corte; they went for S: Seb: and fro thence
to determine theyr corse to Paris, and having seene Fraunce, to
returne home. _____ within this 2 dayes is to departe fro
hence Mr Digges, and Stephan Collimore factor to Mr Jackson in
London, who having ended his pleys, returnes for Sevill to follow
his trade, and Mr Digges (being furnished by him) is gone with
him to stay there some tyme. Mr Persall is shortely
bound for Portugall, so as we shall at all tast many of
English his hence. _____ my L: finding some inconvenience in the
cominge in and out of many spaniardes into his house to those are
Duyelle within him, required a more convenient...
whereuppon was appoynted him, 2 greate and exceeding fayre
houses; towardes the Prado in one of the w...
present, yt was the house of the Duke of Maqueda, for somes
especially, it is very pleasant having a fayre garden and an
excellent vista both to the towne and fieldes; and so
spatious and full of roome it is as my L: having exceeding
large quarters for his owne use, and so very well lodged
all the rest of his house, both given chambers to Mr Tribault
and others, both English and Scottish, w... hath a little
increast the number of those belonging to the house; and
much company hether becomes yt being a little out of the
waye. And thus desyring to your... and all you the likecase
of all health and happynes, I recommend unto your favorable
acceptance the affectionate dearly of

Madrid this 8th of
Aprill 1609 stilonovo: your worshipp most humble servante

                                                    Mathew Bruninge

Syr I have seene a debtor to Mr
Peasole for 40 rials yt all while he
now at his departure was not able
to paye him, but have borrowed of
more and given him a bill to you
for the 3 L 5s w... I pray pay him
out of the 20 L I nowe have written
for, and send me the rest.

63.

Now yor Lo: may see how I was engaged in this business before I was aware under the pretence of tellinge mee good newes, otherwise yf I had guessed yt his speche would have tended to a practise, I had prevented him, for I thancke god I am owner of such a fortune as is able to afford me what I desier, the comfort whereof is so much the sweeter unto me, as I have spent most of my tyme overburthened wth debtes and wantes, and had resolved within my selfe to spend my daies quietly. Now itt may appeare to yor Lo: yt nether my hand, purse, or heade was ether in the actinge or contrivinge of this plott, but beinge lately and unexspectedly fallen into itt, I sought wth all the argumentes I could to disswade itt, ~~yett~~ I what care and charge I have been att to deliver my selfe honestly out of itt, and yt the silence yt I used was only to deliver my selfe from yt infamous brand of an accuser, and to save his life wch in all true rules I was bound to doe, and yt the course yt I held wth them was not only to free his matie and the state from this psent treason, but to shipe them all away yt they might have no meanes left them to contrive any more. Allso may itt please yor Lo: yt besides these demonstrations yt my hart abhorred the treason all other circumstances doe concur to quitt me from this intended treason. For since the knowledge of this acte, I never bought armer, or pistoll, many horses I have swolden, and lessened my house att the least by twenty to ease my charge, and when I went into the country to levy mony for the paiinge of my fathers debtes I made bargaines very neare to the value of three thousand pound, and never tooke penny of them, but only gave daies some to pay on the tenth of this monthe some on the twentieth, and some the next terme. yf I had thought yt the wholl kingedome should have been sett in combustion, I would rather have sought to drawe the mony into my owne handes, then have left itt in other mens. thus havinge acquainted yor Lo: wth my knowledge in these matters I most humbly beseech you yt seeinge yee see wth what minde I have offended only in usinge silence, yt yor Lo: will bee intercessers for me unto his matie yt he will voutsafe to holde me in the number of his true subjectes, wthout the wch my life will not bee to mee a life, and I shall ever be bound to pray for yor Lo: So in all duty I humbly end,

Francis Tresame.

PART OF A LETTER BY FRANCIS TRESHAM

In contrast the handwriting of William Tresham from Paris on 5 November 1602 shows no such similarity, either in relation to the script signed Francis Tresham in 1605, or that signed Matthew Bruninge in 1609.

In fact the stroke quality of the 1602 sample is poor and shows considerable ataxia. Thus quite apart from differences in co-ordination and pressure pattern, it would have been virtually impossible for the writer of the script signed William Tresham, to have produced the lively, coherent movement evident particularly in Francis Tresham's script in 1605, but also in that signed Matthew Bruninge in 1609.

Among several common graphic movements, the following are perhaps most easily identified in the photographed pages:

Francis Tresham *Matthew Bruninge*

Line 4 Line 16

Line 29 *Note* (i) Similarity of 'r' forms
(ii) Similarity of connective link of 'f' to 'o'

Line 1 Line 2

Line 10 Line 7

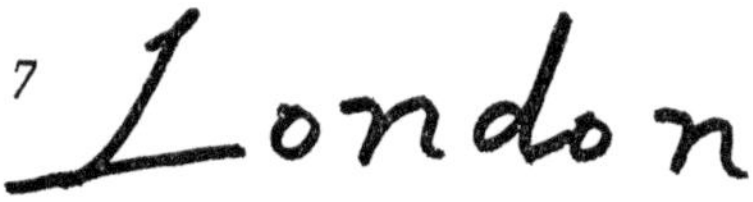

Note (i) Similarity of movement of 'L' form, particularly in the line 2 occurrence.

(ii) The difference in rhythm and form between the two executions of 'London' in the same script, with the stiltedness of over-control very evident in the sample in line 7.

Index

Set in 12 point Van Dijck type.
Text and litho illustrations printed by
W & J Mackay Limited, Chatham
on Guard Bridge Bookwove paper.
Bound by W & J Mackay Limited
using Scholco Brillianta cloth,
blocked with a special design
by Jeff Clements.